WHAT YOUR COLLEAGU

Time and time again, Jarred Amato has proven himself to be an educator who successfully manages to get the most reluctant of students to choose reading and engagement with literature over myriad other forms of entertainment. In *Just Read It*, we get an inside view of his methods and practices presented in ways that are easy to emulate. This book should be required reading for every middle and high school ELA teacher.

—Nic Stone, #1 New York Times Bestselling
author of *Dear Martin*

Without a doubt, books are hope and a location for healing. Jarred Amato recognizes this and many of us across the nation—teachers, scholars, and literacy specialists—have benefited from his teaching leadership and expertise, especially his dedication to promote youth agency, literacy, and brilliance. Jarred Amato's superpower has always been his willingness to listen to young people as experts of their lives and to increase their access to engaging, diverse texts. This is why *Just Read It: Unlocking the Magic of Independent Reading in Middle and High School Classrooms* is such a phenomenal resource. Here, Jarred offers multiple steps for creating a positive literacy culture for students to write, to reflect, to analyze, and to participate across numerous communities. Amato reminds us that we must know our roles as educators, what our data tells us, and how the views of young people can inform our everyday practices. Jarred's expertise is irreplaceable. At last, the great work of Project LIT within his classrooms is shared in a new book for all of us to read!

—Bryan Ripley Crandall, Connecticut
Writing Project Director, Associate Professor
of English Education at Fairfield University, and
co-host of the National Writing Project's The Write Time

Jarred Amato's Read and WRAP method has been invaluable to my literacy efforts with my students. This book is full of incredible ideas and practical activities to help enrich the reading lives of our students while still developing the skills that are most critical in an engaging way. This is a book I will come back to regularly and a MUST READ for any educator.

—Carrie Friday, Media Specialist

Fostering a culture of passion and purpose through independent reading in classrooms empowers students to explore diverse perspectives, fuels their curiosity, and deepens their understanding of the world. Jarred Amato's book helps educators grow their practice to initiate a love of learning to cultivate lifelong readers that actively engage with ideas and contribute to a meaningful society.

—Nikki Healy ("Mrs. G"),
Assistant Principal MNPS Early College High School

Engagement, access, and a love of reading aren't just for elementary school! Jarred Amato will inspire you while carefully guiding you on how to make literacy real for your middle school and high school students. You'll feel his love for teaching, books, and kids on every page, while quietly transforming your practices.

—Tom Marshall, Principal and Author

I first heard about Project LIT Community and the work Jarred Amato and his high school students were doing in Nashville in 2018. What a life changing experience! Every moment of that June Summit I was inspired, incredibly excited and hopeful that my students and I could bring similar energy and love of reading to our high school in Washington. What I've experienced since then: witnessing dozens of my students step into leadership opportunities, participate in authentic and meaningful learning through literacy, connecting with incredible authors and rallying hundreds of others in their community to join in spreading the joys of reading. Jarred Amato has changed many lives already through his unmatched generosity of sharing what works—this book guarantees that what he and his students have done will truly live forever and continue to impact readers, educators, and whole communities in ways that they may have never imagined.

—Kristin Fraga Sierra, Teacher Librarian and
Project Lit Abes Advisor at Lincoln High School in Tacoma WA

JUST READ IT

JUST READ IT

UNLOCKING THE MAGIC OF INDEPENDENT READING IN MIDDLE AND HIGH SCHOOL CLASSROOMS

JARRED AMATO

Foreword by
KWAME ALEXANDER

CORWIN Literacy

FOR INFORMATION:

Corwin

A SAGE Company

2455 Teller Road

Thousand Oaks, California 91320

(800) 233-9936

www.corwin.com

SAGE Publications Ltd.

1 Oliver's Yard

55 City Road

London EC1Y 1SP

United Kingdom

SAGE Publications India Pvt. Ltd.

Unit No 323-333, Third Floor, F-Block

International Trade Tower Nehru Place

New Delhi 110 019

India

SAGE Publications Asia-Pacific Pte. Ltd.

18 Cross Street #10-10/11/12

China Square Central

Singapore 048423

Vice President and
  Editorial Director: Monica Eckman

Executive Editor: Tori Mello Bachman

Content Development Editor: Sharon Wu

Associate Content
  Development Editor: Sarah Ross

Editorial Assistant: Zachary Vann

Project Editor: Amy Schroller

Copy Editor: Lynne Curry

Typesetter: C&M Digitals (P) Ltd.

Proofreader: Rae-Ann Goodwin

Indexer: Integra

Cover Designe: Gail Buschman

Marketing Manager: Margaret O'Connor

Printed in the United States of America

Library of Congress Cataloging-in-Publication Data

Names: Amato, Jarred, author.

Title: Just read it : unlocking the magic of independent reading in middle and high school classrooms/Jarred Amato.

Description: Thousand Oaks, California : Corwin, 2024. | Series: Corwin literacy | Includes bibliographical references and index.

Identifiers: LCCN 2023044236 | ISBN 9781071907245 (paperback) | ISBN 9781071934609 (epub) | ISBN 9781071934616 (epub) | ISBN 9781071934623 (pdf)

Subjects: LCSH: Reading (Middle school) | Reading (Secondary) | Supplementary reading. | Reading promotion. | Academic achievement.

Classification: LCC LB1632 .A63 2024 | DDC 418/.40712—dc23/eng/20231025

LC record available at https://lccn.loc.gov/2023044236

This book is printed on acid-free paper.

24 25 26 27 28 10 9 8 7 6 5 4 3 2 1

Contents

6 FINISHING WITH FINESSE: CELEBRATORY END-OF-YEAR ACTIVITIES 177

PART 3. LEVELING UP AND MAXIMIZING THE IMPACT OF INDEPENDENT READING

For downloadable resources related to *Just Read It*, visit the companion website: **resources.corwin.com/justreadit**

Foreword

I don't remember the circumstances around the first time I met Jarred Amato in person, but I do remember it was in 2017, and I do remember his energy—endless. I do remember his passion—inspiring—and that he was teaching high school ELA in Tennessee. I do remember that he kept going on and on about this Project LIT organization he and his students were starting and how it *aimed to eliminate book deserts and inspire all Nashville children to become lifelong readers.* And, I do remember that two years before that, he'd sent an email via my website:

> *Good afternoon, Mr. Alexander . . . I wanted to thank you for writing books that reach ALL kids . . . I know firsthand that your books (The Crossover and Booked) engage even the most reluctant readers, so I am writing you with a specific ask . . .*

As I was reading his note, I mistakenly read "task" and thought to myself, Wow, this dude is intentional and a little presumptuous. He doesn't know me.

> *I would love to provide all students involved in our project (approx. 50) with a copy of one or both of your novels. Once they read (or in many of their cases, re-read) they will be tasked with passing on the book(s) to other children in their community, who will then do the same . . .*

I remember reading this and thinking this guy is bold. And ambitious. Seemingly eliminating book deserts in a WHOLE city is an indomitable feat, but if you're gonna do it, you gotta believe you can, which means you must be bold and highly enthusiastic. Or naïve. Jarred was all three. Plus, it appeared that his vision was limitless.

> *I envision using your books as a way to hook hundreds of children on the power of reading. Therefore, my question is this: what would be the most cost-effective way to purchase class sets of The Crossover?*

I don't remember how I responded, but I do remember that I did, and it began what has become a near decades-long conversation around literacy and empowerment. I've watched over the years as Jarred's Project LIT has grown in size, scope, and impact. The little project that started at Maplewood High School in Nashville has spread to over two thousand schools across the United States and around the world. I'm proud to say that I was there with Jarred and his students in the early days, that my book *The Crossover* had such impact. And I'm excited to be able to share with you Jarred's first professional book now.

So many teachers tell me the biggest challenge in middle or high school ELA is getting kids excited about reading. I see a lot of kids in a lot of schools, and I want to make it clear: The kids in Jarred's classes are typical kids. They have Snapchat, after-school sports, theater, homework, family drama, and jobs contending for their attention just like the kids in your classes. They come into his room at the start of the year uninterested, disengaged, maybe even with a chip on the shoulder, hoisting whatever baggage they bring from other ELA teachers and classes in years past. Aside from Mrs. Virgil in first grade, I don't remember a single ELA teacher creating an environment that made me WANT to read. But Jarred's students (and some of yours, I'm sure) leave class with a blazing love of reading. Because Jarred has learned—through his own teaching successes and setbacks—how to create the conditions that make reading books engaging, exciting, and even fun! Oh, and it's not just that they become avid readers and begin to appreciate the beauty and power of literature. Oh no, these kids are also achieving better on state tests, getting into good colleges, and creating change in their communities.

Just Read It shows you how he did it. How he does it. How so many Project LIT teachers are taking on the challenge of independent reading—getting kids interested, making space and time in your class periods, and giving kids practice with all the necessary literacy skills they need to master—and he breaks it down into doable chunks. Like so many great teachers who are life-giving and life-saving, Jarred is not only committed to his students, but he has an eagerness to share what he's learned with other teachers.

Jarred's Read and WRAP routines offer practical, do-this-tomorrow ways to get kids reading, talking, thinking, and writing about what they're reading—and you'll even find ways to make room for the occasional whole-class novel and required texts. In other words, in these pages you have all you need to establish independent reading routines AND teach the skills kids need to meet reading and writing standards.

There's no better time for a book like *Just Read It* to be in your hands. We live in a time when choosing what we read is critically important. A time when other people, who lack the imaginations to fully embrace all of our humanity, are trying to limit what our kids read. Ironically, it is through reading that we grow our humanity. The mind of an adult begins in the imagination of child. Right now, our kids need to have space to read and talk, listen and write, think and enjoy, learn and grow. Jarred has given us a road map for this journey. It's not THE answer, but it is an answer. And it's been proven. And, it's a multi-tool you'll use again and again as you keep striving to create the best possible learning experience for the kids in your care. Watch what happens when you make room for independent reading— simply letting kids read books they care about—amidst all the curricular challenges and standards goals.

I don't remember whether I sent Jarred autographed class sets of the books for his students (I sure hope I did, 'cause it makes for a great story, doesn't it?), but I do remember that we became friends. And he changed some lives. And I do think this book will change yours.

—Kwame Alexander
Author, *The Write Thing*

Acknowledgments

To my students. I wish I had the space here to list each and every one of you by name. This book would not exist without y'all, and I am forever grateful. Please know that it was an honor and privilege to be your teacher. Keep reading, keep writing, keep chasing your dreams. I will always be rooting for you.

To Tom Donnellan, Helen Smith, George Swift, and every teacher and coach who believed in me before I believed in myself.

To LaFonda Davis, Carrie Friday, Alex Harper, Tyler Sainato, Kristin Fraga Sierra, and every librarian who continues to defend our readers and our right to read.

To Mrs. G and every teacher who continues to champion our young people and model what it means to "be a good human."

To Julie Travis and every school leader who brings out the best in their teachers and takes this work, but never themselves, too seriously.

To my friends and colleagues at JBMS, MHS, ECHS, and FMS. I have learned so much from all of you.

To Kwame Alexander and Nic Stone. You have changed so many lives, including mine. Thank you for everything.

To our entire Project LIT family—every student, every chapter leader, every author, every community member—I am so incredibly proud of what we have built together.

To Tori Bachman, Sharon Wu, and the entire Corwin team for your trust, support, and expertise.

To mom. You will always be my hero.

To dad. We love and miss you more every day.

To Zack, the best brother in the world. (I don't expect you to read this book, but I'm hoping you'll at least buy a copy or two.)

To Lizzie, you make it look so easy.

To Lucca. Whenever you read this, five or ten or fifty years from now, know that mom and dad love you more than life itself.

And to you, dear reader. Thanks again for the work you do every day. It matters. My goodness, it matters.

PUBLISHER'S ACKNOWLEDGEMENTS

Corwin gratefully acknowledges the contributions of the following reviewers:

Carmen Gordillo
Middle School Language Arts Teacher, Rutgers University
Toms River, NJ

Andy Schoenborn
English Teacher, Clare Public Schools
Midland, MI

Theresa Walter
English Department Chair/English Teacher,
   Great Neck Public Schools
Greenlawn, NY

About the Author

Dr. Jarred Amato is an award-winning English teacher and the cofounder of Project LIT Community, a national grassroots literacy movement. Jarred enjoys reading, writing, and laughing alongside young people every day and collaborating with fellow educators to improve literacy access, attitudes, and outcomes. Jarred is a two-time MNPS Blue Ribbon teacher and the recipient of the Penguin Random House Teacher Award for Literacy and the Inspiring Educator Award from the Nashville Public Education Foundation. Jarred received his BA in English and history from Vanderbilt University, his MAT from Belmont University, and his EdD from Lipscomb University. After thirteen years of teaching middle and high school English in Nashville, Jarred recently relocated to New Jersey, where he and his wife are attempting to keep up with their two-year-old son.

To Lucca, our light and love.

Warm-Up

An Introduction

F or as long as I can remember, I've been a reader. In fact, I recently stumbled upon a letter that I had written near the end of first grade at Underwood Elementary School: *Dear Second Grade Teacher. My name is Jarred Amato. I am 7 years old and My brother is 5. I am good at baseball, basketball, readding [sic], and writing.*

And here I am today, nearly thirty years later, a middle and high school English teacher, an advocate and champion of reading and our readers, and Project LIT Community cofounder, honored to share a bit of my journey with you. I stumbled upon this letter during the summer of 2019 as my brother and I sorted through boxes of our childhood, just after our dad had passed away unexpectedly. Despite his flaws (and we've all got them), my dad was one of my biggest champions (and we all need people who believe in us, no matter what). Gosh, he would have been so proud of me for writing this book. However, my dad was definitely *not* a reader. I wish he had been.

Years ago, my students and I learned that readers tend to live longer than non-readers. We determined there was sufficient evidence to support the claim. From the *Washington Post* (emphasis mine),

> Good news on National Book Lovers Day: A chapter a day might keep the Grim Reaper away—at least a little longer. A recent study by Yale University researchers, published online in the journal Social Science & Medicine, concluded that **"book readers experienced a 20 percent reduction in risk of mortality over the 12 years of follow-up compared to non-book readers."**

The data was obtained from a longitudinal Health and Retirement Study sponsored by the National Institute on Aging. The study looked at 3,635 subjects, all older than 50, whom the researchers divided into three groups: those who didn't read books, those who read up to 3.5 hours a week, and those who read more than 3.5 hours a week.

The findings were remarkable: Book readers survived almost two years longer than those who didn't crack open a book.

Accounting for variables such as education level, income and health status, the study found that those who read more than 3.5 hours weekly were 23 percent less likely to die during that 12-year period. Those who read up to 3.5 hours — an average of a half-hour a day — were 17 percent less likely.

In other words, just like a healthy diet and exercise, books appear to promote a "significant survival advantage," the authors concluded.

I wish my dad could have experienced the joy of getting lost in a great book. I wish he could have cheered for characters the same way he rooted for Mickey Mantle and Derek Jeter. I wish that his story was uncommon. However, with each passing year, more and more of us—young and old—are spending significant time in front of screens and little, if any, immersed in books. We are only just beginning to understand the effects, but as the parent of a toddler and educator of adolescents, I'd be lying if I said I wasn't concerned. And I wish more adults, particularly our policymakers and educational leaders, acknowledged the urgency of the moment. If we do not value reading, if we do not value our readers, the consequences will be dire.

If you are reading this book (thank you!), you probably believe in the power of books to change lives—to save lives. And like me, you probably know that books help us understand ourselves and empathize with others. Books have a unique ability to connect us and comfort us, to challenge us and change us. Books help us heal. Books give us hope.

However, I have to admit: in the years that it took me to complete this book, I often felt hopeless. I found it nearly impossible to focus. I struggled to block out the noise. And, in talking with colleagues in my school and across the country, I know I was not alone. Being an educator in today's climate is not easy—and that's putting it lightly. It wasn't easy before March 2020, and it's infinitely harder now. Somehow, we have been asked to do more with less. Incredible educators everywhere are exiting the profession, or at the very least, seriously considering it. Perhaps you've had your doubts, too; I know I have.

Of course, everyone has their own reasons for leaving, but ultimately, it comes down to this: the "highs" of teaching no longer outweigh the "lows." Low pay. Low morale. Low respect. Most educators aren't leaving because of the students; we are leaving because of the adults. Adults who are using educators and students as pawns in their political games. Adults who continue to pile more and more on our plates without taking anything off. Adults who prioritize programs over people. Adults who find room in the budget for scripted curriculum while forcing teachers to crowdsource for books and supplies. Adults who ban books before reading them. Adults who care more about keeping their job than keeping students and educators safe. Adults who value compliance and control more than creativity and innovation. Adults who don't support us enough. Who don't trust us enough. Who don't respect us enough. Who, in far too many places, don't pay us enough. Educators are finally saying: *Enough*. And I get it. Believe me, I totally get it.

But here's the thing: Our students need you. They need us! Our students don't need martyrs. They don't need saviors. However, our students deserve to have educators who give a damn. Courageous educators, like you, who love and believe in them no matter what. Who have their back in the classroom and cafeteria. Who always seem to know exactly what books to recommend. Who recognize that the little things are, in fact, the big things. Who care about strengthening our communities and building a better future for *all*.

That's why I'm not going anywhere. I am committed to this work for the long haul. At the same time, I believe wholeheartedly that teaching should be sustainable. Teaching should be rewarding. And yes, teaching should be *fun*. Despite the challenges, teaching middle and high school English for the past decade and a half has often been all three of those things for me, which is one of the reasons I decided to write this book. To remind myself—along with all of you—why this literacy work still matters. Why this work is still worth doing.

I also wrote this book for my son, Lucca, who was born in the fall of 2021. He devours books —quite literally. And I hope that he never stops. Because my dream for Lucca is the same dream that I hold for every child in this world. That he is always surrounded by books. All sorts of books. Books that make him laugh out loud. Books that move him to tears. Books that he implores his mother to read to him before bedtime. Books that he wants to stay up late reading under the covers. Books that teach him all sorts of wonderful things about himself and the messy, magical world around him.

My hope is that reading always remains meaningful. That it never feels like a chore or punishment. That when Lucca gets to school, he is showered with an abundance of patience, love, and support from incredible teachers who receive the same. That he can always find refuge and community in the library. That when he returns home, while we are sitting around the kitchen table, he will ramble on in excitement about the stories he's reading and the conversations he's having. That his third-grade teacher will help him publish his first "book" and make him feel like a real writer, the way Mrs. Madsen did for me.

My hope is that Lucca's love for literacy and learning does not fade as he heads into middle and high school, like it does for so many of today's adolescents. That expert educators will encourage him to read widely and read often. To engage with different ideas and perspectives. To find his voice. To pursue his passions.

I wrote this book because I believe, with all my heart, that all of this is possible, not just for my son but for every child. I have a feeling you believe it, too. At the same time, we know there are closeminded people working relentlessly to limit what we read, what we teach, and what we can imagine. We cannot be naïve. Yet we cannot lose hope. It's a delicate balance.

Parenting, like teaching, feels overwhelming, if not impossible, at times. The doubt. The fear. The big questions. *Am I good enough? How can I keep my child safe? How do I sleep at night knowing that I can't?* The small ones. *What in the world are we going to have for dinner? How has he already outgrown that shirt? Why is fruit so expensive?* In these moments of stress, I try my best to be present. To sit on the floor with Lucca as we build a block tower or read *Brown Bear, Brown Bear.* To get outside and play in the sprinkler. To walk to the library. To run around the bookstore. (My apologies to the Barnes and Noble staff for the titles Lucca routinely pulled from your shelves and left scattered across your store during the summer and fall of 2022.)

I try my best to seek out and savor these moments of joy in the classroom, too. In a society where teachers and parents are constantly told what they are doing wrong, I take time to appreciate all that we are doing right. There is no such thing as a perfect parent or teacher. I wrote this book to remind myself, and all of you, that our good is good enough—more than enough.

I also wrote this book to honor and amplify my former students—Adrian, CJ, David, De'Montre, De'Sean, Faith, Gerrick, Jakaylia, Jay, Lauren, Paisley, Rodrea, Sean, Selena, TJ, Ty, and so many more. Young people who rallied an entire community around reading and ultimately transformed a class project into a national literacy movement. The foundation of our work has been a relentless commitment to independent reading, writing, reflection, and relationships. That is the "secret" to our success, and that is what I plan to zoom in on in this book.

Admittedly, the principles of access, choice, time, and community are not new. They have been the focus of countless books; you and I have probably read many of them. Yet, our literacy challenges persist. My students and I took the principles, outlined brilliantly by the likes of literacy giants such as (but certainly not limited to) Nancie Atwell, Kelly Gallagher, Penny Kittle, and Cornelius Minor, brought them to life, day in and day out, year after year. By any measure, we were successful. We have so many moments and memories to share. Even more, we hope to show you that the "magic" can happen in every classroom in this country, no matter the barriers, no matter the obstacles. We promise.

My hope is that this book serves as a resource for schools and ELA teams as we continue to reimagine education. To be clear, reimagining does not mean overcomplicating. Let's keep things simple when we can. Let's get the "easy" things right first and go from there. Over the past fourteen years, I have taught in four schools across six grade levels (seventh through twelfth) and two states. An under-resourced middle school and high school serving primarily Black and brown students. An early college high school serving a small, diverse group of ninth and tenth graders. A suburban middle school serving primarily white students. Each experience was different. However, in many ways, each classroom functioned and felt the same, and that's because of our commitment to independent reading.

Instead of searching for (and often arguing over) the "best" book to teach, trying to write the perfect lesson plan, or finding time to "do SEL," let's focus on establishing a positive literacy culture from day one—and cultivating it throughout the year—one step, one book, and one conversation at a time.

"JUST READING"

Before we get too far in this book, I must make two quick points:

1. **There is nothing wrong when students are "just reading."**

   Shouldn't that be one of our goals? Instead of asking educators, "*Why* are your students reading all the time?," we should be asking, "*How* are you getting your students to read all the time?" Why are we shaming teachers who have successfully managed to get teenagers off their phones and into books? Shouldn't we be asking them to share their strategies and secrets? Why are we making educators feel like they are breaking the rules to provide students with the positive literacy experiences they deserve? Shouldn't we be thanking them for going above and beyond to nurture the next generation of readers? Why are we okay with students "just sitting" in rows listening to a teacher lecture for an hour, "just answering" low-level recall questions from a textbook or TPT handout, or "just Snapchatting" with their friends because they finished their work for the period? Shouldn't we want all students to be engaged and empowered?

2. **Getting to a point where all students are "just reading" (and _actually_ reading) is a lot harder than it looks.**

   If you walk into an ELA classroom and all twenty or twenty-five students are "just reading," it means their teacher has done a lot of wonderful work behind the scenes (work that we will attempt to name and unpack in this book). It means their teacher deserves praise, not ridicule. It's also worth pointing out that our students are never "just reading"—they are thinking critically, asking questions, developing empathy, gaining confidence, relieving stress, setting goals, building stamina, discovering themselves, expanding their vocabulary, connecting with others, improving their concentration, fueling their imagination, acquiring knowledge, sharpening their writing and communication skills, exercising their brain, and so much more.

I have no problem admitting that it took me a long time to get to a point where every student was "just reading." Too long. In fact, there are still plenty of days where we fall short of 100 percent. That's okay! Every student has a different relationship with reading; every student enters our classroom at a different point in their literacy journey. I try my best to meet them where they are and to embrace progress over perfection. And I encourage you to do the same.

WHAT I HOPE YOU'LL GET FROM THIS BOOK

My sincere hope is that the activities, ideas, inspiration, and strategies shared over the next eight chapters strengthen your conviction and empower you to make an even greater impact in your classroom, school, and community. While this book can be read from start to finish, I know that if you are like me, you may want to jump to specific sections, depending on what you need (and how much time you have). Therefore, here is what you can expect to find in each chapter:

PART 1 – THE FUNDAMENTALS OF INDEPENDENT READING

In Chapter 1, I bring you into our classroom and recount our journey with independent reading— our difficulties with the "traditional" ELA approach, the important distinction between literary and literature, how we developed our Read and WRAP framework, what it looks like in practice, and why we continue to stick with it year after year. (WRAP is an acronym that stands for Write, Reflect, Analyze, and Participate.)

In Chapter 2, I outline what it's going to take for all students to establish, or reestablish, a positive reading identity—a strong sense of purpose, a clear understanding of our readers, and a simplified approach (that hopefully includes our Read and WRAP routine).

In Chapter 3, I show how we can transform the principles of access, choice, time, and community into actions. In other words, I offer specific tools and strategies to increase book access (especially on a teacher budget), promote choice, guarantee time, and build community.

PART 2 – STRATEGIES TO SUSTAIN INDEPENDENT READING SUCCESS

In Chapter 4, I walk you through our "Intro to Lit" unit, which includes a wide range of activities, texts, and tasks that help us hit the ground running (or in our case, reading and writing) from day one. From our student surveys and book tasting activity to our "Best Nine" and "Ten Things" writing assignment (along with much more), this chapter includes more than a dozen resources to start the year strong, build community, and invest students in our Read and WRAP routine. My hunch is that you, like me, will return to this chapter each fall.

In Chapter 5, I share our extensive collection of WRAP prompts that help us engage and empower readers day in and day out, week after week. This chapter attempts to answer the question "When the timer goes off and our notebooks come out, what does it look like to WRAP?" Book reviews and narrative continuations, grammar and poetry, character analysis and creative projects—this chapter is jam-packed with prompts varying in length, difficulty, and purpose to help you meet the specific needs of your students.

In Chapter 6, I outline several meaningful end-of-year projects and activities, from "For Every One" and our "Lit Awards" to "My Ten" and our sample "Independent Reading Project," that help us come full circle and end the school year even stronger than we started.

PART 3 – LEVELING UP AND MAXIMIZING THE IMPACT OF INDEPENDENT READING

In Chapter 7, I discuss how to leverage student feedback (via WRAP prompts, one-on-one conversations, quarterly reflections, and formal reading surveys) to fine-tune our Read and WRAP routine throughout the school year.

In Chapter 8, I reflect on our Project LIT journey and invite you and your students to join our movement and launch a "chapter" of your own. It would be an honor to continue leading and learning together.

PART 1

The Fundamentals of Independent Reading

CHAPTER 1

Developing the
Read and WRAP
Framework

At its core, this book is about why independent reading (IR) matters, what it looks like in action, and how we can unlock the "magic" of IR in every ELA classroom, every day. Specifically, we will zoom in on the Read and WRAP *(write, reflect, analyze, participate)* framework that I developed with my students: ten to twenty minutes of independent reading followed by meaningful writing, reflection, conversation, and community building. When we maximize this time, when we protect this time, the rewards and possibilities are endless—for students, for educators, for everyone.

At the same time, we must acknowledge that far too many of our nation's middle and high school students—in small towns and big cities, before and after the pandemic, and due to a wide range of factors—do not

- have access to books they are interested in reading;
- read or write frequently enough (volume);
- identify as readers and/or writers;
- enjoy reading and/or writing;
- feel engaged or empowered in the learning process;
- have authentic opportunities to discuss their reading, writing, and thinking;
- feel connected to their classroom community; and
- have tools to address the various mental health challenges.

While I certainly do not have all the answers, I believe, with all my heart, that creating a solid, daily framework for independent reading in middle and high school ELA classrooms should be part of the solution. Here is how the National Council of Teachers of English (NCTE, 2019) defines independent reading:

Read the full statement on how NCTE defines independent reading.

> a routine, protected instructional practice that occurs across all grade levels. Effective independent reading practices include time for students to read, access to books that represent a wide range of characters and experiences, and support within a reading community that includes teachers and students. Student choice in text is essential because it motivates, engages, and reaches a wide variety of readers. The goal of independent reading as an instructional practice is to build habitual readers with conscious reading identities.

As we continue the process of reimagining education, and reimagining adolescent literacy instruction, one thing is certain—every school should make independent reading a priority. When we do, we begin to address the challenges listed on the previous page (lack of access, volume, belonging, identity, enjoyment, etc.) and increase the number of students who possess the literacy skills to thrive in this crazy thing we call life.

Of course, components of our ELA block can and should change depending on the day and week, lesson and unit, standards and objectives, students and grade level, and school and community. Independent reading, however, should remain a constant. When done with intention and care, independent reading—coupled with our WRAP time that follows—provides significant social-emotional and academic benefits that we will explore in more detail later this chapter and throughout this book. Ultimately, independent reading is an essential practice if we are serious about nurturing a generation of readers, writers, and leaders; if we are serious about educating the whole child; and if we are serious about centering students in our classrooms and schools.

Independent reading is an essential practice if we are serious about nurturing a generation of readers, writers, and leaders; if we are serious about educating the whole child; and if we are serious about centering students in our classrooms and schools.

Educators reap the rewards of independent reading, too. Since committing to our Read and WRAP routine, I have become a more optimistic and empathetic educator. I have become more efficient and effective. I have yet to "burn out" (although I've certainly been close at times) and plan to stay in this profession for the long haul. (This is another benefit of our Read and WRAP routine—it increases the likelihood that schools retain teachers and maintain strong, stable ELA departments.) Before looking too far ahead, however, I think it's important to first look back. To return to the fall of 2015, which turned out to be an inflection point in my teaching career.

MY JOURNEY WITH INDEPENDENT READING

In 2015, I decided to make the "loop" from a middle school to a high school in the same Nashville community, which meant that I had the honor of teaching many of my eighth graders again as ninth graders. I also had the opportunity to work for an incredibly supportive leadership team. For one of the first times in my career, I felt truly empowered. And what a difference it made.

When Ms. Travis or Dr. Jackson walked into our classroom and students were "just reading," they smiled. They knew how much work went on behind the scenes to make that happen. They knew how much our students benefited from this routine. Sometimes they'd turn off their walkie-talkies, grab a book from the shelf, and join us. Not once did they disrupt, doubt, or question. They championed innovation. They championed students. They championed teachers as we worked together to build a schoolwide literacy culture.

There was only one big problem: time or the lack thereof. Our high school ran on a traditional block schedule, which meant that I saw my students for roughly eighty minutes, every other day. When you factor in two weeks for semester exams, another two weeks (at a minimum) for end-of-year state tests, and another day or two each quarter for district-mandated benchmarks, we were already down to 150 school days. Cut that in half and we were at seventy-five days. Not to mention teacher and student absences, field trips and fire drills, pep rallies and assemblies, and (fingers crossed) snow days. Seventy-five days. That's it!

In seventy-five days, there was no way anyone could teach every standard. Well, let me rephrase that: in seventy-five days, there was no way students could "demonstrate mastery" of every standard, especially when many entered high school with significant literacy gaps. In seventy-five days, the "traditional" way of doing high school English was simply not going to work. We tried.

I remember passing out copies of *Lord of the Flies* after we found them in a bin in the back of the library (clearly access was another challenge, but more on that later). We had a few options from there:

- Read the entire book aloud together?
- Have students read it silently in class?
- Assign chapters to read on their own each week? With quizzes?
- Facilitate in-class discussions, even if half the group hadn't done the reading?

Spoiler alert: None of the options were ideal. Even the most enthusiastic readers were hesitant. While some decided to "play the game" like I did in high school (skimming and Sparknoting), many chose to stay on the sidelines, checking out completely. And who could blame them? I certainly didn't. While I didn't poll this particular group of students, consider a survey (example below) I administered to fifty of my ninth graders at the beginning of the 2018–2019 school year.

FALL READING SURVEY

1. How many books did you read independently last year?

   0   1   2   3   4   5   6   7   8   9   10

2. How do you feel about reading?

   1 (hate it)   2   3   4   5 (love it)

   Explain why: _____

3. Reading is boring.

   1 (strongly disagree)   2   3   4   5 (strongly agree)

4. Reading is important.

   1 (strongly disagree)   2   3   4   5 (strongly agree)

5. How often do you read outside of school?

   Never   Rarely   Sometimes   Often

   Explain why: _____

6. What was the best book you read in middle school?

online resources

The findings were significant:

- Fourteen out of fifty reported that they read zero books independently the previous school year. Another fifteen reported reading just one or two.
- Thirty-five out of fifty said they rarely or never read outside of school.
- Twenty-seven out of fifty literally could not name the best book they read in middle school, responding with "I don't remember," "No idea," "None," or a teacher's three favorite letters, "IDK."
- Thirty-two out of fifty reported a neutral or negative attitude toward reading.

To be clear, this was/is an adult problem, not a student one. As I told my students then, and as I tell new groups every fall, I get why they stop reading. In fact, if I were in their shoes, sitting in a classroom without engaging texts to choose from or consistent time to read, knowing that many adults in education simply see them as scores and numbers, I would feel the same way. Shoot, I often do feel that way as an educator.

Every year, more and more of our students are asking, *Why? Why do we have to read this? Can't we do something else? Why don't we have a voice in our education?* Again, these are legitimate questions. We should all be looking for ways to enhance the ELA and school experience for everyone. We cannot continue to do things the way they have always been done, especially when "that way" didn't work particularly well in the first place.

Sometimes we forget that books are competing against several formidable opponents for our time and attention. For better or worse (and probably both), smartphones and social media have changed our lives and our world forever. Teens are turning to YouTube and TikTok, Snapchat and Instagram, for both entertainment and connection. Teens, like all of us, crave acceptance and belonging. They thrive when engaged and empowered. They despise boredom and being told what to do. A student might debate various options:

> Hmmm, I could slog through *Lord of the Flies* for hours on my own or I could use ChatGPT to help me write the essay? I could struggle through Shakespeare or I could spend that time writing my own music? I could complete this "test-prep packet," or I could eat dinner with my family for the first time all week and then hop on NBA2K with my friends to unwind a bit? I could

complete the homework assignment that my teacher probably won't even look at, or I could finally catch up on my sleep?

For a lot of our students, it's an easy decision—whether adults agree with them or not. (And to be clear, I'm not excusing all student behavior but rather trying to explain it.) Instead of judging our students ("Why don't they just . . . ?") or blaming the latest technology (ChatGPT arrived on the scene while I was writing this manuscript), let's take a deep breath and begin to understand where they are coming from. Let's acknowledge that for a young person to a pick a book over a controller, the experience has to be meaningful.

Let's acknowledge that for a young person to a pick a book over a controller, the experience has to be meaningful.

Another factor to keep in mind, our young people are exhausted. The school day is tiring enough on its own, and when you throw in extracurricular activities and after-school responsibilities, it becomes unsustainable. Something has to give. For many of our students, many of the assigned texts, whether we are talking whole-class novels or the steady diet of "close reading" passages and accompanying questions, are not working. We need to recognize that a text is not "rigorous" if no one reads it. A lot of lesson and unit plans look challenging and "complex" on paper, especially if they have the seal of approval from a testing company or district office. However, walk into that ELA classroom and pay attention to the person who is doing all the work—the teacher. Meanwhile, the students are participating passively, at best. Some politely nod along and take notes while others choose to shut down, doze off, or find their own entertainment. (Even in classrooms where students are generally compliant, consider this: when is the compliance the goal of education? We can do better!)

MAKING ROOM FOR BOTH INDEPENDENT READING AND WHOLE-CLASS NOVELS

While we could argue about the merits of *Lord of the Flies* and other ELA department staples, I am not going to waste the time or energy here. I believe that is the wrong way to frame the conversation. In today's climate, people are expected, if not encouraged, to have a "take" on everything. Sports. Politics. Parenting. Education is no exception. *Pick a side. Get off the fence. Yes or no. For or against.* Prior to the pandemic, I occasionally took the bait and engaged in unproductive Twitter spats with strangers. No longer. I spend far less time online and refuse to accept interview requests from those who are looking to perpetuate the reading "war" narrative. The rhetoric is harmful and counterproductive. I am troubled by the lack of nuance. I am troubled by the fact that those outside of the classroom continue to pit educators against one another—either for "clicks" and dollars, or even worse, to sow distrust and undermine public education.

There is too much polarization and not enough collaboration. There is too much teacher shaming and not enough support. To paraphrase a line from Ray Bradbury, there is too much burning and not enough building. Speaking of Bradbury, I recently made a big personal and professional move—from Nashville to New Jersey. My new middle school featured *Fahrenheit 451* in its eighth-grade curriculum. Since I had not taught the book before, I was skeptical.

Ultimately, however, the novel turned to be an overwhelmingly positive experience. We created one-pagers for each of the three sections. We explored powerful themes, such as happiness, technology, conformity, and censorship. We wrote powerful personal narratives and brilliant novel continuations that Bradbury himself would have admired. We spent time observing and appreciating nature and reading poetry from the likes of Mary Oliver and Robert Frost. Inspired by StoryCorps's mission—"to preserve and share humanity's stories in order to build connections between people and create a more just and compassionate world"—we also completed a digital storytelling project where students interviewed family members about their childhood, changes in society, overcoming hardship, immigrating to the United States, career advice, their happiest memories, and so much more.

Which brings me back to this point: there is more than enough room for both choice and the required, whole-class reads, "classic" or contemporary. We do not have to pick one or the other. In fact, when we do choice well, it enhances our experience with the required texts. In Chapter 7, I will detail how we can balance independent reading with our required texts. In the meantime, here is the CliffsNotes version:

- We dedicate the first month to our "Intro to Lit" unit (see Chapter 4) and establishing our independent reading routine, which sets the tone for the rest of the year.

- We are intentional with our whole-class reads. We set clear learning targets and assign relevant, meaningful writing tasks. We read the texts at a quick pace and avoid over-teaching them. We encourage choice, collaboration, conversation, and critical thinking.

- While there is no perfect or magic ratio, we spend roughly two-thirds of our 180 days reading books of our choice. We dedicate the remaining one-third, then, to our required texts. Of course, with some groups, the ratio may be closer to 75:25 or 80:20.

- Whether a choice book or required read, we start nearly every one of our 180 class periods the same way—with our Read and WRAP routine. This ensures that by the end of the year, every student has read often (a minimum of ten to fifteen minutes every day, not including the time outside of school) and read widely (a minimum of five or six genres).

There is more than enough room for both choice and the required, whole-class reads, "classic" or contemporary. We do not have to pick one or the other.

I am not "for" or "against" *Lord of the Flies*, especially without context. I am, however, *for* any text, old or new, that gets our students back into reading and helps our classroom come alive. I am *against* any text, old or new, that pushes our students away from our ELA classrooms. I am *for* whole-class novels when taught with care and intention. I am *against* whole-class novels when taught without students in mind. I am *for* literacy experiences that spark joy and growth, and I am *against* those that cause harm. I am *for* students and educators working together to develop a literacy game plan that makes sense for their classroom, school, and community. I am *against* one-size-fits-all programs and top-down mandates. Finally, and most emphatically, I am *for* a daily independent reading routine, where students in all ELA classrooms and in all schools are encouraged to read and respond to a variety of beautiful, rich, and complex texts.

THE DIFFERENCE BETWEEN LITERATURE AND LITERACY

In 2021, the *New York Times Book Review* asked eight authors under forty to "name the writer or writers who have most influenced your work and explain how." (The article, "The Books That Made Me: 8 Writers on Their Literary Inspirations," could serve as a delightful mentor text to help students write their own "The Books That Made Me" piece.) As I read through the eight interviews, it became clear that each list differed drastically.

However, what did the eight writers have in common? What could we learn from their respective journeys? For me, the biggest takeaway was that all eight read often and read widely . . . eventually. Every author had someone in their lives—whether it was a parent, sibling, neighbor, teacher, or librarian—who ensured they had book access, who respected their reading choices, who built relationships, who understood the importance of representation, who encouraged them. I also found it telling that even our world's most prolific writers tend to succeed in spite of school, not because of it.

For example, Tommy Orange, author of *There, There,* did not finish a single novel in high school and only began reading fiction after college. Orange said, "No one was telling me what to read then, I was out of school and doing it all on my own, so I read what I liked" (Qasim, 2021). Meanwhile, Alyssa Cole spoke about the value of reading broadly: "I'm a multigenre writer, and this is the result of being a multigenre reader — picking up anything and everything I could get my hands on as a child." Cole credited authors such as Stephen King and Toni Morrison for inspiring and influencing her in a multitude of ways. She also credited manga, a genre often dismissed by educators. (Here's one more quote from Cole that's too good not to share: "I think what we read as children — what makes us feel seen or, for marginalized readers, not seen — plants the seeds of the stories that grow in us over years and decades." Wow.)

Read the original article, "The Books That Made Me."

Gabriel Bump grew up reading *Sports Illustrated* "as all mildly athletic teenage bookworms once did." (Guilty as charged.) Eventually, Bump moved from sports writers such as Scoop Jackson and Gary Smith to literary giants such as Hemingway and Baldwin. The key takeaway is that Bump started with what he loved and developed a positive reading identity. Later, with the support of his teachers and family—but notably not his school's ELA department—he began to explore different authors and genres, which is precisely what we should be doing with each student: meeting them where they are, building confidence, and continuing to support them on a reading journey that will hopefully continue long after they leave our classroom. And even if that journey stalls when they move on to the next teacher or the next school, we have done our part. One rich reading year is better than none. One rich reading year can change a student's entire trajectory.

One rich reading year is better than none. One rich reading year can change a student's entire trajectory.

Jason Reynolds, the 2020–2022 National Ambassador for Young People's Literature, understands this intimately. Reynolds admits that he, an award-winning, bestselling author, did not read his first book cover to cover until the age of seventeen. In a January 2018 *Daily Show* interview with Trevor Noah, Reynolds said,

> It's insane obviously, but it's only insane for me because I became a writer. But the truth of the matter is back then, there weren't a lot of books for kids like me. You're talking about the 1980s on through the 1990s. There weren't books about young people living in black communities, especially during the time. . . . In America, you had the crack epidemic, you had hip-hop, you had HIV, and those sort of three huge pillars were never mentioned in books for young people who were living and experiencing that life and things like that, and we just didn't see it.

Watch the full Reynolds interview

For Reynolds, it was hip-hop that gave him voice; it was hip-hop that helped him feel seen and valued. Rap music "let me know that who I already was was good enough because they got to tell the world that kids like me existed, that we walked a certain way and that we talked a certain way, and that we shouldn't apologize for any of that." Today, Reynolds's books have the same effect on young people that Queen Latifah's songs had on him.

In the interview, Noah also posed a question that many of us have been asked frequently over the years: *Why don't kids read these days? Why don't a lot of kids connect with Shakespeare and authors people deem to be "required" reading?* Reynolds's response brought me back to the fall of 2015 when we struggled to connect with William Golding's 1954 novel:

> One, young people are allergic to boredom . . . and that doesn't mean that Shakespeare is boring, it just means that often times the *teaching* of Shakespeare is boring. Two, we have to start really assessing what the literary canon is and whether or not it should remain fossilized and concrete as it is today. It's static. Why not figure out how to expand that canon to be diverse, to be old, to be young? It doesn't mean I want them to only read my books; it's just a springboard, so that they then build relationships not just with literature but with literacy.

Reynolds's distinction between "literacy" and "literature" is an important one, especially when we consider this—approximately 3.7 million US students graduate high school every year, and only forty thousand of them will become college English majors. Put another way: 99 percent of the students we serve in our K–12 classrooms will *not* major in English. They will go on to major in biology and business, engineering and computer science. Others will attend trade school, join the military, or jump straight into the workforce. All deserve rich, relevant, and rewarding ELA experiences during their middle and high school journey.

As I was writing the first draft of this book, Jay, a former student and Project LIT cofounder, was finishing up her sophomore year at Belmont University. In late April 2021, she texted me her grades for the semester: straight As in classes like Human Anatomy and Physiology and Kinesiology. An exercise science major and sports medicine minor, Jay did not read one "classic" novel in high school. Instead, she devoured dozens of books— beautiful, complex books of her choice —and developed the literacy and life skills to thrive at an elite university.

I still remember the video we recorded in May 2018, near the end of her junior year. Inspired by a viral clip from Jimmy Kimmel, students stood took turns attempting to "name a book." Looking through my phone, most clips lasted three or four seconds. And then there is Jay, standing in front of our classroom library, challenged by a classmate to name as many books as she could in ten seconds.

"Okay, you have *Fallen, The Hate U Give, Dear Martin, All American Boys, Solo, The Crossover, Ghost, Sunny, Patina; Everything, Everything; The Poet X* . . ."

There's a quick pause.

"Uhhhhh . . . .ahhhhhhh!"

Jay's arms are out, and she's grinning from ear to ear. The ultimate competitor (she won nearly every trivia competition at book club), Jay's not giving up just yet.

"*The Hunger Games* series, the *Immortal Souls* series, I've read that too. I've read so many series I can't even think."

You can hear Olivia—her future college roommate—in the background throwing out titles. Jay engages. *Long Way Down?* Yes. The Bible? "I don't read the Bible, which is kind of bad." *The Wild Robot?* "I've read that book!"

My favorite moment comes when someone asks about *The Giver*. Jay's perplexed face is priceless. "*The Giver?* What's that? That's a movie, ain't it?" At this point, you can hear me cracking up as I continue filming. "*I've seen the movie. I haven't read the book.*"

The sixty-six-second video ends shortly thereafter, but it's obvious that Jay could have kept going. There's still a huge smile on her face. Reflecting on this moment years later, I can't help but smile, too. Here are a few observations:

- There was so much joy in our classroom that day. We need more moments like this. Joy is good.

- Think about how many books Jay could name in one minute. Shouldn't we want that for all students? On the other hand, how would you feel if every student in your school could only rattle off the same three or four books (because that's all they had an opportunity to read)? Even worse, what if they couldn't name any?

- Jay entered high school with a positive reading identity, but it very easily could have faded, especially if had we followed our district's scripted curriculum, which made no room for novels of any kind. Instead, with daily time to read books of her choice, with relevant and rigorous literacy instruction, with the support of teachers, classmates, and community members, Jay continued to soar—academically, socially, and emotionally.

Clearly, Jay was "college ready," however we want to define that term. She had the stamina, fluency, confidence, vocabulary, and comprehension to push through boring reading passages on standardized tests. (Jay and her classmates crushed the ACT, outperforming their peers by 5.7 points on the English section and 4.4 points in reading.) Jay wrote clearly and compellingly, and she excelled as a public speaker, presenting at local events and national conferences. She cared deeply about her community.

So, what can we learn from Jay, one of the 99 percent who decided not to major in English? I would argue that the ability to read and write proficiently, to think critically, and to communicate clearly is more important than an understanding or appreciation of any specific text, no matter how much you or I may love it or how long it's been in the curriculum. Besides, as Reynolds points out in an interview in *The Guardian* (Knight et al., 2022), offering choice and making room for contemporary novels actually "preserves the classics" because, in doing so, we're creating lifelong readers who will, in time, explore a wide range of novels.

I would argue that the ability to read and write proficiently, to think critically, and to communicate clearly is more important than an understanding or appreciation of any specific text, no matter how much you or I may love it or how long it's been in the curriculum.

I care that all students graduate high school with the literacy skills needed to choose their path in life. I don't care if they've read *The Scarlet Letter*. I care that Jay had daily opportunities to read books that offered refuge from a real world full of mass shootings, natural disasters, and political polarization. Books that sparked writing and conversation. Books that reminded Jay that she mattered when people in power were trying to tell her otherwise.

So, here's my challenge to readers: Watch Jay's joyful video clip with your colleagues. Smile. And then continue the important conversations I know you're having.

View Jay's video clip

How many of our students can "name a book," let alone dozens? Do our students have ongoing opportunities to read books of their choice? If not, how can we make that happen? What skills do our students need for success in the next grade level, in college, and in life? Are we focusing on the right things? What should keep doing? What should we reconsider?

I remember having a similar conversation in the fall of 2015. Sure, we could have made *Lord of the Flies* "work." I know there are incredible teachers all over the country who find ways to bring classic novels to life. (And if you're one of those teachers, please share your secrets!) However, I kept coming back to this. *Was this the best use of our limited time?* No, it was not. *Was there a different way? A better way?* Yes, without a doubt.

DEVELOPING THE READ AND WRAP FRAMEWORK

I knew that I had just seventy-five days to help my students become passionate, proficient readers and writers, to help them navigate the traditional challenges of high school along with the newer struggles brought on by technology and social media. I knew that **every text and every task had to be intentional.** And so, like any good coach, I returned to the drawing board.

I wanted to maximize the time we had together. I wanted to prioritize the most important literacy skills and concepts. I wanted to increase the likelihood that students would choose to make reading and writing a part of their lives on the remaining 290 days of the year (and the following year, and the year after that). I wanted students to feel empowered and connected to our classroom community.

None of that would have been possible if I stuck with *Lord of the Flies* for the next eight weeks, or if I had been forced to follow a scripted curriculum that was not designed with any of our students in mind. At the very least, it would have been a lot harder. What did we do instead? What was our new game plan? The general adjustment was simple:

1. **We dedicated the first ten to twenty minutes of every class period to independent reading.**

2. **Following independent reading, our classroom came alive as we engaged in five to ten minutes of authentic writing, reflection, conversation, and community-building.**

Write
Reflect
Analyze
Participate

At the time, there was no name for this powerful post-reading routine, but I eventually developed an acronym (because educators love acronyms and we don't have enough of them). Daily time to **Read** and **WRAP . . . which stands for Write, Reflect, Analyze, and Participate.** *Let's wrap up our reading. Let's talk and (w)rap about our books.*

Being literate is not simply about reading in a vacuum; it's about reading and thinking and discussing and applying what we've read to our own lives and experiences. This is how WRAP has boosted independent reading in my classrooms. It makes reading a community-building, life-enhancing experience.

One of the reasons schools have moved away from independent reading is the lack of accountability. Students "drop everything and read" while the teacher grades papers. The reading eventually ends (assuming it even began), and the class moves on to the next activity. There are no opportunities to dig deeper or to check for understanding. When "independent reading" looks like this, I understand why schools abandon the practice. That's why the WRAP piece is so critical.

WRAP is where we dig into meaningful writing and analysis. Where we review conflict and point of view and setting. Where we write book reviews, alternate endings, and author letters. Where we craft sonnets and create beautiful one-pagers. Where we appreciate author's craft and gain inspiration for our own stories. Where we learn, once and for all, the difference between a comma, colon, and semicolon. Where we collaborate with classmates and engage in authentic conversations. Where we reflect on our progress and set goals for the future.

Was this revised game plan perfect? Of course not. Was our revised game plan better than the initial one, the one with the kids on the island? Without question. Our Read and WRAP routine was, and remains, one of our most powerful practices because it allows us to do the following:

- Honor the interests and needs of each individual reader
- Build community and create a sense of belonging
- Increase engagement and investment (and ultimately outcomes)
- Hold students "accountable"
- Begin each class period smoothly and calmly
- Establish credibility and earn students' trust and respect
- Serve as a positive reading role model

Furthermore, our Read and WRAP routine helps students:

- Process what they are reading and develop "troubleshooting" strategies
- Deepen their understanding of the text, world, and self

- Get more "reps" and practice with key literacy skills and standards
- Give and receive book recommendations
- Set and achieve personally meaningful goals
- Take charge of their reading and learning
- Experience success and build confidence
- Gain inspiration for their own writing
- Think more clearly, critically, and creatively
- Reset, reenergize, and refocus during what is often a grueling school day

Upon reflection, I believe that establishing our Read and WRAP routine in the fall of 2015 was the best pedagogical decision I have ever made. Since then, I have taught in three schools across five grade levels (8th through 12th grade) and two states. I am constantly making adjustments; units get tweaked, added, and removed all the time. However, Read and WRAP remains, and I now have a decade of evidence—attendance, behavior, reading attitude, writing quality, NWEA/MAP growth, ACT scores, and more— to defend the practice.

By prioritizing access, time, choice, and community, by keeping our students at the center, and by trusting the process, we all continue to get a little bit better every day.

CHAPTER 2

Simplifying Our Approach to Shift Reading Mindsets

Throughout the pandemic, I kept thinking about the parallels between literacy and exercise. For a multitude of reasons, students and educators alike were unable to read or exercise consistently. We lost access to our classrooms and libraries, gyms and studios. Our entire lives were upended, and our schedules were flipped upside down. *What was time?* Mentally, every day was a challenge. We lacked community, camaraderie, and connection.

Consequently, many of us lost the motivation to read (or exercise) and developed different, often less healthy habits and routines. Our goal, simply and understandably, was survival, so we spent our time in other ways. More Netflix binging. More gaming. More scrolling. Beautiful books sat unread on my shelves as I scrolled and stressed and scrolled some more. On my best days, days where I had bursts of energy and glimmers of hope, I opened my laptop and started writing. I tried my best to remain positive and to imagine a better future for students and educators. I kept returning to this thought: We have an incredible opportunity, and I would argue, an obligation, to help all students establish or reestablish a positive reading identity.

---

*We have an incredible opportunity, and I would argue,
an obligation, to help all students establish or reestablish a positive
reading identity.*

If we agree that:

1. Reading, like exercise, helps us live healthier, happier lives.
2. As educators, we want all students to live healthy, happy lives.
3. Every student enters our classroom at a different point in their literacy journey (confidence, experience, interests, ability, etc.).
4. The pandemic disrupted our literacy routines, and in some cases, widened literacy gaps.
5. Too many students, before and after the pandemic, do not read willingly, consistently, joyfully, or proficiently.

Then, this is also true:

6. Every school must make reading, and specifically our students' reading identities, a priority.

ESTABLISHING AND MAINTAINING POSITIVE READING IDENTITIES—IT CAN BE DONE!

Let's start here! Let's make this the goal. Let's do whatever it takes to ensure that every student in our classroom, and in our school, develops and/or maintains a positive reading attitude and establishes (or reestablishes) a consistent reading routine. If we keep this the focus, if we trust and commit to the process, then success—however you or I or "they" want to define it—will inevitably follow. Instead of taking short cuts, let's do this work the right way. Let's be relentless in our effort to move all students, over time, from the left-hand column to the right in the following table.

SHIFTING READING MINDSETS	
FROM THIS . . .	**TO THIS . . .**
"I'm not really a reader."	"Oh yeah, I'm a reader."
"Reading just isn't fun for me."	"Reading brings me so much joy."
"I only read when it's for school or for a grade."	"I read all the time, whether it's for a grade or not."
"Can I stop now?"	"Can we keep reading?"
"I'm not sure what books I like. I don't really read that much."	"Let me tell you about some of my favorite authors and genres!"

SHIFTING READING MINDSETS	
FROM THIS . . .	**TO THIS . . .**
Feelings of anxiety, insecurity, doubt, negativity, etc.	Feelings of confidence, pride, accomplishment, joy, etc.
"I hate reading."	"I love reading."
"Why would anyone want to read?"	"Why doesn't everyone like reading?"
"I don't have time to read."	"I *have* to make time for this, even though I'm busy."
Constantly on their phone	Willing and able to "unplug"
Struggles to navigate a library or bookstore	Enjoys frequenting a library or bookstore
"I haven't read a book since elementary school."	"I can't believe how many books I've read this year."
No interest in discussing their reading with anyone	Excited to discuss their reading with classmates, friends, family, etc.
Sticks with a book too long and/or gives up a book too easily	Knows when to abandon a book and when to push through
Struggles to find "good" books to read	Has "too many" books on their TBR list
Has difficult getting out of a reading "slump"	Has strategies to get back into a reading rhythm
Reluctant to read broadly	Willing to read a variety of genres
Shuts down at the first sign of boredom or difficulty	Willing to push themselves to read "harder" or more challenging books
Lacks stamina to read for extended periods of time	Consistently able to read for sustained stretches

The question, then, is how? Recognizing that this shift doesn't happen on their own or overnight, how can we support all students as they move from the left to the right? I know it's cliché, but it's true: we must have an unwavering belief in young people. Without that foundation, nothing else matters. Over time, we will get better at providing feedback and teaching figurative language. However, from day one, we can and should be one of our students' biggest champions. Here's what one of my favorite X (formerly Twitter) followers, best-selling author, and former educator Serrano (2016) said about teaching (emphasis mine):

> You have to learn the curriculum. You have to learn how to test the curriculum. You have to learn how to manage children who think they're grown-ups (and

how to manage grown-ups that behave like children). You have to learn how to weave differentiated instruction into the lessons you're building and also you have to learn what "differentiated instruction" means. You have to learn how to manage the tiny amount of time you get with each class each day. You have to learn when and how to discipline your students and you have to learn when and how to let them just exist as children, because they are children. You have to learn all of that. Every single piece. It's all important. *But you only ever really have to be good at one thing: Making sure your students know that you absolutely, no question, no doubt, for sure, 100 percent want to be in that particular classroom with those particular kids. If you do that, s*** usually works out.*

That's it. That's what it's all about. Of course, there are also concrete things ELA teachers can do to shift student reading mindsets, and we'll highlight several throughout this chapter. First and foremost, we must **know our purpose, know our role, know our data, and know our readers.** With this foundation in place, we're able to simplify our game plan, ideally with our Read and WRAP routine as the focal point.

KNOW OUR PURPOSE

Because of our nation's obsession with standardized testing, it is no surprise that many educators have lost their passion and purpose. The wrong mindsets and moves have been rewarded (and often, the wrong people promoted). Too many schools and districts continue to rely on the narratives spun by testing companies and outside influencers when making curriculum decisions. They stress over loaded terms like "learning loss" and "Lexile level" without questioning who invented them, what purpose they serve, or how those labels affect their students. They shame students who love graphic novels (along with the educators who support them). They spend money on "test-prep" T-shirts but claim there's no room in the budget for books. They force teachers to commit educational malpractice in the name of "data." They obsess over a mediocre-on-its-best-day standardized test, which leads to "quick fixes" and "fad diets" and, ultimately, disappointment. The programs and companies change, but the results stay the same. At best, there's a neutral effect; often, however, the programs lead to more harm than good. Students lose what little interest they had in reading while educators, without any agency or autonomy, are left feeling even more deflated and defeated.

My advice? Let's not let them reduce us all to numbers. Let's not lose sight of what this whole teaching thing should be about. Let's take time to reflect and reevaluate our values, beliefs, and practices, to remember why we teach.

Here's why I teach. I teach because I believe that all students deserve to become passionate, proficient readers and writers who can choose their path in life. Every day is an opportunity for us to get closer to that goal. I teach because our students deserve as many positive literacy experiences as possible. I teach because literacy transforms lives and unlocks doors. I teach because, as Jason Reynolds says, young people "are the antidote to hopelessness."

I teach for the heart-to-heart conversations and fist-bumps before the bell. I teach for the students who celebrate finishing their first book in May and those who devour a dozen by December. I teach for the quiet moments where the only sounds you hear are pages turning and the air conditioner humming. I teach for the loud moments where students are clamoring for a few extra minutes of reading time.

I teach for the moments of book love and book rage. I still remember when Rodrea, upon finishing *Long Way Down*, called me over to her desk and asked, "How (Jason) Reynolds gonna do me like that?!" When Olivia, in the middle of Tiffany Jackson's *Allegedly*, wanted to know, "So did Mary do it or not?!"

I still remember when Adriana pulled out a copy of Erika Sánchez's *I Am Not Your Perfect Mexican Daughter* from her bag. She had taken it home earlier in the week after spotting it in our classroom library. The beautiful cover and title caught her attention. "I started this yesterday and I'm already on chapter six. Julia's exactly like me. And her mom sounds just like mine." Adriana continued: "I never used to like reading before this year." What's the difference? "You just have better books."

I still remember when Ari pulled out her phone in class. My first instinct was to tell her to put it away and get back to reading. "No, I want to show you this email I sent." And so, as the rest of the class took out their notebooks, I crouched down to check out her phone. Ari had emailed Yale University. Even better, she had already received a response from one of their admissions officers, thanking her for expressing interest. If you have read *Dear Martin*, you've already made the connection. But, if you haven't, Justyce McAllister, the protagonist of Nic Stone's best-selling novel, is a high school senior bound for Yale. And because Ariana could see herself in Justyce, she saw Yale as an option.

Why do I teach? I teach to play a small but not insignificant part in a student's journey, to be that silly English teacher holding up a sign with their name on it, cheering them on from the bleachers. I teach because I love learning alongside young people as we seek to better ourselves and the world around us and because I love bonding with students over great books. I love playing the role of matchmaker and connecting students with books they struggle to put down. I teach for sequences like this one:

Helping Students Select Their Next Book

"Dr. Amato, what should I read next?"

Step 1: Knowing that student, I suggest two or three books I think they will enjoy.

Step 2: Student previews the contenders, picks one, and begins reading.

Step 3: Quick check-in during our WRAP time. "What do you think so far? Want to keep going or try another one?"

Step 4: Student decides to keep reading. (And if not, we revisit our "contenders" or find others.)

Step 5: Student continues to read and discuss the book.

Step 6: Student returns the book, grateful for the recommendation and ready to complete the process again.

KNOW OUR ROLE

On the most successful sports teams (think the 1990s Chicago Bulls or the 2000s New England Patriots), every player and coach understands and accepts their role. Sure, it helps to have a Michael Jordan or Tom Brady as the leader, but winning at the highest level requires contributions from everyone on the roster. In education, we cannot afford to operate with uncertainty. My advice for new teachers (and perhaps some veterans, too) is simple—clarify your role. As you prepare for your first year, confirm the following as soon as you can:

- **What is your daily schedule?** What time are teachers expected to arrive and depart? When is your lunch? When are your prep/planning period(s)?

- **What are you teaching?** What grade level(s)? What subject(s)? How many sections of each course? Are any sections co-taught? What are the anticipated class sizes?

- **How long are your classes?** This is arguably the most important question. Do you see each class fifty minutes every day? Ninety minutes every other day? If the schedule varies, how many minutes do you see each class over the course of a week?

- **What is your school's calendar?** When do you start and end the year? What "off days" and vacations are built into the calendar? How many PD/planning days are there? When are faculty and department meetings scheduled? Are there natural breaks between each quarter and/or grading period? What are the longest "stretches" without a break?

- **What does a student schedule look like?** It's important that we understand what school looks and feels like from our students' perspective, and how our ELA course fits into the bigger picture. How many courses are your students taking at one time? Four? Six? Eight? Is there an advisory period? Intervention block? What electives are offered? What time are they waking up in the morning? What time are they getting home?

- **What are expectations for staff members?** You may get a handbook from your school or district, but be sure to talk to colleagues, too. Ask what is required and what is recommended. Veterans know there is a big difference. Here are a few more questions to pose to members of your school's leadership team:

  - What is the pacing guide and/or scope and sequence?
  - What level of autonomy do teachers have regarding curriculum?
  - What are the school's homework and grading policies?
  - Are lesson plans submitted weekly? Monthly? Not at all?
  - What assessments will students take during the year? When?
  - What coaching and mentorship is offered to new teachers?

KNOW OUR DATA

I recommend that ELA teachers and teams create a "Literacy Dashboard" to capture a more complete picture of each student and to identity grade-level and whole-school trends. The dashboard doesn't need to be fancy (I typically use Google Sheets), but it can/should be comprehensive. Instead of relying on one number, such as the end-of-year state test score, our dashboard includes multiple data points for each student, including but not limited to the following:

- results from our reading attitude survey (administered three times annually)
- attendance (number of absences)
- behavior (number of office referrals and/or suspensions)
- grades (ELA specifically)
- overall GPA (across all classes)
- formal writing samples (scored internally by ELA department according to a 1-4 rubric)
- district benchmark scores (such as NWEA/MAP)
- state assessment scores (TN Ready, NJSLA, STAAR, CAASPP, MCAS, etc.)
- pre-ACT/ACT or PSAT/SAT scores

By the second or third week of school, after we've administered our first reading attitude survey and NWEA/MAP benchmark, our dashboard may look something like this.

STUDENT NAME	STATE TEST SCORE (PREVIOUS YEAR)	NWEA/ MAP RIT SCORE (CURRENT YEAR FALL)	NWEA/MAP PERCENTILE (CURRENT YEAR FALL)	ELA GRADE (PREVIOUS YEAR)	OVERALL GPA (PREVIOUS YEAR)	ATTENDANCE (ABSENCES PREVIOUS YEAR)
Student A	Approaching Expectation	215	43	70	2.5	16
Student B	Exceeding Expectation	247	96	98	4.0	4
Student C	Met Expectation	232	79	95	3.6	7

STUDENT NAME	BEHAVIOR (OFFICE REFERRALS PREVIOUS YEAR)	# OF BOOKS READ (PREVIOUS YEAR)	READING GOAL (CURRENT YEAR)	OVERALL READING ATTITUDE (CURRENT YEAR)	WRITING DIAGNOSTIC (CURRENT YEAR)
Student A	6	8	10	3	2
Student B	0	17	20	5	4
Student C	2	5	8	3	3

It's important to understand that everything is connected. Literacy and SEL. Reading and writing. Attendance and grades. Performance and behavior. All of it matters. We cannot "solve" anything in isolation. My hope is that by creating your own version of a literacy dashboard and discussing the questions in the following table, you and your colleagues are better equipped to address your school's unique challenges. Perhaps students and families are reporting significant mental health concerns. Perhaps there has been a noticeable decline in the quality of student writing. Perhaps there's a growing sense of apathy and indifference. Regardless, it's important for our ELA departments and literacy teams to gather relevant data instead of relying on what we think we're seeing in our classrooms or what we assume to be true about our students.

DATA POINTS FOR ELA TEAMS TO CONSIDER (PART 1)

What percentage of our students
- read proficiently?
- write proficiently?
- have access to high-quality, high-interest books?
- possess a positive literacy identity?
- read and write daily?
- enjoy reading and writing?
- feel connected at school?
- attend school consistently?
- are considered chronically absent?
- enjoy ELA class and participate consistently?
- have regular opportunities to share what they are reading and writing?
- have regular opportunities to process and discuss how they are feeling?
- feel safe, seen, and valued in our school, specifically our ELA classrooms?
- feel stressed and/or anxious frequently?
- believe they're appropriately supported and challenged in school?

The next step, of course, is using this data to inform what we do, primarily in but not limited to our ELA classrooms. For example, how should we respond if attendance is low and many of our students do not feel connected at school? How can our ELA team increase engagement and belonging? What if book access is a barrier? If so, perhaps we should address that first? What if test scores are high but the SEL data reveal that students report feeling extremely anxious and unhappy at school? How can our ELA department begin to improve student well-being? To that end, the following table provides additional questions for our literacy teams to discuss as we review data and develop a schoolwide game plan in both the short and long term.

DATA POINTS FOR ELA
TEAMS TO CONSIDER (PART 2)

- How does our literacy work tie into our school and/or district's mission, vision, and strategic plan?
- How are our students doing—socially, emotionally, and academically? How are we measuring student success?
- What goals and priorities does our ELA department have for the upcoming year? Do they make sense? Is there buy-in?
- What's the overall "vibe" in our school, specifically our ELA classrooms? How do we know?
- What's working in our ELA classrooms? What's not? What specific policies and practices seem to be producing positive results? What policies and practices seem to be causing harm?
- What does our school do to celebrate and recognize our readers?
- How does our school engage families and community members in our literacy efforts?
- Does our budget reflect a strong commitment to literacy?
- How much time do our students spend reading and writing—inside and outside of school?
- How much choice do students have in what they read? What percentage of texts are student-selected, teacher-selected, school-selected, district-selected, etc.?
- What are we doing to address student and staff well-being?
- Are we listening to our students and teachers? Are we making adjustments based on their feedback?
- Do our students and teachers have what they need to succeed? What's getting in the way?
- Are we finding ways to help all students and teachers explore their interests and passions? Are we highlighting students' and teachers' strengths or focusing more on their weaknesses?
- How can the rest of the school support our ELA department's efforts?

KNOW OUR READERS

Every fall, I look forward to the challenge of matching our students with books they don't want to put down. However, even with comfortable seating, ample book access, consistent time, supportive classmates, and a knowledgeable teacher offering recommendations, not all students embrace our reading routine right away. Again, each student is at a different point in their reading journey. **While we can all agree that labels suck, in my experience, many (but certainly not all) students fall into one of three reading categories: instant starters, bike riders, and smart skeptics.**

INSTANT STARTERS

Students in this group take off immediately. In fact, they don't even wait for the timer to begin reading. They know what genres and authors they like, and they have a plan. They can read . . . and read . . . and read without getting bored or tired. Students in this group pick up a new book during first-period English, sneak pages during their math lesson (I have to pretend to support the math teacher when they complain that "_____ never puts their book down"), stop by my room to read more at lunch, and then continue reading at home. When they return the following morning, our conversation sounds like this:

Me: "How's the book?"

Student: "I already finished it!"

Me: "What?! I assume you loved it?"

Student: "Yup. It was so good."

Me: "Did you even sleep?!"

Occasionally, the Instant Starters will ask for a recommendation: "Amato, what should I read next?" And we will head to the shelves and discuss their options. After a few minutes of browsing and chatting, they will return to their seat with a stack of three or four titles. Students in this group also join me in giving impromptu book talks and "selling" their favorites to friends and classmates.

"You have to read this one!"
"Oh, if you liked _____, then you're going to love _____!"

BIKE RIDERS

Many students in this group will tell you they enjoyed reading at one point. They can happily recall positive reading experiences from their childhood. However, as they got older and busier (and reading, for a variety of reasons, became laborious), books no longer fit into their lives. Therefore, it doesn't take much time for the Bike Riders to get back into a reading routine. The conversations, although different for each student, tend to have a similar rhythm. We will walk over to the bookshelves where I will ask a few questions:

"What books did you like last year? Or maybe the year before that?"
"What are some of your favorite books of all-time?"
"OK, so what are some of your favorite movies or TV series?"
"Graphic novels or poetry?"
"Realistic fiction or fantasy?"
"What do you think you are in the mood to read now?"
"Hmmm . . . okay. Here are three that I think you'll like. Check out the summaries and let me know if any of them look interesting."

A few minutes later:

Student:	"I'm gonna go with this one."
Me:	"Sweet! Great choice. Keep me posted. And if you end up changing your mind and want to grab another one, no worries."

It may take a few days or weeks, but eventually students in this group hit their stride. For them, reading is just like riding a bike, and hopefully we can push them to try longer and more challenging trails.

"I forgot how much fun reading could be."
"I haven't read this much since fifth grade!"
"My mental health is so much better now that I'm not on my phone as much."

SMART SKEPTICS

Students in this group are justifiably skeptical: *Why? Why reading? Why are we doing this? What's the point?* When educators say that "reading is important," they refuse to just take our word for it. They don't buy "because I said so." The Smart Skeptics need to see evidence. Students in this group, regardless of their reading ability, choose to spend their time in other ways.

"No offense, but I just don't like reading."
"None of these books are interesting."
"Can I do something else instead?"

Instead of getting frustrated, it's important that we remain patient and flexible with this group. Let's put our own egos aside and acknowledge that our students' hesitation is valid. Let's show our Smart Skeptics that reading is a worthwhile investment. Let's continue to build relationships, offer support, and be ready when they finally come around.

SIMPLIFYING OUR GAME PLAN

Over the past decade, I have learned to accept that there is no "perfect" approach or game plan. For the caregivers of young children reading this book, I recently heard Miss Rachel say that "there is no way to be a perfect parent, but there are a thousand ways to be a good one." The same can be said for teachers. I accept that teaching literacy is an incredibly complex and difficult task. I accept that there is never going to be enough time to read, do, teach, or cover it all . . . and that's okay. I accept that not every lesson will be perfect, and I take comfort in the fact that my students are reading and writing meaningfully every day. Instead of trying to do *everything* well (and thus setting myself up for failure and disappointment), I keep my focus here:

1. **Establish the Read and WRAP routine from day one and ensure that it continues to run smoothly throughout the school year.** This means we are clear in our expectations and consistent in our follow-through. We model an authentic reading lifestyle. We offer ongoing motivation and encouragement. We champion students and literacy daily. We cultivate a sense of belonging and community based on mutual respect. We adjust and adapt as needed.

2. **Maximize the "second half" of the block.** This means we prioritize key literacy skills, standards, and concepts (as determined by our school, district, and/or state). We are intentional with both our product and process. Every text, task, activity, and mini-lesson has purpose. We provide personalized support and intervention to help students achieve short-term and long-term goals (see below).

"FIRST HALF" ROUTINE	
Read	We start class with 10–20 minutes of independent reading.
WRAP	When the timer goes off, signaling the end of our reading, we jump into our WRAP prompt, which we typically try to limit to 3–7 minutes. (Longer tasks, however, may require additional time.)
"SECOND HALF" POSSIBILITIES	
Text Analysis	Analysis and discussion of print and non-print texts (articles, informational texts, speeches, TED Talks, memoir excerpts, poems, short stories, podcasts, charts, graphs, photographs, paintings, video clips, short films and documentaries, etc.).
Article of the Week	Inspired by Kelly Gallagher, the AoW has been a classroom staple for the past decade, and I will share my modified "AoW Sequence" in Chapter 4.
Vocabulary/ Word Study and Grammar Instruction	In Chapter 5, I'll share how we can integrate grammar instruction into our WRAP prompts. However, full transparency: I've struggled to find a way to "fit" vocabulary (and to a lesser extent, grammar) into our ELA block on a consistent basis. I'm open to any/all suggestions.
Targeted Mini-Lessons	Chunks of class time dedicated to teaching/re-teaching specific skills, standards, strategies, etc.
Extended Writing Tasks	In our classroom, students write every day (in addition to our informal quick writes, we're almost always working on a longer, polished piece). We'll share the first extended writing task of the year, "Ten Things I've Been Meaning to Say to You," in Chapter 4. From there, students write book reviews, literary analyses, personal narratives, narrative continuations, fictional short stories (often around "Spooky Season"), op-eds and argumentative research papers, original poems and poetry analyses, author and character letters, objective summaries, and much more. While students work on their drafts, we also study exemplars, collaborate, confer, reflect, self-assess, and more.

By the end of the first week of the school year, if not sooner, here is what our "first half" looks like in action.

STEP 1: WELCOME/GREETING

In the two to three minutes between classes, I stand at the door, greeting students upon arrival. As students enter our room, they find their seat and take out their independent reading book. A couple of students volunteer to pass out our composition notebooks. Once the bell rings and the last person enters, we review the agenda and goals for the day (which are displayed on the screen and written on the whiteboard), share any updates or announcements, and answer any questions from the group. From there, we are ready to jump into our Read and WRAP routine.

STEP 2: READ

My students and I finalize the exact number of minutes. *How much reading time does everyone want today? Think we can handle fifteen minutes? We're working on our argumentative essays, so is it okay if we cut reading time to ten today?* We tend to land between thirteen and seventeen minutes; ten is the minimum and twenty is the max (unless the class "bullies" me into extending it).

Before diving into our books, I usually preview our WRAP prompt, so that students can be thinking about it (character traits, conflict, theme, etc.) or looking for it (author's use of dialogue, figurative language, imagery, etc.) while they read. I dim the lights and set the timer, which is visible to everyone, and hit play on YouTube or Pandora. We prefer "chill," lyric-less music playing in the background, such as Lo-Fi Beats, classical music, "Coffee Shop" jazz, and more. It creates the right reading vibes and helps students who are overwhelmed by complete silence.

Once the timer is going and the music is playing, I circulate the room to make sure everyone is good to go. *Does anyone need a new book? Is someone still talking and distracting others? Does someone have their head down? If so, is there anything I need to know or can do to support?* As soon as everyone has begun reading silently, I find a spot in the middle of the room —where I am visible and able to get to any student quickly if necessary—and I join them in reading.

While there are some fantastic educators out there who prefer to confer with students during this time, I have found that (a) other students in the class are distracted by the noise, (b) I myself struggle to engage in a meaningful conversation while also trying to monitor the rest of the room, and (c) it's more important that I serve as a reading model during this time. For us, the conferring happens during our WRAP time.

Jarred Amato
@jarredamato

"Mr. Amato, I'm mad at you. Why'd the timer have to go off? I wanted to keep reading."
#englishteacherproblems

9:07 AM · Aug 31, 2016 · Twitter for iPhone

STEP 3: WRAP

Once the timer goes off, signaling the end of our reading time, I dog-ear my book, recirculate the room, and get a "status update" from the group.

"How's everyone doing?"
"Does anyone need a bookmark?"
"Who needs to finish the page they're on?"

I pass out sticky notes (our version of a bookmark) while some students attempt to sneak in a few final lines. As I bounce from table to table, my goals are simple:

1. Identify students who may want/need a quick conversation.
2. Provide positive reinforcement and words of encouragement.

"Great job today, y'all. Appreciate your focus and concentration. How are we feeling about our books? Does anyone want to share?"

At this point, students may decide to share out with the group.

"I started this book yesterday, and it's so good. Can I read the summary (or this one paragraph) to y'all?"
"Oh, that sounds interesting! Can I read it next?"
"I just finished _____ and loved it."
"I'm not feeling _____ so far. I may try a new book tomorrow. Does anyone have a recommendation?"

From there, we open to a clean page in our notebooks and dig into our WRAP prompt, which can be thirty seconds or thirty minutes long—and generally somewhere in between. (Chapter 5 outlines a wide range of WRAP prompts to share with your students.) We may **write** a letter to the author or one strong compound sentence

Quick tip: Depending on the class size, feel free to add more "structure" to these conversations, whether it's to "turn and talk" with a partner or a "music-pair-share" protocol that gets students moving and sharing with classmates across the room.

describing a central conflict in our book that uses a comma and FANBOYS correctly. We may **reflect** on our reading progress over the course of the year and revisit our reading goals. We may **analyze** how our respective authors develop a theme or use dialogue to reveal character. We may **participate** in intimate, small-group conversations or in a spirited, whole-class discussion.

READ AND WRAP FAQS

Here are a few common questions—and answers—regarding our Read and WRAP routine.

How do you grade WRAP responses? While a lot of our notebook writing is low-stakes, informal practice, there are times when we're working on longer, more "formal" tasks that may require multiple class periods to complete. I tend to grade the latter but not the former. I also assign a quarterly "Independent Reading" grade based on our notebook checks, teacher observation, teacher-student conferences, and student reflection.

What does a longer WRAP task look like in action? The prompt (for example, a letter/email to the author) is introduced on Monday, where students have an opportunity to write a draft in their notebooks (not graded). Throughout the week, students spend our WRAP time participating in a mini lesson, analyzing exemplars, receiving peer and teacher feedback, making revisions, completing a self-assessment, and so forth as they aim to have their finished product (in this case, a thoughtful, multi-paragraph letter that they could potentially share with the author) completed by Friday. The final draft is graded.

What if my ELA period is only forty-five minutes long? First step: See if you can advocate for a new schedule (especially if your school's data reveal that literacy is a priority). In the meantime, I still think there's room for Read and WRAP. Maybe it's ten minutes of reading with a short, focused WRAP prompt? That still leaves you thirty solid minutes. And maybe you start with three days a week? Again, there are always going to be tradeoffs—by making room for Read and WRAP, we're automatically removing something else (such as classroom discussion, which while fruitful, may not be as valuable).

How do you introduce Read and WRAP to families? Here's a sample letter that you can modify for your community:

Dear families,

We recognize that many of our students are not reading often outside of school—for a number of legitimate reasons. We also recognize that many students (and adults) are spending too much time online and in front of screens. As a school, we believe that one small but powerful way to support our students, families, and staff members, to improve our mental well-being and academic performance, and to reestablish a positive reading culture in our community, is to encourage ten to fifteen minutes of daily independent reading in our ELA classes. Through our Read and WRAP routine, students will have an opportunity to explore a wide range of high-quality, developmentally appropriate books and engage in meaningful writing, reflection, analysis, and participation. We appreciate all you do to nurture your child's reading life, and we encourage you to join us for our upcoming literacy programs and events, such as our book drive, book fair, Lit Buddies, and our community-wide book club. Please do not hesitate to reach out with any questions, and as always, happy reading!

What do you do if your school/district doesn't seem to support Read and WRAP? Keep on reading for the full answer.

SECURING READ AND WRAP APPROVAL

I have a feeling that you already believe in the power of independent reading and our Read and WRAP framework. (If that's the case, my hope is that this book strengthens your conviction and helps you elevate your game.) However, perhaps you or some of your colleagues are still a bit skeptical. (No hard feelings; I get it!)

Yeah, I agree . . . BUT . . .
There's not enough time,
BUT . . .
We just have too much to cover,
BUT . . .
I can't justify doing it every day.
I know independent reading is important,
BUT . . .
our admin just won't allow it.

These conversations need not be contentious. In fact, it is healthy for people to share different literacy visions and philosophies. My hope is that you work in a collaborative environment where folks are open to new ideas and willing to try new things, where folks are "borrowing" and "stealing" freely from one another, where there are "strong opinions, loosely held."

However, I recognize that not all teachers are so fortunate. When asking school or district leadership, "Do I have your support to move forward with daily independent reading in my classroom?," you can anticipate one of three outcomes:

Outcome 1 is ideal. It's an unequivocal YES. Everyone in is on board with independent reading. Everyone recognizes the practice as an integral part of our literacy approach. Everyone is working collaboratively to champion our readers. This is the dream. In this environment, students and educators have the space to flourish. *Clear eyes, full hearts, can't lose.*

Outcome 2 isn't perfect, but it works. It's a hard maybe. In this scenario, there's no consensus and perhaps even some skepticism about our Read and WRAP routine. The good news is that, in Outcome 2, you still have permission to move forward with independent reading, even if other teammates and/or school leaders remain unconvinced. Can it feel a bit awkward in department meetings when we're doing things differently than our colleagues? Sure, initially. Does this put a little more "pressure" on us to produce results? Unfortunately. However, be sure to keep the lines of communication open, continue to share your strategies and successes, and know that many colleagues will come around to independent reading when they're ready (or they won't, and that's okay, too). Regardless, you have a wonderful opportunity to read and write alongside your students—and that is 100 percent worth celebrating.

Outcome 3 is the most frustrating. It's essentially no. The administration states, in no uncertain terms, that there is no room for independent reading in our ELA classrooms. For those who have heard this directive, I am so sorry. And to the school and district leaders who refuse to support (or at least explore) this practice, please reconsider. In this scenario, we're left with three choices: (a) fall in line and accept the mandate begrudgingly; (b) close our door and do our thing anyway; or (c) continue to make our case and hope that we can eventually get permission to "pilot" Read and WRAP and conduct our own action research project.

While I am a fan of "asking for forgiveness, not permission," I recognize that not everyone is wired the same way. I also recognize that it feels much better when we head into a school year knowing we have the green light to move forward with independent reading. To that end, my advice is to explain how the Read and WRAP framework fits into your larger literacy vision and supports the goals/priorities your school and district already have in place. Be prepared to answer questions, alleviate concerns, and clarify misconceptions. Be willing to compromise (within reason) and work to find common ground (there should be plenty). For example, perhaps we stick to just ten minutes or start with three days per week. Perhaps we start every period with Read and WRAP but alternate between self-selected and whole-class texts. Perhaps we agree to collect data and keep the team up to date with successes and challenges.

I've been fortunate to work with school leaders like Mrs. Travis, Mr. Jackson, Dr. Woodard, Mr. Manuel, Mr. Lauricella, and Mrs. Risoli, all of whom leveraged their teacher's strengths, trusted their professional judgement, and empowered them to meet the diverse needs of their students. There were a few times in my career, however, where I had to teach in "defense" mode. I know firsthand how heartbreaking it is to have to do this work in isolation or in secret. How exhausting it is to keep at it without any resources or support. How infuriating it is to know that decisions are being made without students or educators in mind.

Although I empathize with school leaders who feel pressured to "follow orders," I empathize more with students who are repeatedly denied access, choice, and time to read in a nurturing environment. Who struggle to name their favorite book because every single one has been assigned. Who now associate reading with assessment and who only read "for a grade," if at all. If I'm forced to pick a side—doing what's best for students or doing what's convenient for adults —I will choose our students every single time.

CHAPTER 3

Transforming Principles Into Actions

Strategies to Increase Access, Promote Choice, Guarantee Time, and Build Community

Access. Choice. Time. Community. The words function as standalone nouns, but they're even more powerful when coupled with a verb. As literacy leaders, we transform the four principles into actions, day in and day out. We work tirelessly to *increase access* to high-quality titles. We *promote choice* as we encourage students to read often and read widely. We *guarantee time* for independent reading, recognizing the power of this ritual. We *build community* with care and intention.

In this chapter, we will break down these four essential actions or "moves" that allow us to unlock the magic of our Read and WRAP routine and set up our entire classroom for a "winning" school year. Specifically, we will show what it looks like and what it takes for ELA educators and teams to increase access, promote choice, guarantee time, and build community. Let's get right to it.

MOVE 1: INCREASE ACCESS

Access is essential. Without access to books, the chances of becoming an avid reader (or writer) are slim. I still remember reading Wong's 2016 article, "Where Books Are All But Nonexistent," in *The Atlantic*. It was the first time I had heard of the term "book desert," or a neighborhood with limited access to books. Wong cited a 2016 study from Neuman and Moland, who found "intense disparities in access to children's reading resources in Detroit, Los Angeles, and Washington, D.C.—even between a very poor neighborhood and a slightly-less-poor one within a given city." The researchers wrote, "When there are no books, or when there are so few that choice is not an option, book reading becomes an occasion and not a routine (Neuman & Moland, 2016)."

Read Wong's full article

After finishing the article, I was outraged . . . but also inspired. One line stuck with me: "Ultimately, giving kids access to books may be one of the most overlooked solutions." At the time, our district supported Project Based Learning, or PBL, so my wheels began to turn. *How could my students and I analyze the impact of book deserts in our community?* Soon, we were back in the classroom, reading and discussing the article:

- What are book deserts?
- Why are book deserts harmful?
- Why do you think book deserts exist?
- What can we do this year to solve this problem?
- What ideas or suggestions do you have?
- List any places where you currently buy or borrow books.
- List anywhere you go in the community that would benefit from more books.

And with that, Project LIT ("Libraries in the") Community was born. My students began to craft our mission, vision, and logo, and we set out to increase book access and spread a love of reading in our East Nashville community.

Our guiding "formula" was simple but effective: When we increase book access and improve reading attitudes, we see improved literacy outcomes. The opposite is also true. When students do not have access to high-quality books, it is difficult to improve reading attitudes, and thus harder to improve outcomes. Without access, or with limited access, our effort to nurture a nation full of passionate readers (and thus critical thinkers and eventually informed voters) becomes much harder (keep in mind, the "book banners" know this). It's like trying to start a band without any instruments, learning to ski without any snow, or opening a restaurant without any food or appliances.

Our guiding "formula" was simple but effective: When we increase book access and improve reading attitudes, we see improved literacy outcomes.

With access, however, anything is possible. Everything is possible. (The "book banners" know this, too.) Therefore, we must start here. All students deserve access to books. High-quality books. Serious and lighthearted books. Short and long books. Book of all genres and formats. Books that encourage students to fall in love with reading again or for the first time. Books that make students feel seen, heard, affirmed, and valued. Books that ignite imagination and creativity. Books that spark self-reflection and conversation. Books that educate and entertain. Books that promote empathy and action. Books that help young people grapple with big questions and ideas. Books that encourage students to write stories of their own. Books that students choose to pick up over their smartphone. Books they don't want to put down.

The cost of investing in these books, the cost of developing abundant, inclusive classroom and school libraries is nothing compared to the cost of not doing so. For a fraction of what we spend annually on standardized testing (in Tennessee, for example, Questar received $30 million per year to administer the state assessment, TN Ready), prepackaged curriculum, and computer programs, we could flood classrooms, schools, and communities with great books. I wish districts and states would follow the great Dolly Parton's lead. Did you know that one in ten US children under the age of five receive a high-quality, age-appropriate book each month (at no cost to the family) thanks to Parton's Imagination Library? My dream is to extend this initiative throughout elementary school and middle school (and, yes, even high school). However, it shouldn't be Dolly's responsibility. I'd love to see districts, states, nonprofits, and private businesses work together to provide every student, K–12, with a new book every month. My hypothesis is that the short-term and long-term return on this investment—for students, teachers, families, and the entire community—would be massive. (And if you end up piloting a program like this in your community, please keep me posted! I'd love to be involved.)

TIPS FOR INCREASING ACCESS AND "LEVELING UP" OUR CLASSROOM LIBRARIES

Even in the districts and states that continue to protect our students' right to read, there's still much work to be done to increase access. The same way we think about our readers (the instant starters, bike riders, and smart skeptics), I have found that our classroom libraries also tend to fall into one of three categories or levels:

> **Level 1 Library:** New teachers, for example, almost always start here. At this level, there are few, if any, books available for students to check out and read. Perhaps there is an inherited bookshelf full of outdated titles, but most students don't even notice it's there. There's a lack of quality and quantity. Impact on literacy attitudes and outcomes? Zero.

> **Level 2 Library:** Now we're talking! Multiple bookshelves. Wide range of titles. Lots of student favorites. Solid quality and quantity. Positive impact on attitudes and outcomes. Of course, there's always room for improvement, but at this level, independent reading can thrive. There are enough options, especially in tandem with the school library, for students to find *their* book.

> **Level 3 Library:** Hashtag Library Goals. This is where we all want to be eventually! The level 3 library isn't perfect, but it's pretty darn close. Quality *and* quantity. There are books for *every* reader—all beautifully displayed. The library looks and feels majestic. You know a "Level 3" library when you see one. Impact? Maximum.

Note: I think we need to add a fourth category, the "Dystopian Library." No, this library isn't full of dystopian novels like *The Hunger Games, Scythe, 1984,* and *Fahrenheit 451.* It's the library that is boxed up or off limits (with caution tape around it) or removed altogether.

From the *New Yorker* (Bethea, 2023):

> Brian Covey, an entrepreneur in his late thirties, came to pick up his daughter, who's in second grade, and his son, who's in fifth. His kids looked confused. "Did you hear what happened at school today?" his daughter asked. "They took all the books out of the classrooms." Covey asked which books. "All the books," she said.

> Covey went into the school classrooms to see what his children were talking about and found bookshelves papered over to hide the books.

> "Most teachers I know are in disbelief," Covey, who has worked as a substitute teacher, told me. "I can only imagine how heartbreaking it is for career educators to have to take kids' books away and what kinds of threats would have to be passed down to them so they'd feel they had no choice."

Here's the thing about these ridiculous book bans and challenges—even if they don't hold up, they've succeeded in further exhausting our educators and taking up what little time and energy they had left to write grants, coordinate author visits, and create bulletin board displays. They've succeeded in scaring educators. *Is my classroom library going to get me in trouble? Will I lose my job? Will I go to jail?* Tragically yet understandably, many educators have decided "it's not worth it" when considering adding a "offensive" or "obscene" (be sure check out the John Green quote in the sidebar) book to their shelves. *I can't take the risk.* I said it earlier, and I will say it again here—teachers should not feel like they're breaking the rules (or the law) to provide students with positive literacy experiences. This moment calls for courage from all of us, particularly the parents and policymakers who support public education and a healthy democracy.

This moment calls for courage from all of us, particularly the parents and policymakers who support public education and a healthy democracy.

AUTHORS RESPOND TO THE MOST RECENT WAVE OF BOOK BANS AND CHALLENGES

John Green

In *Offline with Jon Favreau* Podcast on April 16, 2023

"The argument is always the same, which is that somehow our children are going to be massively corrupted by encountering the reality of experience in a novel and encountering the reality of feeling. But of course, if anything is offensive in a novel and it's true, what's offensive is the world, not the novel.

I don't particularly think that using the word *f**** is obscene and I don't personally think that acknowledging the existence of human sexuality is obscene. I do think it's quite obscene that we're going to lose so many people to gun violence this year when we know how to reduce the number of people we lose to gun violence because everywhere else in the world has done it. I think that's obscene. And so if we're going to have these different definitions of obscenity, I think that we have to make room for each other and that's what librarians and teachers do. Librarians and teachers are the professionals that we have trained to make these decisions. To make decisions about how to educate our kids, to make decisions about what the books in our libraries should be, and I think we should trust them.

But also on a deeper level, you can't tell other people's kids what to read and then call yourself in favor of liberty. You can maybe tell your kids what to read, although they will reach an age where they decide for themselves, but you cannot order other people's kids to read this or that in school and not read that or this and call yourself a libertarian."

(Continued)

(Continued)

Meg Medina

"Stop the Madness: Book Banning Is Not the Answer" (2021)

"To pull books from a school library because of the discomfort they create in adults is a recipe for disaster. It erodes the trust young people have in the adults in their lives and pushes them to secrecy. It undermines the studied opinion of professional librarians and educators. It supports a false idea that there is one version of life that is acceptable. And, it denigrates the work of authors who are brave enough to name experiences that are difficult and real.

Every parent is entitled to engage with their child about what they read. They are always at liberty to ask for an alternative assignment in classrooms. That's fair.

But that is a far cry from asking libraries to pull material from shelves and to insist that no other child should choose to read a particular title because a parent or group deems something too sexual or vulgar or outside their own comfort or value system.

We are a varied community, with wildly diverse backgrounds, tastes, and experiences. If you find a book objectionable, don't read it. That's your right, and I respect it. It isn't more complicated than that. Just don't assume that you speak for everyone or that you have the right to demand a book's removal."

Ta-Nehisi Coates

PEN America Interview (Tolin & Coates, 2023)

"I think it's really, really, really important that while we highlight what is going on right now, we do not paint America as though there was some golden age of literacy and freedom of speech. I don't believe that has ever existed."

"I would say the enemies of equality, the enemies of freedom, have always recognized that the first thing you attack when you want to strip people of their rights is the imagination, the ability to imagine those rights in the first place. And books are just an excellent, exceptional, maybe our best technology for conveying that. . . .

"People who simply seek comfort, and people who come to education of all things, to seek comfort, don't make for good citizens. And they don't really make for mature adults, honestly. I think maintaining an imagination as it pertains to humanity in the world is the least you can do. And protecting that imagination is the least you can do."

So how do we take our classroom libraries to the next level (on a teacher's salary, no less)? How can we beautify our classroom libraries without going broke? The honest answer: It's not easy. At one point, my classroom library was at or approaching "Level 3," but following the pandemic and a cross-country move, it's closer to a "Level 2." I am 100 percent okay with that. I know that I am doing the best I can, and I am grateful that my students also have access to a wonderful school library. While we're missing out on some of the new releases, we have more than enough to work with.

RECOMMENDATIONS FOR TAKING OUR CLASSROOM LIBRARIES TO THE NEXT LEVEL

First and foremost: Be passionate. Be persistent.

Know what you have and what you need. What titles seem to fly on the shelves and end up in backpacks and homes? What stories and voices are missing from your library? What books are most popular around the country and on social media? Do your students need more comfortable seating options? Better lighting? More bookshelves?

Work with your students to develop your "wish list." Often, I'll create a quick Google Form survey: What books would you like to see added to our classroom library? Then, you can share that list online, in your email signature, and in conversations with friends and family, school and district leaders, businesses and organizations.

While we want to fill our bookshelves immediately, remember to focus on quality over quantity. If the books aren't going to be read, don't bother buying them. With that said, if you can find solid books on the cheap, go for it!

Partner with your librarian. A few questions to pose during your conversations: How can you best support your librarian? How can the two of you collaborate on projects or initiatives? Is there room in the library budget to order additional copies of student favorites? Are there existing partnerships with the local public libraries and/or digital resources that students can access?

Keep school and district leaders in the loop. Outline your literacy vision, explain how it benefits students, and connect it to your district's stated goals and priorities. Present the data in your literacy dashboard. Invite folks into your classroom and continue to share success stories—student reflections, surveys, videos, pictures, writing samples, parent emails, and the like. Ask to be included in the school budget process if you aren't already.

Network. In addition to sharing your vision with school and district leaders, reach out to local businesses, nonprofits, colleges/universities, and so forth. to see if they're interested in a partnership. I recommend developing a list of individuals and organizations in your community that truly care about literacy and young people. Reach out when you're ready and be sure to invite them to your book clubs and literacy events (which we'll get to later).

Have your "ask" ready. When adults and caregivers say, "How can I help?" or "What do you need?," you need to be ready. Maybe it's an online "wish list" with all of your students' favorites. Or maybe you'd like thirty-five copies of four titles. Or maybe you just want adults to donate food (for book club) or bean bags (because the school chairs are unbearable). Whatever your "ask," have it ready! See the graphic for inspiration.

Tell everybody. When you're passionate, people notice. Students will say, "Dr. Amato, that dude's a reader. He loves books." My

FIGURE 3.1 ● How can I support Project LIT Community?

How can I support Project LIT Community?

DONATE BOOKS to local chapters as we strive to build inclusive classroom libraries & secure class sets of Project LIT titles!

PROVIDE FOOD, including breakfast, snacks & refreshments for our book clubs!

CONTRIBUTE INCENTIVES, including prizes for trivia winners (books, gift cards, Project LIT swag, etc.)

INVEST TIME by spending an hour each month discussing a great book with our Project LIT students!

HOST SPECIAL LITERACY EVENTS, including field trips, author visits, book clubs on college campuses, etc.

SHARE YOUR NETWORK by connecting us to educators & organizations passionate about literacy & young people!

Contact your local chapter leader or email us at projectlitcommunity@gmail.com! Follow us on Twitter and Instagram at @projectlitcomm!

friends and family know it, too. Reading has a way of coming up in conversations. And occasionally, someone will even ask, "How can I help?"

Apply for grants. I've found the summer is a good time to write a grant or set up an online fundraiser. Yes, there will be rejections, but, as Wayne Gretzky likes to say, "You miss 100 percent of the shots you don't take." It only takes one or two to say yes to make a huge difference.

Order from First Book Marketplace. I cannot speak more highly of this nonprofit organization, its team, and its mission. First Book is a game-changer for teachers and schools who care about getting great books into the hands of kids.

Empower students in your book access efforts. As part of our PBL to eliminate book deserts and promote a love of reading in our East Nashville community, my students and I launched a book drive. To get support, we wrote emails to local organizations and community members and created a YouTube video that we shared on social media. As donations came in, we kept the quality titles to expand our classroom library and to distribute in our community, and we brought the outdated titles to our local used bookstore, taking the store credit to buy copies of the latest middle grade and YA reads.

Collaborate. Find your people—even if it's just one or two to start. If you're feeling isolated in your building (again, I've been there), try to connect with educators at nearby schools. If all else fails, try joining a social media community. Once you have your team, begin thinking about short-term and long-term goals. What will bring you joy? What's sustainable? What do your students have in mind? For example, here's how a team of four educators across multiple schools can work together to effect real change:

> **Step 1:** Each educator commits to securing a class set (or more) of one title over the summer —whether it's through an online fundraiser or school budget.

> **Step 2:** Each educator starts the year with one title. Students have the option of reading it during our Read and WRAP time (or at home) and discussing it with classmates at a lunchtime or after-school book club.

Step 3: The four educators then meet up at the end of every quarter to swap books and to share ideas, resources, and recommended activities.

Step 4: While each group will be reading the books at different points, it will be easy for the educators to set up cross-school conversations and collaboration throughout the school year. At a minimum, we've given our students an opportunity to read and discuss four incredible books for the price of one. Here's a chart (using four books I love) to help you visualize the "book swap":

	QUARTER 1	QUARTER 2	QUARTER 3	QUARTER 4
Teacher 1	*Born a Crime*	*Long Way Down*	*The Poet X*	*Scythe*
Teacher 2	*Scythe*	*Born a Crime*	*Long Way Down*	*The Poet X*
Teacher 3	*The Poet X*	*Scythe*	*Born a Crime*	*Long Way Down*
Teacher 4	*Long Way Down*	*The Poet X*	*Scythe*	*Born a Crime*

Start small but start somewhere. Change happens one book at a time, and you and your students will enjoy looking back at the journey and being proud of what you accomplished together. Additionally, as you and your students continue to grow as readers, writers, and leaders, the hope is that the adults in power (and in charge of the budgets) step up and support you.

Remain a reader. Knowing our books does not require reading all of them. Start by reading alongside your students. Share your reading journey with students and colleagues. Be "in it" with your readers. They will appreciate your vulnerability and authenticity.

Remember: it's okay to dream big. In an ideal world with an unlimited budget, what would your classroom look like? Take a moment or two to visualize it. (My dream classroom feels like a cozy coffee shop.) Then, think about the steps it will take to get there. Consider all the angles, too: space, lighting, art on the walls, snacks—there's nothing out of bounds.

MOVE 2: PROMOTE CHOICE

Like access, choice is essential. Put simply:

- Many of today's students lack motivation (for a variety of reasons).

- Choice (in particular, the ability to choose from a wide range of high-quality options) increases motivation and engagement.

- When students are motivated, they are more likely to put forth their best effort and to embrace feedback.

- Greater effort, coupled with effective teaching and coaching, leads to improved performance over time.

Note that when I talk about choice, I don't mean a free-for-all where students select books at random. Think of it more as guided or curated choice; at first, we as the knowledgeable adults provide quality, developmentally appropriate options (another reason why access is so critical). As students begin to take ownership of their reading and learning, we can release more of the book selection responsibility to them.

Allowing students choice in what they read is the antithesis of compliance and control that is so often part of traditional instruction. This is not about "Here, read this and answer these questions." Instead, it's about building and sustaining intrinsic motivation, honoring students' reading preferences, and guiding them in ways that nurture critical thinking, creativity, and conversation.

Allowing students choice in what they read is the antithesis of compliance and control that is so often part of traditional instruction.

Yes, there is value in shared texts: poems, plays, short stories, speeches, articles; and whole-class novels when they are done well. However, it is difficult, if not impossible, to improve students' literacy attitudes and identities when they are always required to read the same book at the same pace and respond in the same way, when *every* text and task is determined by their teacher or school.

Many educators ask, "What percentage of texts should be teacher-selected vs. student-selected?" I don't know if there's a perfect ratio. But I do know this: student choice must be part of the equation. I've administered dozens of reading surveys over the past decade, and all graphs look nearly identical to the two you see here. (Note: 1 = strongly disagree and 5 = strongly agree.)

FIGURE 3.2 ● "I like to choose what book I read" Graph

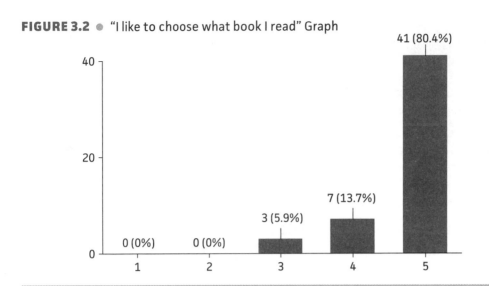

FIGURE 3.3 ● "I like when a teacher chooses what book I read" Graph

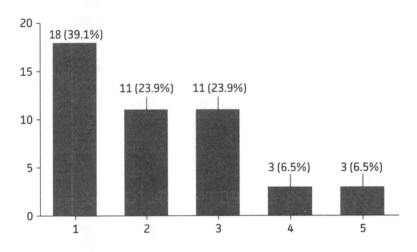

Here are a few additional points around choice worth reiterating:

● We cannot assume that all students know how to choose well. We have a responsibility to help students develop their reading habits (how to preview books, how to push through, when to abandon, etc.) and expand their reading preferences.

● Sometimes we can actually give students "too much" choice. Think about how hard it can be to pick a movie on Netflix or to decide on a restaurant for dinner. What do we do in those situations? Try to narrow our options.

In the classroom, we can put together mini stacks of three to five titles and encourage students to pick one from there. We can display trending titles on bulletin boards. We can feature popular titles prominently in our classroom library.

- Is it okay for students to reread books? Yes! Is it okay for students to read manga and graphic novels? Yes! Is it okay for students to read books "below their level" (whatever that means)? Yes! As we build relationships, establish trust, and instill confidence, students will often expand their interests and begin to read more broadly. Let's not turn them away.

- Can we eventually nudge students to read "harder" books? Can we eventually encourage students to try different genres? Of course!

- Students don't need to read the same text to practice the same skills. Whether they're reading *Pride* by Ibi Zoboi or *Pride and Prejudice* by Jane Austen, students can still analyze literary elements, craft a book review, or rewrite a scene from a different point of view.

- Let's offer students choice in *where* they read (within reason, of course). Think about some of your favorite reading spots at home. Couch? Bed? Hammock? The reading experience should be comfortable, not painful, in both a literal and figurative sense.

What advice would you offer new English teachers? Here's what my high school students in the spring of 2019 said:

- *Let your kids pick books relevant to our lives, what we see and go through every day.*

- *Out with the old and in with the new. (Don't force kids to read the same book you read in high school; give them options to pick from.)*

- *Let your students decide what they should read, but make sure the books have meaning.*

- *Make your kids read more. Give them good books and more options. Read with them and make it fun.*

- *Try to find books that match their interest and/or their personality.*

(Continued)

(Continued)

- *Really get to know your students and let them pick the books. Students won't love reading if they're forced to read books they aren't interested in.*

- *Take your students' suggestions into consideration.*

- *Don't be afraid to go outside the usual reading material.*

- *Read relevant books.*

Notice a theme? I certainly do. Here's one final comment that reminds me, and hopefully all of us, that this work matters. My goodness, it matters. *"Thanks for allowing me to be in Project LIT. You were one of the teachers who cared."*

READ WIDELY, READ OFTEN

One of our classroom mottos is *to read often and to read widely*. Let's start with the first part—*to read often*. We know that good things happen when we (students and teachers) read all the time, so why not make that our focus? Let's be relentless about helping every single person in our school get "back on the bike" and reading often (without worrying too much about what everyone is reading). Then, as students get more comfortable and competent, we can push one another to read more widely and expand our reading palates. We can still honor student choice while encouraging them to explore contemporary and classic texts, poetry and prose, fiction and nonfiction. Ultimately, we want to expose students to a wide range of genres, themes, and perspectives—not only because it will help them succeed in future English classes and perform better on standardized tests (although it will) but also because being a well-rounded reader helps one become a well-rounded individual.

Have students keep track of their "Reading Journey" throughout their middle school and/or high school career. How many books did they read each year? Is the number going up or down, or staying flat? What genres have they enjoyed? How have their reading tastes and preferences evolved? Share Reading Journeys with their next-year teachers, too.

For example, the following table shows a snapshot of one eighth grader's reading over the course of the school year. By June, this student read more than a dozen books across several genres—memoir, mystery, horror, tragedy, drama, dystopian, romance, novel in verse, realistic fiction, graphic novel, and so forth—some old, some new, a few required, many self-selected. All powerful and profound. Will all student lists look this impressive right away? Of course not. However, I don't think it's unreasonable for us to expect all students to get to this point (reading more than ten books per year across multiple genes) eventually. With our guidance, passion, and expertise, we're able to push students to read more frequently, proficiently, and diversely.

AN EIGHTH GRADER'S READING JOURNEY

TITLE	AUTHOR	GENRE
Scythe	Neal Shusterman	Dystopian
Night	Elie Wiesel	Memoir
The Graveyard Book	Neil Gaiman	Fantasy/Horror
I'm Glad My Mom Died	Jennette McCurdy	Memoir
The Sun Is Also a Star	Nicola Yoon	Romance
Fahrenheit 451	Ray Bradbury	Dystopian
A Good Girl's Guide to Murder	Holly Jackson	Mystery/Thriller
Romeo and Juliet	William Shakespeare	Drama
Long Way Down	Jason Reynolds	Novel in Verse
Speak	Laurie Halse Anderson	Graphic Novel
Superman Smashes the Klan	Guen Luen Yang	Graphic Novel
The Inheritance Games	Jennifer Lynn Barnes	Mystery/Thriller
It's Trevor Noah: Born a Crime (Adapted for Young Readers)	Trevor Noah	Memoir
For Every One	Jason Reynolds	Inspirational Poem

This student started the year with *Scythe*, a classroom favorite for years now, before moving into *The Graveyard Book* to celebrate "Spooky Season." Sandwiched in between was *Night*, a required text that we read together over the course of a few weeks in the fall. This student was engrossed with McCurdy's memoir, bringing a copy in from home and then sharing with me and others when they were finished, and loved getting to know Daniel and Natasha in Yoon's contemporary love story. Our class enjoyed analyzing Bradbury's dystopian classic and watching the film adaptation before winter break. In January, this student read *A Good Girl's Guide to Murder* (thanks to several student recommendations) before our class jumped into *Romeo and Juliet* in early February (I intentionally had us read it around Valentine's Day). We had a blast performing the play, reading aloud the modern English version, which was printed side by side with the original.

From there, this student took my suggestion and read Reynolds's *Long Way Down*, which includes so many fascinating connections to Shakespeare's tragedy, including family and friendship, love and loyalty, fate vs. free will, the effects of trauma on the adolescent brain, the power of peer pressure and following "the rules," gun (or sword) violence and revenge, the brilliant writing styles, and so much more.

In March, as we set reading goals for the final trimester, this student decided to branch out and try a new genre, reading two outstanding graphic novels, *Speak* and *Superman Smashes the Klan*. (We also had a blast analyzing poems during our "Poetry Madness" unit that coincided with the NCAA Basketball Tournament.) During April's "testing season," which included unnecessary stress and abbreviated schedules, they opted for a fun, twisty read (*The Inheritance Games*). In May, they loved exploring Trevor Noah's memoir, *Born a Crime*, and in June, we enjoyed a class read-aloud of Reynolds's *For Every One*, one of my favorite end-of-year rituals.

CLASSROOM LIBRARY RECOMMENDATIONS

In order for students to read widely and read often, we need to provide access to a wide range of titles and genres. Students can only read what's available to them; our responsibility then is to place quality options in front of their face (often quite literally). If we don't, telling students to "just read it" becomes a lot harder. The following list is meant to be a starting point—but just that. This list of recommendations for middle and high school readers can also be found on the online companion, too, if you want to print out a quick reference guide.

GETTING STARTED: RECOMMENDED TITLES FOR MIDDLE GRADE (MG) AND YOUNG ADULT (YA) READERS

	RECOMMENDED TITLES
NOVELS IN VERSE	**6–8:** *Alone* by Megan Freeman, *Before the Ever After* and *Brown Girl Dreaming* by Jacqueline Woodson, *Booked* and *The Crossover* by Kwame Alexander, *Full Cicada Moon* by Marilyn Hilton, *Inside Out and Back Again* by Thanhhà Lai, *Land of the Cranes* by Aida Salazar, *Other Words for Home* by Jasmine Warga, *Red, White, and Whole* by Rajani LaRocca, *Starfish* by Lisa Fipps, *The Canyon's Edge* by Dusti Bowling.
	9–12: *Clap When You Land* and *The Poet X* by Elizabeth Acevedo, *Home Is Not a Country* by Safia Elhillo, *Long Way Down* by Jason Reynolds, *Me (Moth)* by Amber McBride, *Punching the Air* by Ibi Zoboi and Yusef Salaam, *Shout* by Laurie Halse Anderson, *Solo* by Kwame Alexander, *White Rose* by Kip Wilson.

	RECOMMENDED TITLES
GRAPHIC NOVELS AND GRAPHIC MEMOIRS	**6–8:** *A First Time for Everything* by Dan Santat, *El Deafo* by Cece Bell, *Frizzy* by Claribel Ortega, *Hoops* by Matt Tavares, *New Kid* series by Jerry Craft, *Play Like a Girl* by Misty Wilson and David Wilson, *Roller Girl* and *When Stars Are Scattered* by Victoria Jamieson (and the latter with Omar Mohamed), *Swim Team* by Johnnie Christmas, and *They Called Us Enemy* by George Takei, Justin Eisinger, Steven Scott, and Harmony Becker.
	9–12: *Almost American Girl* by Robin Ha, *American Born Chinese, Dragon Hoops*, and *Superman Smashes the Klan* by Gene Luen Yang, *Dancing at the Pity Party* by Tyler Feder, *Heartstopper* Series by Alice Oseman, *Maus* by Art Spiegelman, *Speak* by Laurie Halse Anderson and Emily Carroll, *I Am Alfonso Jones* by Tony Medina, John Jennings, and Stacey Robinson, *Hey, Kiddo* and *Sunshine* by Jarrett Krosoczka, *The March Trilogy* by John Lewis, Nate Powell, and Andrew Aydin, *The Prince and the Dressmaker* by Jen Wang.
DYSTOPIAN	**7–12:** *Scythe* and *Unwind* by Neal Shusterman, *Divergent* by Veronica Roth, *Fahrenheit 451* by Ray Bradbury, *Legend* by Marie Lu, *Nineteen Eighty-Four* by George Orwell, *Nyxia* by Scott Reintgen, *Ready Player One* by Ernest Cline, *Shatter Me* by Tahereh Mafi, *The Giver* by Lois Lowry, *The Hunger Games* by Suzanne Collins, *The Marrow Thieves* by Cherie Dimaline, *The Maze Runner* by James Dashner, *Uglies* by Scott Westerfield.
"ALL THE FEELS"	**7–12:** *All My Rage* by Sabaa Tahir, *Aristotle and Dante Discover the Secrets of the Universe* by Benjamin Alire Sáenz, *A Very Large Expanse of Sea* by Tahereh Mafi, *Chaos Theory, Jackpot*, and *Odd One Out* by Nic Stone, *Furia* by Yamile Saied Mendez, *Love from A to Z* by S.K. Ali, *Opposite of Always* by Justin Reynolds, *To All the Boys I've Loved Before* and *The Summer I Turned Pretty* by Jenny Han, *The Fault in Our Stars* by John Green, *The Henna Wars* by Adiba Jaigirdar, *The Sun Is Also a Star* by Nicola Yoon, *The Poet X* by Elizabeth Acevedo, *They Both Die at the End* by Adam Silvera, *Today Tonight Tomorrow* by Rachel Lynn Solomon.
REALISTIC FICTION	**6–8:** *A Good Kind of Trouble* by Lisa Moore Ramée, *Black Brother, Black Brother* by Jewell Parker Rhodes, *Blended* and *Out of My Mind* by Sharon Draper, *Dress Coded* by Carrie Firestone, *Efrén Divided* and *Falling Short* by Ernesto Cisneros, *From the Desk of Zoe Washington* by Janae Marks, *I Can Make This Promise* by Christine Day, *Maybe He Just Likes You* by Barbara Dee, *Stand Up, Yumi Chung* by Jessica Kim, *The Epic Fail of Arturo Zamura* by Pablo Cartaya, *The Remarkable Journey of Coyote Sunrise* by Dan Gemeinhart, *The Shape of Thunder* by Jasmine Warga, *The Stars Beneath Our Feet* by David Barclay Moore, *The Track* Series by Jason Reynolds.
	9–12: *All American Boys* by Jason Reynolds and Brendan Kiely, *Dear Martin* by Nic Stone, *Here to Stay* by Sara Farizan, *In the Wild Light* and *The Serpent King* by Jeff Zentner, *Looking for Alaska and Turtles All the Way Down* by John Green, *Patron Saints of Nothing* by Randy Ribay, *Rez Ball* by Byron Graves, *Speak* by Laurie Halse Anderson, *The Hate U Give, Concrete Rose*, and *On the Come Up* by Angie Thomas, *This Is My America* by Kim Johnson, *We Are Not from Here* by Jennifer Torres Sanchez.

(Continued)

(Continued)

	RECOMMENDED TITLES
CONNECTION TO HISTORY	**6–8:** *A High Five for Glenn Burke* by Phil Bildner, *A Long Walk to Water* by Linda Sue Park, *Clean Getaway* and *Fast Pitch* by Nic Stone, *Finding Junie Kim* by Ellen Oh, *Front Desk* series by Kelly Yang, *Ghost Boys* and *Towers Falling* by Jewell Parker Rhodes, *Ophie's Ghosts* by Justina Ireland, *Refugee* (among others) by Alan Gratz, *The Door of No Return* by Kwame Alexander, *The Parker Inheritance* by Varian Johnson, *The War That Saved My Life* by Kimberly Brubaker Bradley, *We Dream of Space* by Erin Entrada Kelly. **9–12:** *Black Birds in the Sky* by Brandy Colbert, *Born a Crime* by Trevor Noah, *Code Name Verity* by Elizabeth Wein, *Just Mercy* by Bryan Stevenson, *Fever 1793* by Laurie Halse Anderson, *Like a Love Story* by Abdi Nazemian, *Salt to the Sea* (among others) by Ruta Sepetys, *The Black Kids* by Christina Hammonds Reed, *The Book Thief* by Markus Zusak, *The 57 Bus* and *Accountable* by Dashka Slater, *Victory. Stand!: Raising My Fist for Justice* by Tommie Smith, Derrick Barnes, and Dawud Anyabwile, *We Are Not Free* by Traci Chee.
MYSTERY & THRILLER	**7–12:** *Ace of Spades* by Faridah Àbíké-Íyímídé, *A Good Girl's Guide to Murder* by Holly Jackson, *Firekeeper's Daughter* by Angeline Boulley, *Monday's Not Coming* (among others) by Tiffany D. Jackson, *One of Us Is Lying* (among others) by Karen McManus, *Sadie* by Courtney Summers, *Spy School* by Stuart Gibbs, *The Inheritance Games* by Jennifer Lynn Barnes, *Promise Boys* by Nick Brooks, *Truly Devious* by Maureen Johnson.
FANTASY	**6–8:** *Amari and the Night Brothers* by B.B. Alston, *A Wish in the Dark* by Christina Soontornvat, *Healer of the Water Monster* by Brian Young, *Nic Blake and the Remarkables* by Angie Thomas, *The Girl Who Drank the Moon* by Kelly Barnhill, *The Lightning Thief* by Rick Riordan, *The Jumbies* by Tracey Baptiste, *The Marvellers* by Dhonielle Clayton, *Tristan Strong Punches a Hole in the Sky* by Kwame Mbalia, *When You Trap a Tiger* by Tae Keller. **9–12:** *An Ember in the Ashes* by Sabaa Tahir, *Children of Blood and Bone* by Tomi Adeyemi, *Elatsoe* by Darcie Little Badger, *Eragon* by Christopher Paolini, *Legendborn* by Tracy Deonn, *Raybearer* by Jordan Ifueko, *Red Queen* by Victoria Aveyard, *Six of Crows* by Leigh Bardugo, *The Sunbearer Trials* by Aiden Thomas, *This Poison Heart* by Kalynn Bayron.

MOVE 3: GUARANTEE TIME

Our students deserve time. Time to think. Time to write. Time to reflect. Time to dream. Time to laugh. Time to create. Time to read. If we value our Read and WRAP time, if we make it "sacred," students will come to appreciate it, too. Initially, some will find this routine uncomfortable or intimidating and thus attempt to resist. Don't take this personally! (I know I used to.) Instead, remember that there's so much we don't know about their reading journey up to this point in life. And then let's work actively to invite students into the routine. One way is to use a timer and make it visible. We start with ten minutes and gradually extend the time as students develop their "reading legs." I also solicit feedback and adjust accordingly.

"How much time do y'all want today?"

"We've been great with ten minutes; think we should bump it up?"

"Let's take a vote—ten or fifteen minutes? Looks like we're split, so let's go with twelve."

"I'm excited for y'all to finish your projects today! Is it okay if we keep our reading time to ten today?"

"Gosh, this rainy day is perfect for reading. Everyone cool if we just keep going?"

"I noticed we're getting a little distracted lately. How's everybody feeling? Wanna talk about it?"

"Amato, I need to finish this chapter! Five more minutes, please!"

Again, we know that many of our students are not reading consistently, if at all, outside of school. In a seven-hour school day, we can't carve out ten to twenty minutes for independent reading? If not in our ELA classrooms, then when? Of course, we want to make time for all of it—reading, writing, speaking, and listening—but reading volume, a huge predictor of post-secondary success, must be a priority. For those who remain unconvinced, here's a suggestion: observe an ELA class every day for an entire week, documenting a minute-by-minute breakdown. How many minutes do students spend reading? How many minutes do students spend writing? How many minutes does the teacher spend talking or lecturing? How many minutes do students spend engaged (or disengaged) in productive (or unproductive) conversations? How much "down" time is there? This exercise isn't an attempt to place judgment. Rather, it's to show how easily we can "find" ten to fifteen minutes per day in many of our classrooms. (And even in the all-star classrooms where every second is accounted for, it's worth considering where/how to make room for independent reading.)

MOVE 4: BUILD COMMUNITY

We know that independent reading is a silent, solitary activity. We also know that students tend to perform best when they're connected to their classmates and feel part of a community. This is why people join running and biking clubs and participate in group workout classes. It feels good to work hard alongside good people.

What does it take to build community? Gosh, so many things. (Who said this teaching thing was easy?) High emotional intelligence. A sense of humor. Strong communicational skills. Empathy and humility. A willingness to reflect and adapt. The list goes on. **Community-building is more art than science, but I believe that educators who are successful in this area tend to be consistent, intentional, passionate, patient, and respectful.** Let's look at each of these traits in the context of an ELA classroom.

Consistent: Middle and high school students are forced to adjust to a different teacher and different set of rules every period. It's not easy. (Try shadowing a student for an entire school day; it will be an eye-opening experience.) Recognizing that students struggle with mixed messages and inconsistent expectations, it's critical that we set clear and consistent policies and procedures in line with schoolwide norms and our own philosophical beliefs. In our classroom, for instance, our agenda is visible (both on the board and on one of our slides), and we take a moment to review the "game plan" for the period. We start every day the same way—with our Read and WRAP routine—which eliminates potential confusion and anxiety or the dreaded question, "What are we doing today?"

Students also know that there is absolutely no talking during our independent reading time. It's one of our only nonnegotiables. The only sounds you typically hear are the light background music playing, pages turning, and AC humming. Once the timer goes off, though, laughter and lively banter are accepted, if not encouraged. Students don't need each of our classrooms to look and feel the same; they just need each of us to be consistent.

Intentional: Everything we do should have a clear purpose and focus. While this is obviously important in our planning, it also applies to the physical space. While our classrooms don't need to look Pinterest or Instagram worthy, a cluttered, chaotic classroom can be distracting and anxiety-inducing. My goal is to create an inclusive and inviting space, literally and figuratively, where all students can be themselves and be their best. I love spending time in my classroom at the start of each year (and on the teacher planning days we occasionally get before/after a break). I put on a podcast or playlist and start wiping desks, organizing shelves, reorganizing bins, and purging the unnecessary paperwork that has found its way into drawers and cabinets. A few hours later, the room is in a great shape and I feel fantastic.

We all have our own style and approach, but my advice is this— be intentional. If we're serious about creating the right reading environment, what do we want our classroom to look like? Where do we want to set up our bookshelves (and how do we want to organize our books)? Where should we place the teacher desk? How do we want to arrange our student desks and tables?

Do we have comfortable seating options? What lighting and furniture should we look to add? What about our bulletin boards and door displays?

The classroom "makeover" does not need to happen overnight. My room remains a work-in-progress. (This is a personal decision, but I am no longer willing to spend any of my own money on classroom upgrades.) Nonetheless, there are still several ways you and I can transform our classroom space. We can see if there's room in the school budget. We can contact local organizations who may be willing to help out, and we can stay on the lookout for grant opportunities. We can swap out furniture with a colleague down the hall, and we can check in with the fantastic art teacher to see what we can paint. We can reach out to friends and family on Facebook, and we can monitor online marketplaces and local yard sales. Finally, we can also empower our students to see what ideas and suggestions they have.

At a minimum, we can and should be intentional with our bulletin boards and door displays. Here are a few possibilities to help us spark conversation, center students, and establish community:

- **Wall of Fame:** Our young people are so incredibly talented, which is why we need to display their writing and artwork prominently. *"Oh, I can't believe you put this up!" "Let me show y'all my poem!" "Who drew this? It's amazing!"*

- **Author Spotlight:** One option is to highlight a new author each month. The visual would include a picture, brief bio, powerful quote, and their books (along with anything else you and your students would like to add). Another option is to create a permanent display, where students continue adding their favorite authors throughout the year. *"Oh, we have to put _____ on there!" Can I add _____? I just finished their book, and it was incredible." "I didn't realize _____ had written so many books. I need to try one."*

- **Recommended Reads:** We print out the covers (or write the titles on index cards) of all the books we've read and loved (and thus recommend to others). I can't tell you how many conversations this display has started over the years. *"Oh, I've read this one . . . and this one . . . and this one . . . and this one!"* It also helps students determine what to read next. *"Have you read _____? What about _____? Ohhhh, you have to read _____!"*

- **"What _____ Is Reading":** You've probably seen variations of this display, where each faculty member lists the book they're reading at the moment (usually outside their door). Simple but super effective. I've done something similar in the classroom, where I write each student's name on the board, and they come up and write the title of their current read next to it.

- **Book Reviews, One-Pagers, and Book/Character "Faceoffs":** We'll share our list of WRAP prompts in Chapter 5, but three assignments (book reviews, one-pagers, and book/character "faceoffs") work especially well for classroom displays.

- **Book Covers on Lockers:** For those looking to dream big, try beautifying (or should I say "book-i-fying"?) your school's lockers. Shout out to award-winning educator and Project LIT chapter leader Danielle Monock for the inspiration!

PHOTO 3.1

Photo by Danielle Monock

Passionate: Our energy, and specifically our passion for reading and writing, is contagious. Our students may not admit it, but they're paying attention. They notice the way we talk about books—the ones that keep us up past our bedtime and the ones that fall flat. They notice the way we praise our favorite authors and celebrate new releases. They also notice (and lose respect for) those who do not practice what they preach—those who spend reading time grading papers or responding to email. If we want our students to be excited about reading, we sure as heck better be excited, too. Being passionate doesn't mean being perfect. We don't need to read one hunred books a year to model a rich reading life. In fact, students appreciate our authenticity and vulnerability:

"I'm not sure why, but I've been in such a reading slump lately. Do any of you have a recommendation for me?"

"Have y'all ever had a day where you had to go back and reread the same page a few times because your mind was wandering? That just happened to me."

"I've had a really hard time getting into this book. The reviews are excellent, but I think I'm going to abandon it."

"The last book I read just wrecked me. I have no idea what to read next because I don't think anything is going to be as good."

"I hate that I find myself on my phone all the time. I'm really going to try to unplug more over the next month and see how it makes me feel."

Patient: Good leaders attempt to shield teachers from the external pressures, but often, they feel the heat, too. Suddenly, everyone's in a rush. *We've gotta get through the standards! We've gotta show growth! We've gotta look at the data! We've gotta focus on the "bubble" kids! We've gotta give more assessments! We've gotta start "teaching to the test"!* This pressure inevitably trickles into our classroom and, to put it bluntly, kills the vibe. Yes, we should have a sense of urgency in this work, but we also need to be patient—with our students, with our colleagues, and with ourselves. We need to remember that readers aren't born in a day, or a week, or a semester. We need to trust the process and celebrate the small wins and signs of progress along the way.

Respectful: Respect is taking time to call every student by the correct name. Respect is honoring a student's reading choices and restraining from judgment. Respect is forgiving young people when they make mistakes—and acknowledging when we make them, too. Respect is calling out harmful behavior and defusing difficult situations. Respect is explaining the *why* behind our assignments and decisions. Respect is holding students to high expectations and helping them reach their potential. Respect is recognizing and celebrating the assets and strengths young people bring into our classrooms. Respecting is taking time to listen (truly listen) to our students. And yes, respect is treating our students the way we want to be treated.

PART 2

Strategies to Sustain Independent Reading Success

. . . .

CHAPTER 4

Starting Strong

How to Invest Readers
From Day One Through
the "Intro To Lit" Unit

Veteran educators know that if we get the first day and first week "right" in our classroom, then we will reap the rewards the rest of the year. Therefore, the goal of this chapter is simple: to show how we can start the year strong in our middle and high school ELA classrooms and set ourselves up for a winning "season." **Specifically, I will walk you through the "Intro to Lit" Unit, which includes a wide range of activities, texts, and tasks that we can assign during the first few weeks (and beyond) to build relationships, establish community, review key skills and standards, and invest students in our Read and WRAP routine.** This unit—which includes student surveys, fiction and nonfiction texts centered around reading, authentic writing prompts, and more—lays the foundation for what is ideally a fruitful year of reading and writing.

My hope is that you, like me, revisit this chapter every fall as you prepare for another school year. Whether we're teaching sixth graders or high school seniors, these activities help us hit the ground running. The activities are a mix of formal and informal, graded and ungraded, introspective and collaborative. That's by design. In many schools and districts, there's a push for teachers to "jump into content" immediately. On the other end of the spectrum, there's also a push for teachers to spend the first week or two strictly on "relationships," which can also backfire. (After a couple of days of being forced to participate in well-meaning but anxiety-inducing icebreakers in every class period, students are practically begging for some *real* work.) Our "Intro to Unit" attempts to find an appropriate balance between the two—purposeful community-building happening in conjunction with authentic, purposeful learning tasks.

Our "Intro to Unit" attempts to find an appropriate balance between the two—purposeful community-building happening in conjunction with authentic, purposeful learning tasks.

Keep in mind that the "Intro to Lit" unit can be as short (three to four days) or as long (three to four weeks) as needed. Throughout the chapter, I'll be sure to let you know which activities are "essential" and which you can save for a rainy day (or sometime later in the school year). For example, the narrative writing mini unit, lit-focused TED Talks, and picture book study work just as well, if not better, in May or June as they do in August or September.

I will also outline several of our favorite community-building icebreakers and activities that we sprinkle in throughout the unit: sticky-note posters to establish norms and expectations; a "This or That?" icebreaker and "How Well Do You Know Your ELA Teacher?" Kahoot challenge; creative six-word writing challenges; and a recurring "book talk" feature.

While we'll share *a lot* in this chapter, don't try to cram all of it in during the first month. My advice is to pick a few things and do them well. Be intentional with your goals/objectives and the skills/standards you want to prioritize.

I don't want to push students away from our classroom; I want to invite them in and overwhelm them (in the best sense of the word) with authentic literacy opportunities. I don't want to bore students with lectures or syllabi or bombard them with awkward icebreakers. I want to build community gradually and authentically. I want students to reflect on their individual literacy journeys and to recognize the benefits that reading and writing can and should provide for all of us. I want students to get "back on the bike" for the first time in a while, or for those who already love to ride (or read), I want them to continue exploring all sorts of interesting and challenging trails. I want students to set personally meaningful goals and to know that I will do my best to help them achieve those goals. I want them to know, not through my words but through my actions, that their voice matters.

"INTRO TO LIT" UNIT AT A GLANCE

ACTIVITY	PAGE NUMBERS	RECOMMENDED TIME FRAME	HOW ESSENTIAL?
Student Interest Survey	76–77	Day 1 or 2	*****
Reading Attitude Survey	78–80	Day 1 or 2	*****
Book Tasting Activity	81–83	Day 1 or 2	*****
Email Etiquette + Reading Check-In	84–86	Week 1 or 2	*****
Best Nine	87–88	Week 1 or 2	***
"Ten Things I've Been Meaning to Say to You" Letter	89–90	Week 1 or 2	****
Why We Read + List Writing	91–93	Week 1 or 2	****
Article of the Week Text Set – "Reading about Reading"	94–100	Flexible	****
Lit-Focused TED Talks	101–102	Flexible	**
Reading Identity – Personal Narrative Mini Unit	103–104	Flexible	***
Picture Book Study	105	Flexible	***
Reading Goals	106	Week 2	****
Authentic Icebreakers	107–112	Flexible	*****

STUDENT INTEREST SURVEY

Recommended Time Frame: Week 1

Estimated Time Length: 20–30 Minutes

How Essential? *****

Overview: This is a simple but comprehensive interest survey, which my students complete electronically on the first or second day of the school year. I switched to Google form in recent years, and it has made reviewing and sorting results much easier. At the same time, there is value in completing this the old-fashioned way with pencil and paper, too. As students work through the survey, I usually read the questions aloud and chime in with my own answers. This survey is super helpful as we begin the relationship-building and book-matching process. From day one, the goal is to get to know our students— their hobbies, interests, likes, dislikes, and so forth— so that we can help them find the "right" book and begin the year with a positive reading experience.

I also use many of the survey questions to inspire longer writing tasks and WRAP prompts throughout the year, too. Additionally, we can encourage students to complete student "surveys" or "profiles" for a character in their current read. See Chapter 5 (page 151) for the full WRAP prompt.

online resources

STUDENT INTEREST SURVEY

Welcome to Dr. Amato's English course! I'm looking forward to a great year and getting to know all of you. Thanks for taking the time to answer the questions below.

- First Name:
- Last Name:
- Email Address:
- I prefer to be called:
- My birthday:
- My favorite subject(s) in school:
- It makes me happy when…
- Some of my talents and hobbies are…
- My favorite candy and/or snack(s):
- My favorite restaurant(s):

- My favorite song(s) and/or artist(s):
- My favorite sport(s) and/or team(s):
- My favorite movie(s):
- My favorite TV show(s):
- My favorite board/video game(s):
- My favorite book(s):
- If I could change one thing about the world, it would be…
- I am afraid of . . .
- I am annoyed when . . .
- My dream vacation:
- My favorite color:
- I think that this year at school is going to be . . .
- Three adjectives to describe me are . . .
- I think that Dr. Amato is going to be . . .
- One of my goals is . . .
- If I could have dinner with three people, I would pick . . .
- This year, I plan to . . .
- Something you should know about me is . . .
- I learn best when . . .
- What question(s) do you have for Dr. Amato?
- Is there anything else you'd like to share about yourself that will help Dr. Amato best teach you this year?

READING ATTITUDE SURVEY

Recommended Time Frame: Week 1

Estimated Time Length: 20–30 Minutes

How Essential? *****

Overview: Like the student interest survey, this reading survey is an incredibly valuable preassessment. How do our students feel about reading heading into the school year? Who are they as readers? How can I best meet their needs? Students complete the survey on day two or three, so we can capture the results in real time and use the data to adjust our approach and game plan for each class. Administering the survey electronically saves a ton of time and makes it easier to share results with students and colleagues (and potential grant application reviewers). To that point, I administer this survey three times (beginning, middle, and end of school year) so that we can track and celebrate student progress and adjust and refine as needed.

How It Works: We learn a lot about a student based on their responses. For example, we should make note of the students who reported reading zero or one book the previous year along with those who read more than ten books. We should make note of the students who struggle to answer questions eight through ten and those who can effortlessly list off their favorite books, authors, and genres. We should make note of those who list reading as a hobby and those who do not—yet. Time permitting, we should also compare students' survey results to their data from the previous year (ELA grades, NWEA/MAP scores, state assessment, etc.). When we do, we can attempt to place students into one of four quadrants:

Negative Survey Score, High Grades/Test Scores	Positive Survey Score, High Grades/Test Scores
Negative Survey Scores, Low Grades/Test Scores	Positive Survey Scores, Low Grades/Test Scores

The top right quadrant, "Positive Survey Score, High Grades/Test Scores," is obviously the goal. How many of our students are starting the year here? On the contrary, the bottom left quadrant, "Negative Survey Score, Low Grades/Test Scores," is the least ideal outcome. How many of our students are starting the year here? On the surface, both quadrants make sense—enjoyment and achievement (either positive or negative) are in alignment.

For students who fall in the two remaining quadrants, the top left and bottom right, we may need to dig a bit deeper. Why do some students enjoy reading but perform poorly? Why do some perform well but seem to dislike reading? It's also important that we identify trends in each ELA class/section. Does my first period fall primarily in the top right quadrant? Does my third period fall primarily in the bottom left? Are students split equally across all four quadrants? Again, this exercise allows us to design a game plan that best meets the needs of the learners in our room.

READING ATTITUDE SURVEY

Welcome to Dr. Amato's English course! I'm looking forward to a great year of reading. Thanks in advance for taking the time to answer the questions below. Please be honest!

1. How many books did you read independently last year? (Rough estimate is fine! And it's okay if you didn't read many at all!)

   0   1   2   3   4   5   6   7   8   9   10+

2. In general, how do you feel about reading?

   1 (hate it)   2 (don't like it)   3 (okay)   4 (like it)   5 (love it)

   Explain why:

3. Reading is boring.

   1 (strongly disagree)   2   3   4   5 (strongly agree)

4. Reading is important.

   1 (strongly disagree)   2   3   4   5 (strongly agree)

5. Reading is cool.

   1 (strongly disagree)   2   3   4   5 (strongly agree)

6. I consider reading to be a hobby.

   1 (strongly disagree)   2   3   4   5 (strongly agree)

7. How often do you read outside of school?

   1 Never   2   3   4   5 (all the time)

   Explain why:

8. Generally, what books do you enjoy reading? (genres, subjects, themes, series, authors, formats, etc.?)

(Continued)

(Continued)

9. What was the best book you read last year?

10. What is one of the best books you've ever read?

11. I like when students have choice in what we read in class.
    1 (strongly disagree)   2   3   4   5 (strongly agree)

12. I like when students have time to read during the class period.
    1 (strongly disagree)   2   3   4   5 (strongly agree)

13. I am confident in my reading ability.
    1 (strongly disagree)   2   3   4   5 (strongly agree)

14. How do you feel when everyone in the class reads the same book? When everyone chooses their own book?

15. How would you describe yourself as a reader? How have your reading habits/routines changed over the past year, if at all?

16. How can Dr. Amato help you improve as a reader/enjoy reading more? What would you love to see in our class? In your opinion, what makes a successful and enjoyable English class?

BOOK TASTING

Recommended Time Frame: Week 1

Estimated Time Length: 45–60 Minutes

How Essential? * * * * *

Overview: I have two main goals on day one and throughout week one of the school year:

1. Begin to form positive relationships with each student and create a positive classroom community

2. Introduce students to the books in our classroom/school libraries and establish our Read and WRAP routine

The "book tasting" activity helps us achieve both goals. To be clear, there are several variations on this activity (depending on class size, quality of classroom library, availability of school library, etc.), but the general goal is simple—to expose students to a wide range of high-quality reading options. We want every student to start the year excited about their book selection.

With a "Level 2" or "Level 3" library, the book tasting can take place in our classroom.

How it works: Students walk around the room (I try to get students up and moving every day) and grab books from our shelves to preview. I also place stacks of popular books on desks and tables, so that they are even easier for students to access.

The book tasting activity also works well in the school library, especially if your classroom library is a work in progress. Reach out to your school librarian in advance to schedule a time for your classes to visit and work together to plan the activity. Whether we are in the classroom or school library, I always start by modeling (before students get out of their seats and start walking around). I grab a book from the shelf or stack. I comment on the cover. I identify the title and author. I read the summary on the back or inside flap. I pay attention to the genre and format. I read aloud the first few lines. I share my initial ranking (one to five stars) along with a brief explanation. I give directions:

> Now, it's your turn to preview as many books as you can. If you find one, like I just did, that you want to start reading, great! Write it down. Hold onto it! Still, try looking at a few more so you can add them to your "TBR" list, which we will keep in our notebooks. Does anyone know what TBR stands for? Yup! To Be Read. . . . Ultimately, here's my

goal for this activity: I want everyone to leave today with at least one book that you are excited to start reading! I'll be walking around if you want any recommendations, but I have a feeling that you're going to find something good. And don't worry if it takes you a little longer to pick one. Sometimes it takes a while for me to figure out what show to watch on Netflix or what book to read next. Any questions before we get started?!

One final note: This activity is worth repeating throughout the school year, especially at the beginning of each quarter and/or the first day back from an extended break.

YOU CAN'T JUDGE A BOOK BY ITS COVER . . . OR CAN YOU?

DIRECTIONS: Take some time to preview some of the books in Dr. Amato's classroom (front and back cover, first page, etc.). Then, give each book an initial ranking (1 – no interest in reading this book, 5 – can I start reading this now?!).

TITLE	AUTHOR	INITIAL RANKING (CIRCLE 1)					EXPLANATION
		1	2	3	4	5	
		1	2	3	4	5	
		1	2	3	4	5	
		1	2	3	4	5	
		1	2	3	4	5	
		1	2	3	4	5	
		1	2	3	4	5	
		1	2	3	4	5	

REFLECTION QUESTIONS

Share your thoughts on this activity. How did it go for you? _____

_____

_____

_____

What book do you plan to read first, and why?_____

_____

_____

*Don't forget to add other interesting titles to the "TBR" page in your notebook.

If you're still undecided, how can Dr. Amato help you find the right book? _____

_____

_____

_____

Were there any books, authors, genres, topics, and so on missing from our library that you'd like for us to order? _____

_____

EMAIL ETIQUETTE + READING CHECK-IN

Recommended Time Frame: Week 1 or 2

Estimated Time Length: 30 Minutes

How Essential? *****

Overview: Instead of lamenting the fact that "students today don't know how to send proper emails," let's take time to teach and practice the skill early on. Here's a step-by-step breakdown of our brief but important "email etiquette" mini lesson that also encourages students to reflect on their current read (two birds, one stone).

How It Works:

Step 1: Teacher reviews the definitions of *formal*, *informal*, and *tone*.

Step 2: Teacher facilitates a class discussion around the following: *When to use a formal (F) vs. informal (I) tone?*

- Text Messages (I)
- Social Media (I)
- Email to Teacher (F)
- Poetry (F or I)
- Literary Analysis (F)
- Book Review (F)
- Research Paper (F)
- Lab Report (F)
- Personal Narrative (F or I)

(Note: To get students up and moving, the left side of the room could be formal, and the right could be informal.)

Step 3: Teacher shows email etiquette video (there are several quality options available on YouTube) as students take notes.

Step 4: Students write a brief email following these guidelines:

1. **Use a specific subject** (e.g., Reading Check-In)

2. **Begin with a polite greeting** (paying attention to comma placement)

3. **Explain briefly why you are writing** (share the title and author of the book you are currently reading along with your thoughts thus far)

4. **Ask a direct question** (related to the course, book, upcoming assignments, etc.)

5. **Wrap up your email** with a "thank you," closing, and your full name plus class period

---

CRAFTING A "READING UPDATE" EMAIL

Step 1: Use a specific subject (e.g., "Reading Check-In" or "Reading Update")

Step 2: Begin with a polite greeting

Step 3: Explain briefly why you are writing (share the title and author of the book you are currently reading along with your thoughts thus far)

Step 4: Ask a direct question (related to the course, book, upcoming assignments, etc.)

Step 5: Wrap up your email with a "thank you," closing, and your full name plus class period

---

Student Examples

Dear Dr. Amato,

Currently, I am reading *I'm Glad My Mom Died* by Jennette McCurdy. So far it is an insightful memoir retelling the disturbing tale of McCurdy's life as a young actor being pressured by her mother to be perfect. I am enjoying the short-paced chapters, the reliability of being an anxious child, and the interesting character style in which McCurdy shares her childhood thoughts and reactions.

What is your goal for the number of books read this school year?

Best,

Name, Grade 8

Good Afternoon Dr. Amato,

My book, *The Hate U Give* by Angie Thomas, focuses on the character Starr Carter, who witnessed her friend being harassed and eventually shot and killed by the police. So far, Starr is being questioned by the police and Starr is questioning

(Continued)

(Continued)

her own friendship with her long-time best friend, Maya. I was wondering if you have read any other books by Angie Thomas?

Thank you.

Sincerely,

Name, Grade 8

Good afternoon,

I am currently reading A Good Girl's Guide to Murder by Holly Jackson. I am really enjoying the book so far and find it very intriguing. I am very happy about my book choice, and I look forward to find out who actually murdered Andie Bell. As of now, I really believe that Jason Bell murdered her, but I also think Naomi is a little suspicious too. If you have read the book, who did you think murdered Andie before finishing it? Thank you for taking the time out of your day to read my email.

Sincerely,

Name, Grade 8

BEST NINE

Recommended Time Frame: Week 1 or 2

Estimated Time Length: 60–90 Minutes (to create and share)

How Essential? ***

Overview: Every December, there are digital apps that allow people to share their "best nine," or nine most popular Instagram photos from the year. I decided to take that concept and turn it into a back-to-school assignment where students share nine facts from their life that they'd like for their classmates and teacher to know. This activity works great as a community-building activity and prewriting strategy for our "Ten Things . . ." letter.

How It Works:

Step 1: I share my example with students on the first day and let them know they will soon be creating something similar. It is incredible how much we learn about each other through this activity. For example, here is what students learn about me:

- Lucca (my son) and Lizzie (my wife) are the loves of my life.
- I have one brother, who lives in Arizona and recently got married.
- I love being outdoors.
- I recently moved from Nashville, TN.
- I graduated from Vanderbilt University (and later Belmont University and Lipscomb University).
- I love reading and bringing my son to the bookstore.
- I am a huge sports fan, and my favorite basketball team is the Boston Celtics. I was born in Rhode Island and spent my childhood in Massachusetts.
- I love to cook and gain a lot of inspiration from the Food Network.
- I try my best to stay active and recently joined the Peloton community.

Step 2: I then encourage them to do the same. Students have time to work on their "Best Nine" in class and at home, first brainstorming on a graphic organizer (download from the online companion) and then completing the final product with their Chromebook or a free phone app such as PhotoGrid. Students can also use some of their responses from the interest survey as inspiration.

Step 3: Once published, students share their "best nine" with classmates. We start by sharing with partners before moving to optional whole-group presentations. We also print and display them in our classroom—putting them side-by-side in a giant grid makes for another great bulletin board. It also helps us introduce the concept of identity. *Who am I? Who are we? What do we all have in common? What makes us unique?*

Step 4: Not only does the activity help us build community; it also serves as a great prewriting activity for our "Ten Things . . ." assignment, which we will outline in more detail shortly. (And later in the year, we can also have students create a "Best Nine" for one of their favorite characters.)

"BEST NINE" DIRECTIONS: Create a "Best Nine" that best represents who you are. See Dr. Amato's example for inspiration, but feel free to make yours unique! A few things to keep in mind:

- Select nine pictures, images, logos, and the like that best represent YOU.
- Think about your interests, hobbies, values, favorites, friends, family, and so on.
- Feel free to scroll through your phone (at home) for inspiration.
- Create via PhotoGrid or an app of your choice.
- Pay attention to the order/arrangement of your images. For example, what do you want to be in the center of the grid?

"TEN THINGS I'VE BEEN MEANING TO SAY TO YOU"

Recommended Time Frame: Weeks 1–2

Estimated Time Length: Multiple Class Periods

How Essential? ****

Overview: This is one of my favorite assignments, hands down. First, we read aloud Jason Reynolds's "Ten Things I've Been Meaning to Say to You," published in 2018, and then we use the letter as a mentor text for our own writing. Letter writing is extremely powerful, particularly at the start of the year where students may cringe at the thought of an "essay" but have no problem writing 750 words in the form of a list. This authentic "preassessment" helps me get to know my students as both writers and people. Whether you go with "Ten Things..." or a more traditional letter, I highly recommend starting the year with a personal piece.

Read Jason Reynolds's letter

How It Works:

"Ten Things..." Writing Prompt: We have just read Jason Reynolds's letter and Dr. Amato's example in class. You can also use Nic Stone's "Letter to My Younger Self" (2018) for even more inspiration. Now it's your turn to write your own version of "Ten Things..." This is a creative assignment, but here are some tips and suggestions to keep in mind while writing:

Read Nic Stone's letter

- **Step 1:** Think about your **audience**. Who do you want to write to? Your teachers, your classmates, a family member, a younger sibling, a younger version of yourself, and so forth.

- **Step 2:** Think about your **purpose**. What do you want to say? What's on your mind? Do you want to share things about yourself? (beliefs, hobbies, interests, goals, questions, fears, dreams, pet peeves, wishes, hopes, memories, etc.) Or do you want to offer advice and inspiration to others? Or a combination of the two?

- **Step 3:** Think about **tone.** Do you want to write in a more formal or informal tone? Playful or serious? Sentimental or inspirational? You will be writing in first person, so it's okay for your authentic voice to shine through in this letter.

- **Step 4:** Incorporate at least *three* examples of **figurative language** (simile, metaphor, alliteration, hyperbole, idiom, etc.) somewhere in your letter. Identify your figurative language examples at the bottom of your letter.

- **Step 5: MLA Format.** Size 12. Times New Roman. Double-spaced. Your title can be the same as Jason's or something different. Then, be sure to write your letter in the same style (as a list with numbers 1 through __). Reminder: you don't need to include exactly ten items in your letter.

- **Step 6: Proofread** for grammar, usage, and mechanics issues prior to submitting. Aim for approximately 500 words. It is okay if it is a little under or a little over.

Here's a sample grading rubric:

- MLA Format: 10 points
- Figurative Language: 15 points (5 points per example)
- Conventions (grammar, usage, and mechanics): 10 points
- Word Count (minimum 500 words): 5 points
- Content and Style (what you say and how you say it): 60 points (30 content, 30 style)

Possible Topics: For those who need more support getting started with their list/letter, I remind students they can write about any/all of the following:

- Favorite Season
- Hobbies/Interests
- Favorite TV Shows/Movies
- Favorite Sports/Teams
- Favorite Music (Genres, Songs, Artists, etc.)
- Favorite Books
- Favorite Colors

- Favorite Foods/Restaurants
- Adjectives to Describe Yourself
- What Brings You Joy?
- What Frustrates You?
- How Do You Learn Best?
- Random Facts About Yourself
- Brief Stories/Memories From Your Life

The companion website provides two completed "Ten Things" letters—one from a student and one from Dr. Amato. There are also two traditional back-to-school letter activities that you could substitute. See resources.corwin.com/JustReadIt.

WHY WE READ + LIST WRITING

Recommended Time Frame: Week 1 or 2

Estimated Time Length: 20–30 Minutes (longer with extension)

How Essential? ****

Overview: I strongly recommend "Why We Read" as a WRAP prompt during week one or two. The goal is to help students brainstorm why reading is important. It's awesome to see how many "reasons to read" and "reading benefits" we can come up with—first individually, then in small groups, and finally as an entire class. Students typically start with a list of three or four on their own, and by the end, they have dozens—their entire notebook page is full. Through the process, we show students the power of both reading *and* collaboration. After reviewing our complete lists, we bring out the flair pens and sharpies and have students write their favorite reasons on index cards before displaying them on our WHY WE READ bulletin board or door. The "Top Ten" list writing is an awesome extension (time permitting, of course).

How It Works:

Step 1: In their notebooks, students spend two to three minutes silently brainstorming as many "reasons to read" and "benefits of reading" as they can.

Step 2: Students get into small groups to share their respective lists, adding their partners' responses to their notebook.

Step 3: Teacher invites students to move around the classroom, continuing to find new partners and add to their lists.

Step 4A: Teacher invites students to return to their seats and review their complete lists. *How many reasons do you have? Who wants to share their complete list? What did we learn from the activity?*

Step 4B (Optional Extension): For those who want to introduce the research process, here's an idea: *Students, now let's take out our Chromebooks and see what additional "reading benefits" we can find online. What key words should we include in our search? What do we know about reliable and unreliable sources?* Students will then find and share helpful articles/links, ultimately adding to their respective lists.

Step 5: Teacher encourages students to select their favorite (most important?) reason and write it neatly/creatively on an index card to be displayed in the classroom.

Step 6 (Optional Extension): Students can use their notes to create their own "Top _____ Reasons to Read" list and/or infographic. (For example, this is an awesome opportunity to introduce Canva.)

Step 7: Along with their reading list, it's also a great opportunity for students to create a second listicle (think BuzzFeed list-articles) of their choosing, based on their own interests. A few examples:

- Top 10 Pieces of Advice for _____ (Teachers, Parents, Athletes, Siblings, Friends, etc.)
- Top 10 Reasons I Love _____ (Soccer, Gymnastics, Cooking, Taylor Swift, Fall, etc.)
- Top 10 Reasons to Join _____ (a specific team, club, organization, etc.)

One final note: this activity is super easy to modify. Instead of ten reasons, we can create "Top Five" lists. We can also extend the assignment by having students write introductory and concluding paragraphs or adding explanations for each of their points. Lots of options here!

Student Examples: "Top Ten Reasons to Read"

SAMPLE A	SAMPLE B
1. To disappear to a different place.	1. Reading improves my mental health.
2. To open your mind to new things.	2. Reading fuels my imagination.
3. To relax and de-stress.	3. Reading makes me a better writer.
4. To expand your vocabulary.	4. Reading brings me joy.
5. To learn something new.	5. Reading helps me sleep better.
6. To become a better reader.	6. Reading inspires me to be a better person.
7. To walk in someone else's shoes.	7. Reading is a form of entertainment and self-care.
8. To perform better in school.	8. Reading helps me connect and communicate with others.
9. To remain hopeful.	9. Reading sharpens my focus and concentration.
10. To hopefully live a little longer.	10. Reading prepares me for life.

WHY DO YOU
ENJOY READING? WHY
IS READING IMPORTANT?

PROJECT LIT FOUNDERS, SPRING 2019

- I really enjoy reading because it helps me get away from the world while educating me at the same time.
- Reading helps you step outside of your surroundings and learn what life is for other people.
- Reading helps expand your vocabulary, widen your imagination, and free your mind.
- I enjoy reading because it gives me a chance to live a life that isn't mine for a little while.
- Reading increases our knowledge, and knowledge leads to success.
- Reading takes me to another place and truly relaxes me.
- Reading makes you think differently and stimulates your brain.
- I love learning new information.
- I enjoy reading because it helps me when I'm in bad place. I love books where I can visualize everything that's happening.
- I enjoy reading because it sends you to another world where you can be and do whatever you want.
- Reading helps you understand more of how the world is and what it could be.
- I read because it's a way to stay sane.
- I read because it's great way to relieve stress and get in my comfort zone.
- If you can't read, you're going to struggle.
- Reading is important because it helps you grow as an individual.
- Reading makes it easier to comprehend the world around us.
- I read because it opens my mind to new opportunities.

ARTICLE OF THE WEEK
TEXT SET: "READING
ABOUT READING"

Recommended Time Frame: Ongoing

Estimated Time Length: 1–2 Hours Per Week

How Essential? ****

Overview: The "Article of the Week," or AoW, has been a staple in our classroom for the past decade—thanks again to Kelly Gallagher and Dave Stuart, Jr., for their inspiration. While I have modified the AoW protocol slightly over the years, the goal remains the same—to encourage students to read and respond to nonfiction texts every week. Over the course of the year, our AoWs will cover a wide range of topics, including but not limited to technology, social media, climate, health, and education (literacy, in particular).

How It Works: In the beginning of the year, as I introduce our AoW protocol and kick off our "Intro to Lit" unit, I intentionally select articles from our "Intro to Lit" text set. By reading informational texts and op-eds about reading (as opposed to articles about the pros and cons of Mars exploration or artificial intelligence, the benefits of sleep, or the conflict in Ukraine), we're able to review AoW expectations while also further investing students in our Read and WRAP routine. Again, two birds, one stone.

Before assigning the AoW to students, teachers will do the following:

1. Select an article to read, discuss, and analyze with students—from Kelly Gallagher or Dave Stuart Jr.'s websites, NewsELA, CommonLit, the New York Times Learning Network, and the New York Times Upfront or *Scholastic Scope* magazine, along with other sources.

2. Read through the article and make sure it is appropriately challenging, relevant, and engaging.

3. Format the article: leave space for annotations, number the paragraphs, include a visual, and identify and bold vocabulary words.

4. Create two to three immediate discussion questions to generate thinking and conversation. (To save time, feel free to keep these consistent with every AoW.)

5. Develop a few text-dependent questions that are aligned to standards and/or curriculum (think about what is worth noticing, analyzing, teaching, reteaching, etc., in this specific text).

6. Develop an extended response prompt, whether it's one paragraph or one page. I typically have students complete an objective summary (paragraph one) and personal reflection (paragraph two).

7. Optional: Create a brief assessment (perhaps three to five multiple-choice questions) similar to what students will see on a standardized test.

Let's review how the AoW process plays out in our classroom using a Walter Dean Myers op-ed from our "Intro to Lit" text set.

SAMPLE AOW ASSIGNMENT

DIRECTIONS: Read and annotate the article, making notes and defining key vocabulary in the margins. Annotation is part of the grade. There should be evidence of your thought process via annotations. **(5 pts)**

"Where Are the Children of Color in Children's Books?"

By Walter Dean Myers, *New York Times*, Opinion, 2014

IMMEDIATE REACTION (3 pts)

- What did you learn from this text?

- What thoughts and feelings arose while reading?

- What questions do you have after reading?

TEXT-DEPENDENT QUESTIONS (12 points)

1. What is the central claim, or main argument, that Myers is trying to make in this opinion piece?

2. Revisit paragraphs 1–6. How did the author's reading identity change over time? Be sure to cite evidence from the text in your response.

3. Describe the effect that James Baldwin and "Sonny's Blues" had on Myers's life, citing evidence from the text in your response.

4. How would you describe the author's tone in paragraph 12? Why?

(Continued)

(Continued)

5. When looking at paragraph 14 specifically, what was Walter Dean Myers's purpose for writing?

6. What is the desired effect of the final sentence? What does Myers mean by the line, "there is work to be done"?

OBJECTIVE SUMMARY: In a well-written paragraph, summarize the main points from the beginning, middle, and end of the text. Reminders: include the title and author, remain objective, write in third-person point of view, keep verb tense consistent, and use transitions to help your writing flow smoothly. (15 points)

PERSONAL RESPONSE: In your second paragraph, share your personal reaction to Myers's piece. What did you find most interesting or thought-provoking? What sections stood out? How would you describe Myers's reading and writing identity, possibly in comparison to yours? Why is representation important? (15 points)

Sample Grading Rubric

*   Annotations 5 pts

*   Immediate Reaction 3 pts

*   Text-Dependent Questions 12 pts

*   Objective Summary 15 pts

*   Personal Response 15 pts

AOW WEEKLY SEQUENCE

Once we've selected and formatted our text and developed our learning tasks, here's a look at how the AoW can be rolled out in the classroom over the course of the week:

Day 1

*   Read and annotate the text (individually, in groups, or whole class).

*   Initial discussion (using the "Immediate Reaction" questions).

Day 2

*   Vocabulary practice (with the bolded words from the article).

*   Complete text-dependent questions (individually, in groups, and/or whole class).

Days 3–4

- Extended writing—students submit the objective summary and personal response via Schoology/Google Classroom (teacher modeling and providing mini lessons if/when necessary).

Day 5

- Culminating discussion—how have our opinions been strengthened/challenged/changed over the course of the week?
- Students receive peer and teacher feedback, self-assess, revise, finalize, and submit.

A few final AOW reminders:

- Typically, I introduce/assign the AoW on Monday and have it due by Friday (or Sunday), allowing students to work at their own pace throughout the week.
- Make the AoW work for your students and schedule. Don't stress if you can't get to it *every* week, but it does pay off to make it a consistent part of your classroom routine.
- While some of the AoW can be completed as homework, try to give students class time, as well, especially in the beginning.
- Feel free to add/subtract AoW components as you see fit each week. For example, if we're short on class time, we may cut out the text-dependent questions and have students focus on writing the two paragraphs (or vice versa). Some articles lend themselves to rich in-class debates and discussions while others encourage individual reflection.
- You can assign the same article to all or offer two to three articles that students can choose from. Students can also select their own AoW (just be sure to review how to detect bias and select credible sources beforehand).
- When in doubt, keep it simple. Be intentional about the skills and concepts you want to prioritize.
- Remember the ultimate goal of the AoW: to expose students to more nonfiction and informational texts, to review key standards and concepts, and to engage students in meaningful reading, writing, talking, and thinking about a variety of topics.
- There are also opportunities to incorporate the AoW in our science and social studies classrooms (or to read science- and history-focused texts).
- Here's one more reason I love the AoW so much: it ensures that, at a minimum, students are reading and responding to high-quality nonfiction and fiction (through our Read and WRAP routine) every week.

POSSIBLE AOWS—"READING ABOUT READING" TEXT SET

In our "Intro to Lit" unit, students read at least one, but often two or three, texts as we introduce our AoW protocol that will become a staple throughout the year. Here is a partial list of options, and you can find a more comprehensive list with hyperlinks on the online companion:

- "Where Are the Children of Color in Children's Books?" by Walter Dean Myers; *New York Times*, Opinion, 2014

- "Where Books Are All But Nonexistent" by Alia Wong; *The Atlantic*, July 14, 2016

- "How a Kid Who Didn't Read a Book until He Was 17 Grew Up to Become a Literary Star" by Nora Krug; *The Washington Post*, October 23, 2017

- "6 Scientific Reasons Reading Is Amazing for Your Health" by Sadie Trombetta; *Bustle*, March 16, 2016

- "People Who Read Books Live Almost 2 Years Longer, Study Finds" by David Nield; *Science Alert*; August 11, 2016

- "The Truth about Teens, Social Media and the Mental Health Crisis" by Michaeleen Doucleff; NPR; April 25, 2023

To clarify, students will read at least one of the "Reading about Reading" articles and complete the protocol: annotation, discussion, vocabulary, text-dependent questions, objective summary, personal response, revision, and reflection. However, if there's time and interest (or perhaps students need a bit more "convincing" to embrace our Read and WRAP routine), we can assign three "Reading about Reading" AoWs course of a few weeks. Here's what this looks like in action, starting at the end:

"READING ABOUT READING" CULMINATING TASK

Here's the culminating task that students will complete:

Part I: We have read and discussed several articles during our "Intro to Lit" unit. For this assignment, you will submit three objective summaries. Revise your first drafts as needed so that they include the following:

- *Topic Sentence:* introduce title (in quotations), source (in italics), author, and main idea
- *Supporting Details:* highlight the key points from the beginning, middle, and end of the text in a clear and compelling manner
- *Sophisticated Syntax and Vocabulary:* varied sentence structure, appropriate transition words, strong verbs, and so forth
- *Objective tone and consistent verb tense*
- *Aim for approximately seventy-five to one hundred words per summary*

Part II: Write a personal reflection (approximately 250 words) that draws connections between the three articles. What are your major takeaways? What big ideas and questions are you thinking about? What problems and/or solutions were addressed in the three articles? How did the articles change your thinking? How did the articles connect/relate to your reading identity? Be sure to demonstrate critical thinking and analysis.

Note: The online companion contains a downloadable self-assessment and rubric students can use before submitting their final drafts.

Student Example

Here is an example of "Part II" (the reflection and synthesis), written by a ninth-grade student in September 2019:

Student Reflection

After reading these three articles, I discovered the true importance of reading. Reading doesn't just improve your vocabulary; it can also mentally improve your stance as a human being. Reading is a fundamental part of development and each article adds to this notion. The first text was eye-opening. As it brought up the problem of book deserts and how prevalent the issue is, I grew to comprehend the need for books. The author really brought the necessity of books to the forefront of my mind. She made me think about how privileged I am to have access to books, even if it's not the best, because there are kids who don't have any access at all.

Walter Dean Myers then took me on a reading voyage. He used books to find himself, and when those books no longer

(Continued)

(Continued)

corresponded with him, he lost the will to read and continue his literary identity. I find that raises the question of how many other children have lost their want to read after feeling left out of their favorite stories. I never really put myself within the actual shoes of a character, but there are times when reading about someone like me definitely would have helped with my self-acknowledgement.

The last article really cemented my opinion on reading. I previously thought reading was something people did to pass time, but I was scientifically proven wrong, kind of. Reading literally changes the way that your brain works. That is scary but cool. I read a lot, but now I have a concrete purpose as to why I want to continue reading. All the books I've read have added up, making me—in certain aspects—the person I am today. That's a pretty nifty idea to ponder.

LIT-FOCUSED TED TALKS

Recommended Time Frame: Anytime

Estimated Time Length: 30–60 Minutes per TED Talk

How Essential? ***

Overview: My colleagues and I turned to TED Talks even more frequently during remote learning in 2020–2021; we appreciated that students could watch, pause, rewind, listen, and read along via the transcript. We assigned TED Talks in lieu of or in addition to the traditional Article of the Week, and they have remained a staple post pandemic. Like the AoW, there are several approaches and possibilities with TED Talks. Here are several reading-focused TED Talks that work well at any point in the school year, especially during our "Intro to Lit" unit, that students can watch and discuss together and/or on their own.

Recommended TED Talks

1. "The Danger of a Single Story" by Chimamanda Adichie
2. "The Windows and Mirrors of Your Child's Bookshelf" by Grace Lin
3. "What Reading Slowly Taught Me about Writing" by Jacqueline Woodson
4. "How a Boy Became an Artist" by Jarrett J. Krosoczka
5. "A Guerilla Gardener in South Central LA" by Ron Finley (for those interested in comparing book deserts with food deserts)
6. "The Healing Power of Reading" by Michelle Kuo
7. "12 Truths I Learned from Life and Writing" by Anne Lamott
8. "How Books Can Open Your Mind" by Lisa Bu

For those looking to extend beyond an AoW format, here are three options:

1. Encourage students to use their notes from their graphic organizer to write a multi-paragraph analysis, assessing the overall effectiveness of the TED Talk. You can access a downloadable TED Talk Analysis graphic organizer at resources.corwin.com/JustReadIt.

2. Have students craft an essay that compares and contrasts two of the TED Talks (theme, structure, rhetorical appeals, strengths and limitations, purpose, intended audience, impact, etc.)

3. Go big and push students to write and deliver their own TED Talk, inspired by Chimamanda Adichie, Jarrett J. Krosoczka, Grace Lin, Jacqueline Woodson, and other authors. Possible topics include but are not limited to the following:

- the need for book access
- why representation matters
- the danger of a single story and stereotypes
- the importance of "mirrors and windows"
- the power of reading, writing, and storytelling
- why we should invest in literacy and arts education
- reading and/or writing identity
- a significant/memorable literacy experience
- an unforgettable teacher or librarian
- book banning and censorship

READING IDENTITY: NARRATIVE WRITING MINI UNIT

Recommended Time Frame: Anytime

Estimated Time Length: Multiple Class Periods

How Essential? ***

Overview: Because many of our "Intro to Lit" WRAP prompts encourage students to reflect on specific literacy memories and moments from their childhood, we have a wonderful opportunity to turn their notebook responses into a polished personal narrative. To help us get there—moving from an informal quick-write to a published piece—we analyze several mentor texts, excerpts from a few of our favorite memoirs.

How It Works:

Step 1: Promote reflection via our WRAP prompts

Before writing a narrative, we want students to reflect and respond to some (but probably not all) of the following prompts:

WRAP Prompts – Reading Identity

- Who am I as a reader? What and why do I read? How would I characterize my reading identity?
- Who am I as a writer? What and why do I write? How would I characterize my writing identity?
- When and where do I prefer reading? What is my ideal reading environment? When and where am I most relaxed and comfortable? Are there are any specific places that come to mind?
- When and where do I prefer writing? What is my ideal writing environment? When and where am I most relaxed and comfortable? Are there are any specific places that come to mind?
- What individuals shaped the reader, writer, and person I am today?
- What literacy experiences/memories (positive or negative) stand out in my life?
- How have I changed (perhaps evolved or regressed) as a reader and writer? Why?
- How would I describe my relationship with reading and writing? What role do they play in my life?
- Why are reading and writing important?
- How does reading affect our physical and mental health?
- Why is book access important?
- How would you define a "book desert"? Why do you believe book deserts exist?
- Why does representation matter in media?
- How do access and representation, or the lack thereof, shape our identity?

Step 2: Mentor Text Analysis

As students continue to reflect on specific literacy moments and memories from their own lives, we also take time to read excerpts from some of our favorite memoirs, including Laurie Halse Anderson's *Shout* and Trevor Noah's *Born a Crime*. Feel free to pick a few of your favorites (based on length, objectives, grade level, etc.) to read and analyze together. You could also set up a gallery walk where students move from one text to the next (reading several excerpts in a short amount of time). Or you could have students work in pairs/groups to analyze one excerpt and then present/share their takeaways with the class.

No matter how you decide to read them, a simple two-column graphic organizer helps students identify specific craft "moves" and narrative techniques in each excerpt. For example, in the left-hand column, students write the words, phrases, sentences, and paragraphs that stand out in the mentor text. Then, in the right-hand column, they explain/analyze the writer's "move" or technique. *What makes this line effective? What can I "borrow" in my own narrative writing?* (See the online companion for a downloadble organizer.) The purpose of the mentor texts, of course, is to provide students with ideas and inspiration for their upcoming personal narrative.

> ### Memoir Excerpts Exploring Reading Identity
>
> - *Between the World and Me* by Ta-Nehisi Coates (pp. 30, 46, 48)
> - *Booked* by Kwame Alexander ("Ms. Hardwick's Honors English Class," "Read Aloud," and "Out of the Dust")
> - *Born a Crime* by Trevor Noah (p. 68)
> - *Shout* by Laurie Halse Anderson ("Lovebrarians")
> - *The Poet X* by Elizabeth Acevedo ("Ms. Galiano," "Final Draft of Assignment 1," and "Every Day after English Class")
> - Many of the personal essays in *Hope Nation*, edited by Rose Brock: Angie Thomas, Ally Carter, Romina Garber, Nic Stone, Jason Reynolds and Brendan Kiely, Jeff Zentner, and so on.

Step 3: Culminating Task

After reading and analyzing exemplary excerpts from several authors, students have an opportunity to do the same, zooming in on a memory, moment, person, or event that reveals an aspect of their reading and/or writing identity.

PICTURE BOOK STUDY

Recommended Time Frame: Any time

Estimated Time Length: Multiple Class Periods

How Essential? ***

Overview: In the fall of 2022, before my son was born, I made frequent trips to the local used bookstore (shout out to McKay's), stocking up on beautiful board books and picture books. Suddenly, I had an idea. What if I brought some of these books into our classroom to help us build community and review literary elements? After all, our students loved participating in our "Lit Buddies" program (reading aloud to local elementary school students) before the pandemic. I prepared a few guiding questions to kick off the activity, which then evolved into a mini-unit of sorts:

- What books do you remember reading and loving as a child?

- What books do you think my son and I will enjoy reading together?

- And more broadly, What makes a good story?

How It Works:

- Give students an opportunity to browse the picture book collection and read several titles aloud with their group members.

- Select at least one picture book to read as a class and pair it with a video or audio reading. We read *Hair Love* by Matthew Cherry and then watched the animated short film, comparing and contrasting (and celebrating) the two. We also watched a scene from Pixar's *Luca*, "Silencio, Bruno!," that allowed us to review the five elements of the plot diagram—exposition, rising action, climax, falling action, and resolution—along with literary elements such as dialogue, conflict, setting, and theme.

- Each student (or group) selects one picture book from the class collection (or one they brought in from home) to read and analyze.

- Students complete a graphic organizer. (Feel free to use the blank Picture Book Analysis graphic organizer found on the online companion, resources.corwin.com/JustReadIt.)

- Students use their notes to write a multi-paragraph response—a clear summary of the picture book followed by a thoughtful critique. *What are the major points and observations you want to make about this book? What made it unique? What were its major strengths and/or weaknesses? What did you appreciate most? Who is the intended audience? How did it make you feel?*

READING GOALS

Overview: Once we have established our Read and WRAP routine and settled into a nice rhythm, it is important to help students set personalized reading goals for the year. Keep in mind that this will be the first time many students have ever been asked to do so. Therefore, it's important that we take time to model and brainstorm as a class. *What does a reading goal look like? What are some examples that y'all can think of?* Here's what we typically come up with:

Types of Reading Goals

- Read ____ books by ____ (end of the quarter, semester, school year, etc.)
- Read ____ pages per ____ (day, week, month, year, etc.)
- Read ____ minutes per ____ (day, week, month, year, etc.)
- Read ____ different genres
- Read every book by a specific author
- Finish an entire series
- Deeper thinking/analysis while reading
- Review/share books with an online community (Instagram, TikTok, YouTube, etc.)
- Track your reading online and/or in a notebook
- Build a book collection/library at home
- Steward a little library in your neighborhood
- Join/start a book club

After our discussion, students complete this reflection:

- What reading goal(s) do you have for yourself this quarter?
- Why is this goal important to you?
- What potential challenges do you anticipate?
- How do you plan to overcome these challenges?
- How do you plan to monitor your progress? How will you know if you're still on track to meet your goal?
- What can your teacher do to help you achieve your reading goals?

Students write their goal on an index card, which makes for another excellent bulletin board display. Throughout the quarter, I set aside time to check in with students about their goals and their progress. Over time, as we build relationships and gather data about our students' reading habits and performance, we can provide more support and encouragement:

"Oh, I think you can push yourself even more this quarter! Soccer season just ended, right? How would you feel about making that goal a little higher?"

"You're way too hard on yourself! You're already reading a ton. And you have so many things on your plate. I recommend keeping your goal the same this quarter?"

AUTHENTIC ICEBREAKERS

The following pages highlight five of my go-to icebreakers and activities that help us establish rules and expectations and build community. Feel free to sprinkle them in whenever and wherever you see fit.

STICKY-NOTE POSTERS

Overview: When it comes to setting classroom norms and expectations, one of my go-to activities is super simple. All we need are some chart paper and sticky notes (preferably in a variety of colors). Instead of reading through a syllabus or reviewing a list of rules and procedures, we discuss the following prompts:

- Our classroom should be _____ every day.
- In order to make our classroom great, I plan to . . .
- Dr. Amato can help us succeed by . . .
- Respect means . . .
- Reading is important because . . .
- Writing is important because . . .

The prompts can be discussed all at once or rolled out over a few days.

How It Works:

Step 1: Share the first prompt with the group. *Our classroom should be _____ every day.*

Step 2: Students write their response on a sticky note.

Step 3: Brief discussion. Students share out answers (either from their seat or as a move-pair-share).

Step 4: Students then place their sticky note on the designated poster.

Step 5: Repeat with the next prompt.

"Our classroom should be ____ every day" helps us visualize and verbalize the kind of community we all want to be part of. Then, the next two prompts help students name how they plan to contribute ("I'm going to be held accountable for my actions") and how I can best support them ("it looks like Dr. Amato is going to listen to us and support us.")

The posters stay up in our room for a while, and we revisit them often. Generally, we have found they are more powerful and aesthetically pleasing than the "No _____ (talking, gum, cell phones, etc.)" posters found in many spaces. For example, if the vibes are off, we can take five minutes to review the posters and reset expectations, like this:

We all agreed that our classroom should be calm, relaxing, fun, and respectful.... Does it feel that way right now? Why do the vibes seem to be off at the moment? Let's see what all of us committed to doing to make our classroom great.... Are we all honoring those commitments? What else do you need from me?

"THIS OR THAT?"

Overview: One community-building activity that our students always seem to enjoy is "This or That?"

How It Works:

- Students first record their answers on a handout.

- Then, we put one "This or That?" statement on the board/screen at a time, and students move to one side of the room or the other. A spirited conversation typically follows.

- There's also an option to turn the activity into an argumentative writing task. For example, students pick one of the prompts and write one strong persuasive paragraph (why fall is the best season, why football is the best sport, why dogs are the best pet, etc.)

THIS or THAT?	
Beach	Mountains
Starbucks	Dunkin'
Reading Outside	Reading on the Couch
Breakfast	Dinner
Netflix	Disney+
Graphic Novel	Novel in Verse
Cake	Ice Cream
Basketball	Football
Standalone Book	Book Series
Pizza	Tacos
YouTube	Instagram
Historical Fiction	Thriller
Batman	Spider-Man
Cats	Dogs
Winter	Summer
ELA	Math
Bonus: Come up with your own categories, too!	

Overview: Years ago, I created a "How well do you know Dr. Amato?" Kahoot challenge that I still update and use on occasion. The goal is for students to learn a little more about me, most importantly that I am a human being with a variety of interests who cares deeply about their academic and emotional wellbeing.

HOW WELL DO YOU KNOW DR. AMATO?

- *What subject do I teach?* (**ELA**, Math, Social Studies, Science)

- *This is my _____ year of teaching.* (5th, 10th, **14th**, 100th)

- *Where did I receive my bachelor's degree?* (**Vanderbilt**, Belmont, Boston College, UCLA)

- *In what state was I born?* (**Rhode Island**, Tennessee, Massachusetts, Maine)

- *In what state did I get married?* (Rhode Island, Tennessee, Massachusetts, **Maine**)

- *In what state did I spend my childhood?* (Rhode Island, Tennessee, **Massachusetts**, Maine)

- *What are some of my hobbies?* (Cooking, Reading, Playing Sports, **All of the Above**)

- *What is my favorite food?* (Tacos, Buffalo Wings, Pizza, **All of the Above**)

- *What is my favorite sports team?* (New York Yankees, **Boston Celtics**, New England Patriots, Nashville Predators)

- *How many children do I have?* (0, **1**, 2, 3)

- *What do I love most about teaching?* (The grading; The pay; The clout; **Helping students achieve their goals**)

- *What is my favorite TV show of all time?* (**The Wire**; Breaking Bad; Friday Night Lights; Paw Patrol)

- *What is my dream vacation?* (**Italy**; Hawaii; South Africa; Australia)

- *Which one of these statements is true?* (**I am a three-time tater tot eating champion**; I speak three languages; I have been skydiving three times; I have three pets)

- *What club would I love for you to join this year?* (**Project LIT Community**; Debate; Model UN; Yearbook)

Overview: This activity would also fit with our collection of WRAP prompts in Chapter 5, but it's shared here because it helps us build a community of readers and writers from the get-go. It shows students that ELA class can be fun and challenging at the time; the two aren't mutually exclusive. Specifically, students quickly learn that it's harder to be concise and that we can, in fact, say more with less. The six-word writing challenges are endless, but here are four possibilities:

1. **Six-Word Memoir:** Students try to capture a bit about who they are and/or how they're feeling as they head into a new year.
   Examples:

   Teacher, dad, husband. Love all three.

   Always anxious to start new year.

   Ready for fresh start. Let's go.

   New year. Same person. That's okay.

   Stop. Look. Inhale. Exhale. Listen. Learn.

2. **Six-Word Reading Identity:** Students describe their reading identity, journey, background, and/or mindset in just six words.
   Examples:

   Life's hard. When in doubt, read.

   Proud book nerd. Always have been.

   Me and books are like PB&J.

   Up and down like a rollercoaster.

   Books provide comfort during darkest storms.

   I've always been allergic to books.

3. **Six-Word Book Summary:** Once students have had time to dig into their first book (at least a week and probably longer), we can push them to summarize it in exactly six words.
Examples:

Dear Martin, I can't do it.

Xiomara's parents control her too much.

The rules matter when you're down.

Claudia's looking for her best friend.

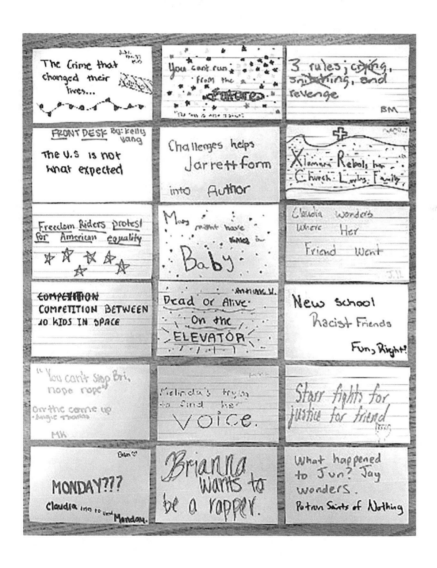

4. **Six-Word Book Critique:** Then, to introduce or review the difference between summary and critique, encourage students to share their thoughts on the book in exactly six words.

   Examples:

   Summary: *Three siblings, now orphaned, terribly unlucky.*

   Critique: *Dark, delightful, and most definitely binge-worthy.*

   Summary: *Santiago's journey to pursue his destiny.*

   Critique: *Worth the hype. Follow your dreams.*

CLASS BOOK TALKS

Overview: They may not admit it, but our students are listening—most of the time, anyway. Frequent "book talks," whether impromptu or rehearsed, have tremendous value. While there are several ways to incorporate book talks, here's an easy one: Every Friday, one person (teacher or student) spends a minute or two "hyping, pitching, selling" their current/recent read to the rest of the class. To learn more about the graded, formal "book talk" assignment, be sure to check out Chapter 5, specifically page 176. In the meantime, here are a few additional thoughts:

- It'd be great if students and staff members had opportunities to share their book talks more widely—on the morning announcements, in the newsletter, on the school's social media accounts, and so on.

- I can't tell you how many times a student comes to my desk, days or weeks after I've given a book talk, and says, "Do you still have a copy of _____? I remember you read it recently, and it sounds really good." My response? "Yup! It's right here. Can't wait to hear what you think about it." Never underestimate the power of a book talk.

- When possible, try to have multiple copies of a book you plan to pitch. If you sell it well, students will be begging to borrow it.

- Use a Book Talk Tracker so there's record for the entire classroom. The tracker includes four columns/tabs—the date of the book talk, the name of the person delivering the book talk, the title and author of the book they're discussing, and any helpful links/resources (article, book trailer, author interview, etc.) related to the book. You can download a Tracker from the companion website, resources.corwin.com/JustReadIt.

REVIEWING OUR "INTRO TO LIT" UNIT

Now that you've had a chance to look through the complete list, I wanted to share how I approach the "Intro to Lit" Unit. In our classroom, we make room for the first seven items—the two surveys, book tasting activity, email etiquette and reading check-in, best nine, "Ten Things..." letter, and "Why We Read" brainstorm—every year without question. We always read at least one, if not more, of the recommend texts as we establish our Article of the Week routine. If time permits, we may watch and discuss a TED Talk or two, but if not, we save them for our argumentative/op-ed unit later in the year. The same goes for the personal narrative mini unit. We respond to many of the reading identity prompts during our WRAP time, but we typically hold off on the longer piece until our personal narrative unit. The picture book study is a new addition, and I think it's a fantastic way to establish community and review literary elements (but it also works well at any point in the year).

The "sticky-note posters," "This or That?" icebreaker, "Reading Goals" exercise, and six-word writing challenges are yearly staples. While book talks have always been an integral part of our classroom, I'm hoping to be even more consistent and intentional with them moving forward.

And that's the final point I wanted to make—our "Intro to Lit" unit is constantly evolving. It's not meant to be a finished product, but rather a starting point for all of us. Instead of slogging through the first few weeks, with students participating passively as the teacher reviews rules and passes out the first assigned read, this unit puts our young people at the center from day one—right where they belong. The hope is that we hit the ground running (or, in our case, reading and writing) and never look back.

CHAPTER 5

Maintaining Momentum

Everyday WRAP Prompts to
Engage and Empower All Readers

While it is easy to imagine what our independent reading time looks like—students and their teacher scattered across the room, engrossed in their books, timer counting down, lights dimmed, instrumental music playing softly in the background—this chapter will zoom in on the second part of our routine. What happens when the timer goes off and students take out their composition notebooks and open to a clean page? We WRAP—or Write, Reflect, Analyze, and Participate. Instead of just "dropping everything and reading," purposeful WRAP prompts help students deepen their understanding of the text and self, develop a wide range of literacy skills, and strengthen their connection with classmates.

Purposeful WRAP prompts help students deepen their understanding of the text and self, develop a wide range of literacy skills, and strengthen their connection with classmates.

Whether we have two or twenty minutes, dedicating daily time to WRAP is invaluable. We don't want students to close their books and move on to the next activity without having a chance to WRAP. Doing so is a missed opportunity. Doing so is malpractice. We want students to revisit powerful passages, to reflect on what they've read and how they've grown, to write analytically and creatively, to learn and apply new things, and to engage in authentic conversation. Our students' daily responses, whether written or verbal, serve as valuable formative assessments that supplement the data in our "Literacy Dashboard" and help us address our students' specific needs.

WRAP prompts allow us to do the following:

- address students' academic and social emotional needs
- check for student understanding
- help students process what they're reading
- hold students accountable for their reading
- increase student effort and engagement
- nurture reflective readers and writers
- promote conversation, collaboration, creativity, and community-building
- push students to engage more deeply and critically with the text
- review and reinforce specific literacy skills and concepts (such as distinguishing between a summary and critique, comma and semicolon, and internal and external conflict)

What does WRAP time look like in action? The short (and not entirely helpful) answer is this: It depends! On the day, week, lesson and unit objectives, curriculum, grade level, and of course, our students. It's important that we tailor our WRAP prompts to best support the readers and writers in our classrooms and to align with our goals as a school and ELA department.

In this chapter, we will outline several WRAP prompts and "collections" that ELA teachers and teams can add to their playbook. You will notice that the prompts vary in purpose, length, and difficulty. Some prompts reinforce literature standards such as characterization, conflict, and point of view while others facilitate student reflection and conversation. Some address one specific concept while others address multiple skills. Many can be "dressed up" (longer and more rigorous) or "dressed down" (shorter and less formal) as needed. Prompts can be repeated throughout the year (weekly, monthly, quarterly, etc.) or assigned just once. You can also design WRAP "choice boards" or "independent reading projects," where students select one or more tasks from a menu of options.

Given that our students' needs are ever evolving, I imagine my approach to WRAP time will continue to evolve, too. Every fall, I review the full list and determine where and how each prompt may fit (or perhaps may not fit) into my plan for the upcoming school year. Here are some of the questions I ponder:

> Based on the data at our disposal, what should we prioritize during our WRAP time? What does this specific group of students need most? What do I want students to learn and accomplish over the course of a week? What skills do I want students to develop over the course of 180 days? Which WRAP prompts will keep students engaged and help us achieve our goals?

Sure, it'd be "easier" for me to run back the same prompts in the same order, year after year, but it wouldn't be fair to my current group of students. What worked one year may not work the next. What worked with one block may not work with the next. For that reason, you will not find the prompts listed in sequential order (Day 1, Day 2, Day 3 . . . Day 180, etc.). Instead, you will find twenty of our "greatest hits"—prompts that continue to inspire rich conversation, creativity, and critical thinking in our classroom.

I recommend that you and your ELA teammates take time to review the full list and customize a sequence that makes sense for your school. The key, of course, is intentionality. We maximize our WRAP impact when we know what we want to accomplish. Do we want our WRAP time to feel collaborative and conversational? Do we want students to engage in literary analysis? Do we want students to examine authors' craft to inspire their own narrative writing? Do we want to use our WRAP time to incorporate poetry, authentic grammar instruction, or SEL competencies? Do we want students to reflect on their reading? All of the above?

If your answer is "all of the above," then here's what a typical week could look like:

- **Monday:** Introduce a grammar concept—say semicolons or appositive phrases—that we want students to apply in their own writing.
- **Tuesday:** Assign a "lit analysis" prompt, where students dig into characterization, conflict, plot, point of view, setting, and/or theme.
- **Wednesday:** Review our grammar concept and facilitate a quick classroom conversation.
- **Thursday:** Encourage students to complete a creative task, such as a character profile, playlist, or poem.
- **Friday:** Have students submit an individual "check-in," reflecting on what they read, learned, and accomplished over the course of the week.

We could then follow the same structure the following week, simply selecting a new grammar concept, "lit analysis" focus, discussion prompt, and creative task (and changing the wording slightly on the Friday reflection). Or the following week could feel entirely different. For example, our students may spend several class periods working on an author letter, book review, compare-contrast essay, narrative continuation, or research project. (You will notice that I tried to group the longer WRAP prompts near the end.)

Remember there's no "perfect" approach. If your students are reading, writing, speaking, thinking, creating, sharing, reflecting, and ultimately improving, then you are doing it right.

As advised with the "Intro to Lit" unit, don't try to get to every prompt in year one. Pick a few and do them well. Be clear and consistent. Keep things simple. (And if you have "a lot to cover" in the second half of your ELA block, it's okay to keep things short.) While our Read and WRAP time should be meaningful, it shouldn't feel overwhelming for students (or us). Don't burn yourself out trying to grade every quick write. Give students the benefit of the doubt. Extend grace. Trust your instincts. Ask yourself, *what prompts would I appreciate if I were a student in this class?* Remember there's no "perfect" approach. If your students are reading, writing, speaking, thinking, creating, sharing, reflecting, and ultimately improving, then you are doing it right. Whether the WRAP tasks are formal or informal, graded or ungraded, completed in five minutes or over the course of five days, they all add up (and compound). And whenever you're doubting the impact, flip through a student composition notebook and see how much brilliance is in there. Finally, remember that this chapter is only a starting point. When the timer goes off and the notebooks come out, the possibilities are endless.

WRAP PROMPTS AND POSSIBILITIES AT A GLANCE

ACTIVITIES	PAGE NUMBERS
Quick Conversations: 8 "go-to" conversation starters when WRAP time is limited	120
Reading Check-ins: 2 opportunities for students to provide an update on reading progress	121–122
Choice Board Options: 12 possible tasks spanning a wide range of skills and standards	123–124
Reading Reflection: 12 prompts that promote deeper thinking and feedback	125–126
Poetry Prompts: 5 ways to sprinkle in poetry throughout the school year	127–134
Grammar Prompts: Strategies to incorporate authentic grammar instruction	135–139
Current Mood: An example of how to integrate literacy and SEL standards	140
Seasonal and Trendy Prompts: 4 prompts to use during specific seasons or riffing off pop culture trends	141–143
100-Word Responses: Several prompts that require students to write with precision	144–147
Character Analysis: 6 questions to help students analyze character(s) and develop deep understanding of their reading	148–149
Character Letters: 6 variations that help students examine perspective and point of view	150
Character Interview or Profile: A chance for students to write creatively while demonstrating comprehension	151–153
Lit Playlist: A creative opportunity to step inside a character, plot, mood, or setting with music	154–155
Literary Matchups: A creative writing prompt that allows a deep dive into character analysis	156–157
Compare-Contrast Writing: 2 prompts for identifying similarities and differences between books and/or characters	158–159
Author Letter and Spotlight: 2 prompts that could be short or lengthy, allowing students additional time for research and writing	160–163
Connect and Extend: A research project inspired by students' independent reading across a semester or year	164–165
One-Pager: A powerful activity to showcase understanding, creativity, and critical thinking	166–167
Narrative Writing: 2 prompts that help students hone their skills using mentor authors and texts, either with scene analysis or narrative continuation	168–171
Book Review: 3 solid options any time during the school year	172–176

QUICK CONVERSATIONS

Overview: The eight prompts outlined here work well if/when our WRAP time is limited (say two to three minutes) and we're still looking to spark authentic conversation and build community. Have students jot down a quick response in their notebook or, more likely, display one or two of the prompts on the screen and jump straight into a small-group or whole-class conversation (after giving students thirty seconds to process on their own). For example, with these prompts, we can circulate the classroom and get "real-time" feedback from every reader:

- "Oh, it looks like a lot of us are holding four or five fingers up. I love to see it. Does anyone want to share why? How about you take thirty seconds to share with a partner?"

- "Oh, I see a good amount of ones and twos. How much longer do y'all plan to keep reading? Let's discuss briefly with a partner. When do you think it's okay to abandon a book? How many pages in?"

- "It looks like fifteen out of twenty of us are giving a thumbs up, which is awesome. Quick math question: What does that look like as a percentage? Now, who wants to share why they gave their book a thumbs up? Does anyone want to share why they gave their book a thumbs down?"

1.	Who is really invested in/excited about their current read and wants to share why?	5.	Thumbs Up or Down: Based on what you've read thus far, would you give your current book a thumbs up or thumbs down, and why?
2.	Who is struggling to get into their book and wants to share why? How much longer do you plan to read before abandoning?	6.	What book(s) do you plan to read next? What's on your TBR? Do you plan to continue a series? Explore a similar genre or theme or try something different?
3.	What genre are you reading right now? Is anyone in the group/class reading a graphic novel? Novel in verse? Nonfiction? Fantasy? Mystery? Is it possible for a book to fall into multiple genres?	7.	Who needs inspiration for their next read? Share what type of book you're in the mood for, and we'll see if someone can help you out with a recommendation.
4.	Fist to Five: On a 0 (fist) to 5 (all five fingers) scale, what would you rate your current read, and why?	8.	Without spoiling anything for the rest of us, what predictions do you have for your book? How do you see things unfolding and ultimately getting resolved?

READING CHECK-INS

FIGURE 5.1 ● Sticky Note Tweet

Sticky note quick-writes are a great way to check in with ALL students (and get them moving) after independent reading. I can then sort comments to see what students I should catch up with the next day. 📚
📓 #ProjectLITchat

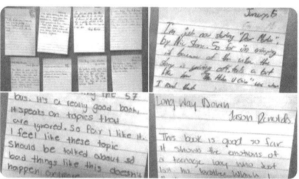

Overview: The two reading check-ins here show how easily our WRAP prompts can be "dressed down" or "dressed up" depending on our time and objective. Both prompts have value; they just serve different purposes. In Option A, students spend a few minutes jotting down their thoughts on a sticky note. This is obviously ungraded—the goal is to get instant feedback and to get students moving. Meanwhile, in Option B, students apply several skills (when to use quotes vs. italics, distinguishing between a summary and critique, MLA format, complex sentence structure, etc.) in one strong paragraph. This prompt will be graded.

Option A: Sticky Note Check-In

Prompt: On a sticky note, share a quick update on your current read.

Student Example

I've been reading The 57 Bus. *It's a really good book, it speaks on topics that are ignored. So far I like it. I feel like these topics should be talked about so bad things like this doesn't happen anymore.*

(Editor's Note: This was written on a sticky note, but it was typed here to make it easier to view.)

(Continued)

(Continued)

Option B: Official Check-In

Prompt: Think about the book you're currently reading (or one you have finished recently) and write one strong paragraph (approximately 8–10 sentences) that accomplishes the following:

- Includes the title (in *italics*) and author.
- Provides a brief synopsis (1–2 sentences). Remember, the primary goal of this response is to highlight YOUR analysis and critical thinking.
- Shares your assessment of the book thus far (strengths and/or weaknesses, what makes it interesting/compelling/ enjoyable and why, target audience, why others should/ shouldn't read it, how it's changed/challenged your thinking, what you've learned, what the author does well and/or poorly, etc.)
- Writes with the audience (Dr. Amato and classmates) in mind.

Reminders:

- Incorporate a variety of sentences (simple, compound, complex, etc.) and strong transition words, adjectives, and verbs.
- MLA Format (including an original title).
- You do not need to cite textual evidence directly, but the response should demonstrate a close reading and deep understanding of the book.

CHOICE BOARD OPTIONS

Overview: The twelve prompts shared here all work well as standalone activities—we can easily share one prompt per day over the course of two to three weeks. For example, in a given week, students could respond to "Driving Question," "Setting the Scene," "Digging into Dialogue," "Word of the Day," and "Character Traits." However, we can also group X number of the prompts into a "choice board." I recommend that we select four of five prompts that most align to our current goals and objectives and then encourage students to pick one (or more) to dig into on their own.

WORD OF THE DAY	DRIVING QUESTION
Find a word from your current read that stands out as particularly interesting and/or previously unknown. Using context clues, what does it mean? Why did the author choose this word? What effect does it have on the sentence and/or story? Create your own original sentence that includes your "word of the day." (Bonus points if you can draw a picture, too!)	What is the big question in your current read?! What are you, as the reader, trying to figure out? For example: • *Why is Monday gone, and where is she?* • *Is Will going to continue the cycle?* • *Will Daniel and Natasha get their happy ending?* • *How is Starr going to overcome her fear of speaking out and get justice?* • *How and why do Romeo and Juliet ultimately die?*
FAVORITE LINES	**"WANT-BUT"**
What are some of your favorite quotes/lines from your current read? Write down at least one quote in your notebook, being sure to include the page number. Then, explain why you found it particularly beautiful, interesting, profound, significant, etc. (Bonus points if you write and "decorate" the quote on an index card for our classroom display.)	What does the main character in your novel WANT more than anything in the world? Who and/or what is getting in their way (conflict)? Feel free to use the following stem to frame your response: _____ *wants* _____, *but* _____
FIGURATIVELY SPEAKING	**PAINTING A PICTURE**
Find and share an example of figurative language from your current read. Be sure to name the type (simile, metaphor, personification, hyperbole, etc.) and explain its impact and/or significance.	Find an example of imagery from your current read. What character, scene, setting, etc. stands out? What can you visualize in your mind? Write down the excerpt in your notebook, being sure to include the page number. Then, explain why you found it particularly vivid. (Bonus points if you can draw the scene or character, too!)

(Continued)

(Continued)

SETTING THE SCENE

As you think about the setting of your current read, respond to some (but probably not all) of the following:

- Where does your current read take place? How do you know?
- When does your current read take place? Is your book set in the past, present, or future?
- Could the story take place anywhere or does it take readers to a specific time and place?
- Are there multiple timelines or just one?
- How does the story's setting affect the plot? Does the setting play a major or minor role in the story? How so?
- What senses (sight, taste, smell, etc.) are evoked as you read?

DIGGING INTO DIALOGUE

As you pay attention to the author's use of dialogue, respond to some (but probably not all) of the following:

- Does the author use dialogue in the story? If so, how frequently? What do you notice about how the dialogue is punctuated?
- Does the dialogue sound realistic? Why, or why not?
- What purpose does dialogue serve in the story? Does it propel the plot forward? Does it reveal character?
- What are some of the most memorable conversations that stand out from what you read today? (Bonus: Try reading aloud some of the best dialogue from your book, recruiting a partner to join you if necessary!)

CHARACTER TRAITS

Step 1: Select one character from your current read and write their name in the center of your notebook page. Put a box around it.

Step 2: Draw three lines out from the character's box. At the end of each line, write a strong, specific adjective to describe that character (for example: driven, empathetic, and outgoing). Then, circle each of the three adjectives.

Step 3: Provide evidence and examples from the text to support each adjective (what makes them driven, empathetic, and outgoing?).

Step 4 (Optional Extension): Use the bubble map to write a strong paragraph or multi-paragraph essay.

PAGE TO SCREEN

Step 1: Identify three or four of the most defining scenes/moments from your current read. (In other words, if your book was turned into a movie, what scenes would *have* to be included?)

Step 2: Write (or draw/sketch) a summary of each and explain its significance (why you found it particularly important, interesting, memorable, etc.)

Step 3 (Bonus): If your book was adapted for the screen, who would you cast for the major roles, and why? And if the book has already been brought to the screen, have you seen it? If so, how did it compare to the book? If not, do you plan to watch it? Either way, how do you feel about the casting choices?

INEVITABLE CONFLICT

Discuss the difference between internal and external conflict. Then, look specifically at your current read. What are the major internal and/or external conflicts in the book? How do you predict the conflict(s) will be resolved?

PLOT DIAGRAM

After reviewing the plot elements (exposition, rising action, climax, falling action, resolution) as a class, complete a plot diagram for your current/recent read. Where would you chart each of the story's major moments? Be ready to share with classmates!

READING REFLECTION

Overview: This collection of prompts encourages students to reflect on their reading and/or provide feedback on our Read and WRAP routine. While some prompts work well during the first few weeks (you will recognize a few from our "Intro to Lit" unit in chapter 4), my advice is to revisit them throughout the year. It's powerful to see how our students' responses change and crystalize. Here's one more suggestion: set aside consistent time (perhaps every other Friday) for students to reflect. For example, here's what I may write and share with students during our WRAP time:

Happy Friday, y'all!

Thanks for your hard work this week. It looks like many of us are in a reading groove lately, which is great to see. For today's quick write, select at least one (but possibly two or three) of the prompts below to respond to in your notebook. Feel free to focus on your current book or discuss your reading more broadly. Additionally, please know that your feedback is always appreciated. Have a great weekend, and as always, happy reading!

Dr. Amato

WRAP PROMPTS: READING REFLECTION

1. What should your teacher know about your reading lately? What would you like to share? What support do you need this week?

2. What book are you reading currently? What page are you on? When do you anticipate that you will finish it? What do you plan to read next?

3. What books do you find yourself gravitating toward lately? Do you plan to stick with that genre or try something different? Do you need any recs?

4. On a 1–5 scale, how would you evaluate your reading performance? (For the sports fan, 1 = "ice cold" and 5 = "on fire.") Be sure to explain why. Are there any tweaks or adjustments you can make to improve your reading performance? What support do you need from your teacher?

5. On a 1–5 scale, how are you feeling about your current book? (1 = "I'm ready to abandon it" and 5 = "I can't put it down.") Be sure to explain why.

(Continued)

(Continued)

6. On a 1–5 scale, how are you feeling about our Read and WRAP time? Be sure to explain why. Feedback and suggestions are appreciated!

7. To borrow a line from Goldilocks, does your current read feel too easy, too hard, or just right for you? How so?

8. Approximately how many pages do you find yourself reading per day? Per week? Are you happy with your pace? Is there anything you can do to get more "steps in" (or "pages in") per day/week?

9. How do you feel about the length of our reading time? Too short? Too long? Just right? Briefly explain why.

10. Who are you as a reader? How would you characterize your reading identity?

11. How have you changed (improved, progressed, stagnated, regressed, etc.) as a reader over the course of the year? How so?

12. Why is reading important to you? What role does it play in your life?

POETRY PROMPTS

Our WRAP time allows us to sprinkle in poetry throughout the year in addition to or in lieu of a full poetry unit. Here are five of our favorites—BioPoem, haiku, acrostic, free verse, and sonnet—along with several student examples.

OPTION A: CHARACTER BIOPOEM

Overview: The "BioPoem" has been a classroom staple for years. Initially, it was an effective way to get students to introduce themselves. Later, we added a twist—write a second BioPoem from the point of view of a character. While I provide a template (see below), I also give students license to write more creatively if they desire. Students write the first draft of the poem on day one and spend the second day revising, polishing, and sharing.

Character BioPoem Template

First Name

3 adjectives to describe them

A significant relationship (family, friendship)

Setting/Location (literal or figurative)

Pick several of the "Who _____" below or come up with your own verbs

Who loves

Who fears

Who needs

Who wants

Who misses

Who feels

Who fears

Who dreams

Who believes

Who would like to see

Last Name

Student Example
(Inspired by *Not Your Perfect Mexican Daughter* by Erika Sanchez)

Julia

rebellious, bold, and unique

Born in Chicago

a sister

who loves her sisters

who believes she is misunderstood

who fears nothing

who wants peace with herself

who wants her sister Olga to come back

who overcomes a loss

who misses her sister

who feels like God isn't real

who dreams to be the best writer

who speaks her mind

who hopes to prove that not everything is her fault

Reyes

Student Example
(Inspired by *Long Way Down* by Jason Reynolds)

Hello, my name's William

Depressed, confused, and scared

A loving brother and son, the last living one

Who loves his family more than anything

Who feels sad, mad, depressed, and angry

Who needs love, a hug, and comfort from the man above

Who remembers too many lives lost to bullets

Who fears the life I live and the people I once called friends

Who wants answers to why Shawn was shot dead in the streets

Who believes Riggs killed my brother, I'm sure but not positive you see

Stuck on an elevator so confused I can barely think

Holloman

OPTION B: HAIKU

Overview: This quick yet challenging prompt is an effective way to introduce or review haiku. Students appreciate the brevity and structure. Here's how it looks in action:

Step 1: Share a few famous haikus on the board and encourage students read them aloud.

Step 2: As a group, review the definition of haiku.

Step 3: Encourage students to write at least one haiku inspired by their current read in their notebook. *Write a haiku (5 syllables, 7 syllables, 5 syllables) inspired by your current read. Feel free to be creative. Your haiku can summarize the book, offer a judgement, describe a character or conflict, convey a key theme, etc. You could also write the poem from the point of view of a character. In other words, what could you see that character writing for this assignment?*

Step 4: Turn and share with partner.

Step 5: Whole-class share-outs.

Overview: As a child, I remember writing acrostic poems all the time. I'm still a fan of acrostic poems today. There are several variations that allow for students at all skill levels to experience success. Here's one possibility: Have fun writing an acrostic poem that uses the book title or a character name. Try to push yourself to write more than one word per line and be sure to demonstrate deep understanding of the book and/or character.

Student Example
(inspired by *The Hate U Give* by Angie Thomas)

Handsome boy

Only if I could have done something

Never thought this would happen

Ova what? Why did he pull the trigger?

Really?

Killed, in front of me

How am I supposed to deal w/this?

Adding this to seeing Natasha being killed

Lately everything is changing

I need some help

Long live Khalil

Student Example
(inspired by *The Crossover* by Kwame Alexander)

Basketball Stars

Balling like I'm Durant

Assisting like I'm Rondo

Shooting like I'm Curry

Kicking my legs up when I dunk like I'm Westbrook

Elevating my teammates like I'm CP3

Talking trash like I'm Garnett

Blocking like I'm Ibaka

Athletic like I'm Lebron

Lefty like I'm Harden

Losing like I'm the Lakers

OPTION D: WRITER'S CHOICE

Overview: In this prompt, students have the option to write in a style, structure, and form of their choice. Rhyme or no rhyme. One long stanza or multiple stanzas with an equal number of lines. The only requirement is that students demonstrate deep understanding of their current read.

Below are three student examples inspired by Angie Thomas's *The Hate U Give*. The first is an authentic, powerful poem written from the point of view of Khalil, Starr's childhood best friend. I still get chills reading it. You will notice that the student underlined the rhyming words for effect. The second, written with an AABBCC rhyme scheme, captures Starr's thoughts and the novel's core themes and conflicts perfectly.
The third poem is equally brilliant; it's a student's take on "Mother to Son" by Langston Hughes (which we had read earlier in the school year). She wrote the poem from the point of view of Maverick to his daughter Starr. Amazing, right?

Student Example

T.H.U.G

Grandma lost her job + has chemo

So she's getting <u>weak</u>

I can't just sit here + let it happen

I can't take a <u>seat</u>

So I'm out here on this corner

24 hours, 7 days a <u>week</u>

Going through hardships

So I hit the <u>streets</u>

Money so good I'm paying bills

+ got the new J's on my <u>feet</u>

No mom or dad so I'm the man of the house

I gotta put food on he table so fam can <u>eat</u>

Saw my friend Starr at a party

I had to <u>speak</u>

Shots go off at the party

We ran to my <u>jeep</u>

Cops pull us over told me to get out the car

He feeling on my <u>jeans</u>

He went back to the car, I go and check on Starr

POP! POP! POP! I got tears of blood

Coming down my <u>cheek</u>

Student Example

THOUGHTS

Should I speak or keep quiet

If I do will it start a riot?

Police just keep wilding

Garden Heights is just violent

Now that Khalil is gone

I feel all alone

Student Example

Daddy to Starr

Well, Starr, I'll tell you

Life for me ain't been no walk in the park

It has had guns in it,

And kings,

And communities torn apart,

And places with little sunshine,

Cold

But threw [*sic*] it all

I found my light,

And achieved my dreams,

(Continued)

(Continued)

And beat the system

And Starr

Now it is your time to shine

I didn't name you Starr by accident

Life for me ain't been no walk in the park

OPTION E: SONNET

Overview: Students enjoyed crafting their own sonnets as we concluded our whole-class read of *Romeo and Juliet*. Their first task was to write an epilogue in the same style as the prologue ("Two households, both alike in dignity/In fair Verona, where we lay our scene"). The second task was to write a sonnet of their choice, whether it was to profess their love of a sport, food, family member, friend, season, or instrument. The results were incredible! However, you don't need to read Shakespeare for students to write a sonnet. Simply review one or all of the possible forms (for example: ABAB CDCD EFEF GG), share a few examples ("Shall I compare thee to a summer's day?"), and encourage students to give it their best shot. *Write a sonnet that summarizes one of your recent reads or one from the point of view of a character. Bonus points if you can stick to iambic pentameter (10 syllables per line).*

GRAMMAR PROMPTS

Overview: Inspired by Dave Stuart Jr.'s article "Mechanics Instruction That Sticks" (https://davestuartjr.com/grammar/), I started to wonder: *Is there a way we can incorporate authentic grammar instruction into our Read and WRAP routine?!* Yes, yes we can. While many schools and districts have understandably moved away from direct grammar instruction, I have found there are ways we can incorporate valuable mini lessons into our Read and WRAP routine. By ignoring run-on sentences and incorrect comma usage, we are ultimately doing students a disservice. Here is how we can address these gaps:

Step 1: After the timer goes off, signaling the end of independent reading, I briefly introduce/review a grammar concept/skill (for example, appositive phrases) that either:

a.   I would like to see students include or apply more frequently in their writing.

b.   I have noticed many students struggling with recently.

c.   I am required to teach as part of our district's curriculum map.

Possible Mini Lessons

- Active vs. Passive Voice
- Adjectives and Adverbs
- Apostrophes
- Appositive Phrases
- Colons and Semicolons
- Commas
- Consistent Verb Tense
- Dashes, Hyphens, and Ellipses
- Dependent vs. Independent Clauses
- Fragments and Run-Ons
- Parallel Structure
- Parts of Speech
- Prefixes/Suffixes
- Pronoun-Antecedent Agreement
- Punctuating Dialogue
- Quotes vs. Italics
- Simple, Compound, Complex, and Compound-Complex Sentences

(Continued)

(Continued)

- Subject-Verb Agreement
- Synonyms/Antonyms
- Troublesome Word Pairs
- Verb Tense and Consistency

Step 2: Before the lesson, I find an example of an appositive phrase from a high-interest MG/YA novel. Then, during the lesson, I share the example with the group. We discuss. *What do we notice about this sentence? Where is the appositive phrase? What is it describing? What would happen if we took it out? Would the sentence still make sense? Where are the commas? Why do we need them?*

Step 3: During our reading time, students keep an eye out for an appositive phrase in their respective books. Then, when we WRAP, the hope is that a few students can share their example with the group. *Who thinks they found an appositive phrase in their book? Anyone want to share? Feel free to go back to the text and see if you can spot one. What should we be looking for again?*

Step 4: From there, I encourage every student to write one strong sentence—related to their current read—that includes an appositive phrase. We can also try to incorporate a literature skill/concept into this sentence (multiple birds, one stone). For example:

> **TODAY'S WRAP PROMPT:** *Write one strong sentence describing the protagonist in your current read. Be sure to include an appositive phrase!*

As students practice in their notebooks, I circulate the room, offering feedback and support. *This sentence looks great—well done! Don't forget your commas. If we took out the appositive phrase, would the sentence still make sense? Go back and underline the appositive phrase if you haven't done so already.* We wrap up the mini lesson with small-group and/or whole-group share-outs along with any reteaching/clarification.

Here's another one of my favorite grammar prompts/mini lessons that reviews several skills in a matter of minutes:

Me: Quick review, y'all. What do we know about compound sentences?

Student: A sentence that has two or more independent clauses.

Me: Perfect! And how can we correctly combine two independent clauses?

Student:	With a semicolon.
Me:	Without a doubt. A semicolon is strong enough to combine two independent clauses. Any other ways?
Student:	A comma and a conjunction?
Me:	Awesome. A comma is too weak by itself, so it needs backup. And what's the acronym for the group of coordinating conjunctions?
Class:	FANBOYS!
Me:	Exactly. What are they again?
Together:	F is FOR. A is AND. N is NOR. B is BUT. O is OR. Y is YET. S is So.
Me:	Sweet. Now, how can we define conflict again?
Student:	A problem.
Me:	What types of conflict do we typically see in literature? Character vs. . . .?

Students share out answers (character vs. character, self, nature, technology, supernatural, society, etc.).

Me:	Well done, y'all. Think we got them all. Do any of you ever face conflict?
Together:	Of course. All the time.
Me:	Any school-appropriate conflicts y'all want to share quickly? *Possible discussion.*
Me:	Conflict is inevitable. Think about a TV show or movie you've watched recently. Why do you keep watching it? *Possible discussion.*
Me:	Now, think about the book you're reading. I guarantee there's conflict. Conflict drives plot. The main character is almost always attempting to overcome a problem, or series of problems. Usually, we're rooting for someone, right? What's the fancy name for that character again?
Student:	Protagonist?
Me:	Yup! If we're PRO Lakers, what does that mean?
Student:	We're rooting for them.
Me:	What if we're against something? What prefix do we use?
Student:	Anti?
Me:	Yup! Anti-bullying. Anti-racism. Antibiotics help us fight against bacteria. So what's the fancy word for the "villain" in a story?

Student:	The antagonist?
Me:	Perfect. And does the antagonist have to be a person?
Student:	Nope! *Possible discussion.*
Me:	Okay, now let's get back to our prompt and the books we're reading. Every one of our stories is different. Yet, I guarantee they all have something in common. Any guesses?
Student:	They all have characters.
Me:	True! Anything else?
Student:	They all have conflict.
Me:	They sure do. So, that's your task now. What is one of the major conflicts in your story? What does your character want? What is getting in their way? Is the conflict internal or external? Think about it for a minute . . . Now, try writing one strong compound sentence. That's it! Just one sentence. What should we see in a compound sentence?
Student:	Two independent clauses with a FANBOYS in the middle of them.
Me:	Great. And what do we want in front of the conjunction?
Student:	A comma?
Me:	Exactly! Everyone, does the comma goes before or after the conjunction?
Together:	Before!
Me:	What if we wanted to use a semicolon to combine the two independent clauses? Would we need a conjunction?
Student:	No, we either use the comma and FANBOYS or the semicolon.
Me:	Exactly. The semicolon is strong enough on its own. Okay, back to our assignment: write one strong compound sentence describing a conflict in your current book. That's it!

From here, I'll circulate the room, checking in with students as they write in their notebooks. Depending on time, we'll have two to three students share out with the group (or with their tables). I may share my example on the board, too, especially if I sense that students need a little more guidance.

Me: Great work, y'all! Who wants to share their sentence?

Student shares.

Me: What do we notice about this example? What do we like about it? Why is it correct? Okay, great. Do we have another volunteer?

Second student shares. Conversation continues.

I like this prompt for several reasons:

- We reviewed several key grammar concepts, including a few that will show up on the ACT, in a short amount of time. Lots of birds (independent clauses, conjunctions, commas, semicolons, conflict, protagonist, anti, antagonist, etc.) with one stone.

- We connected reading, writing, and grammar instead of trying to teach skills in isolation.

- Our students came away with a deeper understanding of their book and stories in general. They also improved as writers.

- We made it easy to engage. One sentence—that's all we needed from everyone. As a result, all students could experience success.

- It was easy to provide feedback. I bounced from table to table, scanning students' sentences. *Check. Check. Check. Great work, y'all. We're ready to move on.* Meanwhile, if I sensed that several of us were struggling, we could return to the board. *Okay, y'all. Here's my example. What do you notice? Exactly right. Now, let's go back to your sentence and revise. Remember, two independent clauses combined with a comma in front of a conjunction.*

- We held students "accountable" without killing their love of the book.

Finally, here's a fun prompt that helps students review some of the most troublesome word pairs.

TODAY'S WRAP PROMPT: *Write a brief review of your current/recent read using at least six of the following troublesome words:* to, too, two; **they're**, **their**, **there**; it's, its; **you're**, **your**; hear, here; **accept**, **except**; bare, bear; **board**, **bored**; weather, whether; **then**, **than**; who's, whose; **affect**, **effect**; break; brake; **definitely**; **defiantly**; lose; loose. *Use the example below as a guide.*

You're not going to be bored if you read *Long Way Down* by Jason Reynolds; in fact, it's almost impossible to put down. The novel in verse follows the story of William Holloman, who's struggling to accept the loss of his brother. Will believes he knows who murdered Shawn—except that he doesn't. Whether you are a teenager or an adult, the heartfelt, lyrical story will definitely keep you hooked from the first page to the last.

CURRENT MOOD

List of Feelings
handout

Overview: This prompt, where students attempt to pinpoint how a character in their current read is feeling before doing the same for themselves, shows how we easily and effectively we can integrate Social Emotional Learning (SEL) and literacy skills into our WRAP time.

Here's what this mini lesson looks like in action:

Step 1: Students review the "List of Feelings" handout (via Hoffman Institute). The teacher places copies on each desk/table.

Step 2: Teacher encourages students to select two to three words to describe how the protagonist in their current read is feeling in the moment.

Step 3: Students explain why they selected those words (either in their notebook or in a group conversation).

Step 4: Teacher encourages students to find the word(s) to describe how they are feeling today.

Step 5: Students explain why they selected their respective words.

Step 6: Students select one gratitude prompt from the slide (see below) to respond to in their notebook.

Step 7: Group share-outs.

FRIDAY GRATITUDE PROMPT

- I am grateful for _____ because . . .
- I appreciate _____ because . . .
- A lesson I am learning is . . .
- An area I've seen myself grow is . . .
- I feel seen and supported by . . .
- I'm proud of the fact that I . . .
- I recently accomplished . . .
- A strength of mine is . . .
- A memory I am grateful for is . . .
- A space/place I feel safe in is . . .
- I'm grateful _____ has taught me about . . .

SEASONAL AND "TRENDY" PROMPTS

Overview: The first two options, which encourage students to show "gratitude" and "love" toward their favorite books and authors, work well near Thanksgiving and Valentine's Day respectively. The third and fourth prompts show how we can lean into the latest pop culture trends, such as Wordle or Spotify Wrapped, and incorporate them into our WRAP time.

OPTION A: SHOWING GRATITUDE

Prompt: Before Thanksgiving break, I encourage students to create four boxes/squares in their notebook (or on a blank sheet of colored paper if we're planning to display them). In box one, they list five authors they are grateful for. In box two, they list five books they are grateful for. In box three, they list five foods thy are grateful for. Students select their fourth and final category —their "top five" songs, artists, athletes, sports teams, video games, board games, products, superheroes, and so forth. (Lots of extension possibilities here, too.)

OPTION B: LIT LOVE

Prompt: Here's a similar version that works well on/near Valentine's Day. Students create a four-square grid and list five characters, books, and authors they "love" in the first three boxes. Students select their fourth and final category. (Bonus: Have students write brief notes/messages "showing love" to one of their favorite authors.)

OPTION C: WORDLE

Prompt: During the Wordle craze, we had a lot of fun with this one. You can see the directions and student examples below. While this specific task may lose its luster, I will continue to find ways to incorporate the latest trends (especially when they're tailor-made for ELA classrooms) into our WRAP prompts.

> **Step 1:** Come up with at least six five-letter words related to your current read (think character, theme, conflict, setting, tone, etc.)
>
> **Step 2:** Decide on the most important word. It will go on the sixth and final line—in green.

Step 3: Fill in the first five lines with the appropriate colors—yellow (right letter, wrong place), green (right letter, right place), or blank (wrong letter).

FIGURES 5.2 – 5.3 ● Student Examples 1–2

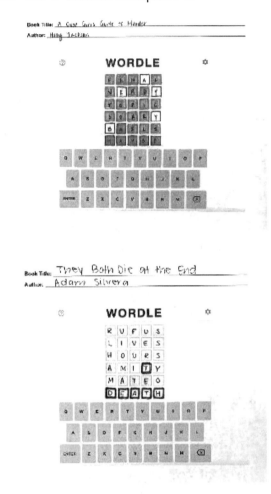

OPTION D: "BOOK WRAPPED"

Prompt: During homeroom one December morning, students were discussing their Spotify "Wrapped" with excitement, which got my teacher brain thinking: *How could we apply this concept to reading?* For those who are unfamiliar, Spotify tracks its users' "listening behavior" (songs, artists, podcasts, total minutes, etc.) from January to October 31. By early December, users can access their personalized "Wrapped" in early December and share it with friends and followers on social media. Inspired by Spotify's description of their viral marketing campaign, I created my reading-focused version, "Book Wrapped":

"Book Wrapped" is a celebration of the school year gone by and an invitation to join in on the fun. . . . We know that no two readers are alike, so Book Wrapped encourages you to gaze into your vibrant literary kaleidoscope and show it off to the world.

Spotify also developed a variety of "Listening Personalities," such as "The Replayer," "The Specialist," and "The Adventurer." How cool would it be if our students created their own "Reading Personalities"? *The Rereader, The Adventurer, The Speed Reader, The Crier, The Mystery-Lover, The Picky Eater, The Fantasy Fan, The Thrill Seeker, The Emo-Reader, The Abandoner*—what am I missing? Additionally, as we close out a semester or school year, we can have students reflect on their favorite authors, books, and genres and estimate the number of pages or minutes read. We can also create a class or schoolwide graphic, inspired by Spotify's "Most-Streamed Artists Globally" chart, that includes our Top Five "Most-Read Books" and Top Five "Most-Read Authors."

BOOK WRAPPED

This school year . . .

- I explored _____ different genres
- My top 5 genres: _____
- My top genre was _____
- I read _____ books
- My top 5 books: _____
- My top book was _____
- I read an estimated _____ pages
- I read for an estimated _____ minutes

As a class . . .

Our Top 5 "Most-Read Books" were _____

Our Top 5 "Most-Read Authors" were _____

100-WORD RESPONSES

Overview: I have found there is an added level of focus and engagement when we're pushed to write an exact number of words, whether it's six, ten, or one hundred words. I actually stumbled upon the one hundred-word prompt while getting a pair of glasses at Warby Parker. I remember reading their origin story, "Warby Parker in 100 Words," and immediately started thinking of the classroom possibilities. Here are a few that we have since used in our classroom:

- Summarize your book in one hundred words.

- Write a review of your book in one hundred words.

- Write: "My Life in 100 Words."

- Share a personal story in one hundred words.

- Describe your reading journey in one hundred words.

- Capture Project LIT in one hundred words.

Here is one more variation that worked extremely well with our whole-class read of *Night*:

> **Prompt:** In precisely one hundred words, try to capture the essence of *Night*. You will write from a first-person point of view (as Elie). However, the style, tone, and format is up to you. You are free to use words and quotes from the memoir. It can be written in verse (poetry) or in traditional prose. You can write chronologically (like Elie) or more erratically. You will also decide how to format the memoir visually on the page. For example, you can include art in the background. We're looking for creativity, craft, and deep understanding of the complete text. Consider both the WHAT (what you decide to write) and HOW (style, visual, presentation, display, spacing, etc.). You have the option of working with a partner or individually.

Student Examples

Night in 100 Words

1941.

Almost thirteen, deeply observant.

The race toward death had begun.

Growing darkness.

"Forward! March!"

I already felt so weak . . .

"Men to the left! Women to the right!"

Was I still alive? Was I awake?

NEVER SHALL I FORGET that night.

Never shall I forget those flames that consumed my faith forever.

A-7713. I had no other name.

"Where is merciful God, where is He?"

Night was falling rapidly.

"Evacuation."

So we were men after all?

"Faster, you filthy dogs!"

"Don't think, don't stop, run!"

We had transcended everything.

Heavy snow continued to fall over the corpses.

I was sixteen.

And here is how two of our student founders described Project LIT:

Project LIT in 100 Words

Putting project lit in 100 words

Would be very hard

I don't know which words would describe

(Continued)

(Continued)

Such a powerful ORGANIZATION

That's spreading across the NATION

This summer will be a CELEBRATION

In the DEFLATION of book deserts

And the inflation of KNOWLEDGE

More people will enroll in COLLEGE

To make something of the lives

For success they'll strive

Some may ask why?

Why do we do what we do

That's because we want these kids to go to school

To gain knowledge

Chances of success would be high

We're project LIT and we're here to change lives

Project LIT in 100 Words

One classroom had a vision

We made it our mission

To end book deserts

In communities where there was drought

There are more liquor stores than libraries

This was our sad reality

We wanted to change that

We started building little libraries

and relationships

One book club with just a few people

Turned to a family with returning members

We now have (2,000) chapters in (48) states

And we met authors face to face

It has been challenging and tough

But we knew that one kid having one

good book isn't enough

We accomplished our mission

Project LIT was born

CHARACTER ANALYSIS

Overview: The six questions here, all designed to help students analyze a character in their current read, work well as a quick write or formal response. Feel free to assign the same prompt to all or encourage students to pick one (or more) that will allow them to demonstrate deep understanding of both their book and character. Numbers one and four, in particular, can be extended into a multi-paragraph essay. For example, students can easily generate a strong thesis that examines character transformation or analyzes three of the character's most admirable/heroic qualities.

Prompt: Think about a book you have finished recently or the one you are currently reading. From your perspective, what character stands out the most? Choose any character that you find particularly interesting and important; it doesn't have to be the protagonist. Once you have selected a character, write one strong paragraph that addresses one (or more) of the following questions:

1. How does the character change and/or grow over the course of the novel? Trace the character's journey/arc/evolution from the beginning to the end.

2. What were some of the critical moments and/or turning points in the character's journey?

3. What major conflict(s) does the character face in the novel? Is the character's struggle primarily internal or external? How so? How do they overcome the conflict(s)?

4. What adjectives would you use to describe the character, and why? What evidence and examples can you provide to support each trait/characteristic?

5. In what ways can you relate/connect/identify with the character? In what ways are you different?

6. What do you value, respect, admire, appreciate, and so on, most about the character? (On the other hand, what aspects of their character do you find frustrating?) Would you consider them to be heroic? Why, or why not?

Reminders:

- Be sure to include the character name, book title (italicized), and author.

- Incorporate a variety of sentences (simple, compound, complex, etc.) and strong transition words, adjectives, and verbs.

- MLA Format (including an original title).

- You do not need to cite textual evidence directly, but the response should demonstrate a deep understanding of the book and character.

Student Example (completed as an informal quick write): "My favorite character is Starr Carter from *The Hate U Give*. She showed me that even if you go through a traumatic experience and feel like there's no hope, justice can still be served. Starr showed compassion and empathy due to the loss of her childhood friend. No matter how hurt and broken she was, she still fought and made sure people would hear her voice. She got through many opsticles [*sic*] and still found happiness in the end of it all. Starr is the strongest and most empathetic character I've ever read about in a book."

CHARACTER LETTERS

Overview: Year after year, students respond well to letter writing. Below are six variations of this prompt, which include writing a letter to a character, writing from the point of view of a character, and writing from one character to another. While the responses can remain informal quick notes, students can easily turn them into longer, published pieces.

Prompts:

1. **Write a thoughtful letter/email to a character in your current/recent read as if they were a friend or classmate.** Feel free to offer advice, comment on a conflict they're going through, share how you can relate, ask questions, etc.	4. **Pick one compelling character from your current/recent read and write a letter from the future (one, five, ten years later, etc.)** What is their life like after the novel ends? What are they up to? Where do they live? How have they changed over time? What do they remember about their childhood? Who are they still in touch with?
2. **Write a letter or diary/journal entry from the point of view of a character in your current/recent read.** What have you been up to lately? What is on your mind? How are you feeling, and why?	5. **Write a letter from one character to another (or feel free to write two shorter letters – one from each character).** The characters must be from the same book. What could you see them sharing and discussing with one another?
3. **Pick one compelling character from your current/recent read and write a letter from their past (one, five, ten years earlier, etc.)** What was their life like before the novel began? What's their backstory? What event(s) shaped the person they are in the novel?	6. **Write a letter from one character to another (or feel free to write two shorter letters – one from each character).** However, the two characters must be from different books. What could you see them sharing and discussing with one another?

Student Example: Letter to Character (Xiomara from *The Poet X* by Elizabeth Acevedo)

Dear Xiomara,

You and I are pretty different but also have many similarities. I know what it's like to have a father "present but absent." When he was present, he would be drinking and arguing with us for no reason. . . . I also know what it's like to try to not share your writing with others. I choose not to share my writing because I'm afraid that people will laugh at my work. I write about my feelings, and if people laugh about my writing, it's as if they're laughing at my feelings which isn't a good feeling. Trust me, I know . . .

CHARACTER INTERVIEW OR PROFILE

Overview: The following prompts—a character interview, generic character profile, and fictional Instagram page—allow students to showcase their creativity while also demonstrating deep understanding of the text.

OPTION A – CHARACTER INTERVIEW

Prompt: Students create a fictional interview (podcast, newspaper, magazine, TV show, etc.) with a character in their current read. First, they will take the role of interviewer, host, reporter, or producer and come up with approximately six to eight thoughtful questions to pose to the character. For example: *How did it feel when . . . ? Do you ever regret . . . ? What's it like to . . . ? What's something most people don't know about you? Can you explain why . . . ? Who do you turn to when . . . ? What advice would you offer someone who . . . ?* Then, they will take the role of the character and come up with thoughtful answers to those questions.

To clarify, students are coming up with both the questions and the answers in the "interview." While the task could easily be completed individually in one or two class periods, it could also be worthwhile for students to work with a partner and hone their speaking and listening skills. For example, Student A interviews Student B, who answers the questions from the point of view of their favorite character. Then, they switch roles, with Student B posing the questions to Student A. Students can conduct the interviews "live" in front of the class or record them via audio or video. (Bonus points for anyone who decides to dress in character!)

OPTION B – CHARACTER PROFILE

Prompt: Inspired by our student interest survey, which was shared in chapter 4, this prompt pushes students to complete a profile from the point of view of their character. There's a high level of creativity and critical thinking involved, and while many of the prompts will not have a right or wrong answer (such as the character's favorite song or dream vacation), students should be ready to defend their responses.

CHARACTER PROFILE

Answer the questions below from the point of view of a character in your current book (or one you have read recently).

- Name:

- Some of my talents and hobbies are . . .

- Three adjectives to describe me are . . .

- My favorite subject(s) in school:

- My favorite song(s) or artist(s):

- My favorite sport(s) or team(s):

- I am afraid of . . .

- I am annoyed when . . .

- My favorite food:

- My dream vacation:

- My favorite book:

- One of my goals is to . . .

- If I could have dinner with three people, I would pick . . .

- Something you should know about me:

OPTION C –
CHARACTER INSTAGRAM PROFILE

Prompt: Students select a character in their current read and create a fictional Instagram profile for them. *What could you see this character posting and sharing on social media? How are they feeling at specific moments in the book?* Specifically, students find (via a Google image search) or take (with their own phone/camera) three photos that they could envision their character posting online. Then, they write a caption from that character's point of view. *Would they write in a formal or informal tone? How would the character punctuate their captions? It is more than acceptable if your captions are not grammatically correct; try to match your character's authentic voice.* In *Fahrenheit 451*, for example, I could see Clarisse McClellan taking a picture somewhere in nature and posting a Mary Oliver poem in the caption. In *The Crossover*, I could see Filthy McNasty posting a picture from basketball practice along with a freestyle poem in the caption. (One final technical note: In lieu of creating an actual Instagram account for the character, students should submit their "posts" via Google slides. On the left side of each slide, students will include the photo, and on the right, they will write the caption.)

LIT PLAYLIST

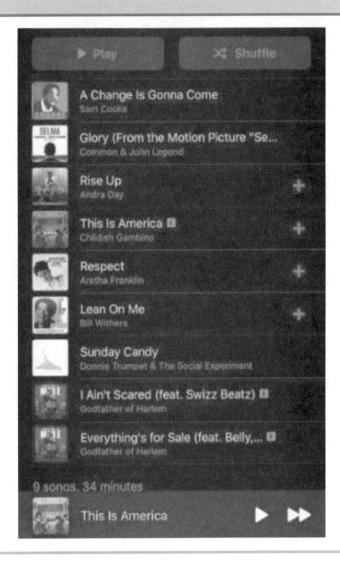

Overview: This prompt is great for the music lovers in our classroom. In the "short and sweet" version, students spend five to ten minutes curating a playlist inspired by a specific character and/or book. For example, what songs could you picture Josh Bell listening to before a basketball game? What songs would you include in a *Fahrenheit 451* or *Romeo and Juliet* soundtrack? Of course, while students are working on their lists, be sure to pull up YouTube and play some of their school-appropriate selections. Suddenly, everyone is singing aloud and analyzing lyrics and requesting the next song. Our classroom is alive.

There are several logical extensions for this task, as well. We can have students defend and explain each of their song choices (and present them to classmates). Students can also create an interactive slideshow that allows the audience to listen to each of the tracks while reading through their insightful analysis.

Prompt: Create a music playlist—minimum of five songs—for one of the characters in your current/recent read. What songs could you picture your character listening to, and why? What songs reflect the character's personality? Are there specific lyrics that the character would know by heart? Another option is to create a soundtrack for the book as a whole. What songs best represent some of the book's major conflicts, characters, and/or themes? Be sure to provide a brief explanation for each.

LITERARY MATCHUPS

Overview: In these two options, students place two of their favorite characters or books side-by-side and attempt to determine a "winner."

OPTION A: CHARACTER "FACEOFF"

Prompt: Students pick two characters to "face off" in a literary matchup. Students can create their own categories, or we can assign them. Possible categories include name, approximate age, hometown, friends and family, best attribute, toxic trait, talents and interests, pet peeves, core desire, and core fear. Some responses have a clear right/wrong answer while many encourage students to make creative inferences. Ultimately, students will choose a "winner" and write a strong paragraph explaining why _____ is the superior character. They can use a simple chart like the one below to organize.

	CHARACTER 1	CHARACTER 2
Name		
Approximate Age		
Hometown		
Friends and Family		
Best Attribute		
Toxic Trait		
Talents and Interests		
Pet Peeves		
Core Desire		
Core Fear		
Create Your Own Category		
And the winner is…		
In one strong paragraph, defend your decision!		

OPTION B: BOOK "FACEOFF"

Prompt: Like Option A, students pick two books to go "head-to-head" in a literary matchup. Possible categories include character development, plot, writing style, "binge-ability", and emotional impact. However, be sure to encourage students to come up with their own categories, as well. Note that the final task, where students defend their selection, can easily be dressed down (as a brief, handwritten response on the bottom or back of the graphic organizer) or dressed up (as a typed, multi-paragraph response). This activity also makes a great display; we can post the completed "Book Faceoff" posters on our classroom and hallway bulletin boards.

COMPARE-CONTRAST WRITING

Overview: In the two prompts below, students identify similarities and differences between two characters they have "met" or two books they have read during the semester (or school year). Students first complete a graphic organizer and then use their notes to write one to two strong paragraphs. We can easily extend the assignment, too, with students writing a four-paragraph essay that includes a brief introduction (including a thesis statement), two strong body paragraphs (two major similarities, two major differences, or one key similarity and one key difference), and a brief conclusion.

OPTION A:
COMPARE-CONTRAST CHARACTERS

Prompt: You have read several books this year and "met" all sorts of interesting characters. For this task, pick two of the most memorable. The characters can be from the same book or from different ones. They can be protagonists or antagonists, enemies or friends—or perhaps star-crossed lovers. Using a graphic organizer of your choice, brainstorm the major similarities and differences (traits, values, characteristics, motivation, etc.) between the two. Then, take your notes to write a strong paragraph that demonstrates strong understanding and analysis of both characters and includes relevant details and examples; has a clear thesis or topic sentence; includes the *Book Title(s)* and Author Name(s); features at least one appositive phrase; uses appropriate transition words/phrases.

OPTION B:
COMPARE-CONTRAST BOOKS

Prompt: Review every book you have read this year and pick two of the most memorable. Using a graphic organizer of your choice, brainstorm the major similarities and differences (title, author, genre, point of view, characters, conflict, theme, plot and pacing, setting, writing style, author's craft, overall rating, etc.). Then, take your notes to write two strong paragraphs that: demonstrate strong understanding and analysis of both books; elaborate on some of the most significant similarities and/or differences; includes relevant details and examples to support your claims; includes the *Book Titles* and names of both authors; features at least one appositive phrase; uses appropriate transition words/phrases.

Student Example (Option A)

Comparing Two Strong Female Leads

Marigold, the protagonist in Tiffany Jackson's latest best-selling novel *White Smoke*, and Daunis, the lead in Angeline Boulley's debut thriller *Firekeeper's Daughter*, share several similarities. Both characters are strong and resilient, attempting to overcome past traumas. For Mari, she moves to a new town looking for a fresh start, only to find her house haunted. Meanwhile, Daunis works with the FBI to uncover secrets about her community. Interestingly, both towns play a major role in the conflict. In *White Smoke*, Mari recognizes that evil is lurking in Maplewood as Jackson explores the effects of greed and gentrification. The evil in Daunis's community takes a different form, and she is determined to discover the truth. Like Mari, Daunis has a strong sense of fairness who is frustrated by the inherent injustices in the world. Despite the external challenges and their own imperfections, the two fierce female protagonists ultimately succeed in "solving" their respective mysteries and inspiring readers everywhere to do what is right. Both Jackson and Boulley deserve credit for crafting such complex and courageous characters.

AUTHOR LETTER AND SPOTLIGHT

Overview: In the first prompt, students write a letter (or email) to the author of a book they have read recently. Ideally, the author is still alive and able to receive correspondence, but it is not required. Reminder that the task can be as formal or informal as we'd like; it can be a quick heartfelt message on an index card or a typed two-page letter. (And please do not mandate that students receive a response from the author to get full credit.) The second prompt, which can be dressed up or down, works well in conjunction with Option A (since it's helpful to research the author before writing a letter) or as its own task. In the simplest version (questions one and two below), students spend a few minutes "getting to know" the author of their current read. In the more elaborate version (questions three through five), students conduct research from a variety of sources and present their findings in an "Author Spotlight" poster or slideshow.

OPTION A: AUTHOR LETTER

Write a letter/email to the author of a book you have read and enjoyed recently. Be sure to write in a conversation and respectful tone. Here are a few tips and guidelines to consider:

- Briefly introduce yourself (what would you like the author to know about you?) and the book you read.
- Share some of your major thoughts and takeaways from the book.
- What did you specifically enjoy and appreciate?
- Favorite character(s), and why?
- Favorite scene(s), and why?
- What other books, movies, series, and the like could you connect it to?
- What tweaks or changes would you recommend?
- What questions do you have for the author?
- Don't forget to provide a brief closing remark.

Student Examples

Dear Jason Reynolds and Brendan Kiely,

My name is _____ and I am a junior from Nashville, TN. Recently we read *All American Boys* for our monthly book club. I fell in love with your book. It's one of my favorite reads of the year; the book felt so real, like it was based off a true story. It seems like it was just on the news (which is sad to say). The world we live in is so violent and crazy. I respect both of you for going against the grain and using your position in the media to bring awareness to the problems we are facing. Thank you for such a great read.

Dear Angie Thomas,

My name is _____, and I am currently a junior at _____. *The Hate U Give* was a beautiful story. I loved every single part of it. I didn't dislike anything, except the fact that I finished it. My favorite part, hands down, has to be when Starr stands on the police car at the end. It was powerful to me because she finally spoke out and stood up for what she believed in.

I am very curious as to what made you write such a powerful story? Was it a past experience? I learned a lot from this book. Mainly that change starts with yourself. I enjoyed this book so much, and I appreciate you writing it.

OPTION B: AUTHOR STUDY OR SPOTLIGHT

Prompts:

1. Who is the author of your current read?

2. Is there an "author bio" featured in the book? If so, what can you learn from it?

3. Now, using your computer, can you find the author's website? If so, take a few minutes to browse. Then, record some of your major findings and takeaways.

4. What other reliable sources (interviews, articles, videos, podcasts, etc.) can you find to learn more about your author? Continue to take notes.

5. Using your research notes, create an "Author Spotlight" poster (digital or by hand). Feel free to include the following: name of author,

location (where they grew up and/or where they live currently), books written, primary genre(s), awards and accolades, fun facts, inspirational quotes, helpful links (their website, articles, essays, interviews, podcasts, videos, etc.), and at least one photo/headshot. Be sure to check out the example below.

 There is a downloadable Author Spotlight template on the companion website, resources.corwin.com/justreadit.

AUTHOR	KWAME ALEXANDER
Childhood	Born in NYC, Kwame grew up in Virginia (surrounded by books)
Books Written	39 books, including *The Door of No Return, Becoming Muhammad Ali, The Crossover, Rebound, Booked, Undefeated, Solo, Surf's Up, Out of Wonder,* etc.
Bio	Poet, educator, speaker, producer, performer, and bestselling author
Awards & Accolades	The Newbery Medal, the Lee Bennett Hopkins Poetry Award, the Coretta Scott King Author Honor, three NAACP Image Award Nominations, the Inaugural Pat Conroy Legacy Award, etc.
Advice for Young Writers	From his website: "TS Eliot said, 'Immature writers imitate. Mature writers steal.' The way we become good writers is by reading. My advice to young writers is to read. Learn what other writers have done right and wrong. This will help you find your own voice. Also, SAY YES!"
Favorite Writers	Kwame mentioned "Alice Walker, Langston Hughes, Pablo Neruda, Nikki Giovanni, Percival Everett, Jacqueline Woodson, Mo Willems, ee cummings, Gordan Korman, Kate DiCamillo, Nikki Grimes, and my parents, to name a few . . . "
Did you know...?	Did you know that . . . Kwame helped turn *The Crossover* into a TV series, which you can now watch on Disney+? Kwame has performed on five continents? Kwame's favorite sports are tennis and basketball? Kwame cofounded LEAP for Ghana, an international literacy program?
Website	https://kwamealexander.com/
Interview Links	https://www.kennedy-center.org/video/education/literary-arts/saying-yes-to-whats-possible-a-conversation-with-kwame-alexander/ https://www.oprahdaily.com/entertainment/a40137063/kwame-alexander-author-interview/ https://www.sikids.com/kid-reporter/author-kwame-alexander-speaks-about-hoops-teamwork-and-hard-work

AUTHOR	KWAME ALEXANDER
Inspirational Quotes	"Children's literature should help young people imagine a better world. The mind of an adult begins in the imagination of a child. What better way to inspire that imagination than through the pages of a book? I believe that children's book authors—like teachers and librarians—have a sacred responsibility, and we have to honor that. Sure, our goal is to create page-turners, we want kids to read these books, but it's more than just entertainment when you're writing for children—it's inspiration, engagement, and, ultimately, it's empowerment." —a 2022 OprahDaily.com interview "Basketball rule #3 Never let anyone lower your goals. Others' expectations of you are determined by their limitations of life. The sky is your limit, sons. Always shoot for the sun and you will shine." —The Crossover

CONNECT AND EXTEND

Overview: This prompt challenges students to make connections between all the books they have read over the course of a semester or school year. Here are some guiding questions for students to consider in their notebook response:

- What connections can you draw or make between the books you have read this year?

- What themes, topics, and issues do they explore?

- What genres have you explored this year?

- What are some of the major similarities and differences between the books you read this year?

- What will you remember most from each book?

- What characters stand out the most, and why?

- What are you still wondering or thinking about? What areas or topics would you like to explore further?

To extend this assignment, encourage students to use their independent reading as a springboard into the research process—developing a research question, conducting research from reliable sources, formulating a thesis statement, developing an outline, writing a

DEVELOPING A RESEARCH TOPIC INSPIRED BY OUR INDEPENDENT READING			
	TITLE	**AUTHOR**	**KEY EVENTS, TOPICS, THEMES, ISSUES, ETC.**
Book 1			
Book 2			
Book 3			
Example	Long Way Down	Jason Reynolds	Gun violence, peer pressure, adolescent and generational trauma, family, grief, following the "rules," etc.
Example	Fahrenheit 451	Ray Bradbury	Censorship and book banning, technology, happiness, knowledge vs. ignorance, control, conformity, etc.

formal research paper, creating a reference page, and so forth. Here's a sample sequence:

Step 1: Students select three of the most impactful books they have read this year.

Step 2: Students brainstorm key events, topics, themes, issues, etc. explored in each book.

Step 3: Students use their notes to begin brainstorming potential research questions.

Step 4: Once their question is approved, students will begin conducting their research. (The answer to that question will become their thesis.) Here is a sample timeline:

Week 1	Finalize research question and submit research project proposal
Week 2	Take notes from at least two or three credible sources
Week 3	Review and organize notes to develop an outline and/or first draft
Week 4	Feedback, revision, works cited page, final draft, etc.
Week 5	Presentations!

ONE-PAGER

Overview: There are lots of variations on the "one-pager," and I am a fan of pretty much all of them. For our whole-class read of Jason Reynolds's *Long Way Down,* we listened to the audiobook and created a one-pager for every chapter, or "floor." My freshman seminar class did the same thing while listening to Trevor Noah's *Born a Crime.* For those looking to structure the one-pager, you will find several tips and templates with a quick Google search, but as always, don't hesitate to adapt for your group. My favorite templates come from Now Spark Creativity (2018), who writes that "one-pagers are becoming increasingly popular as a way to help students process what they have read in one powerful activity. Like sketchnotes, they combine visuals with text to make ideas come alive in students' minds and memories." For example, during our whole-class read of *Fahrenheit 451*, students created a one-pager at the conclusion of each part ("Hearth and The Salamander," "The Sieve and The Sand," and "Burning Bright") according to the following guidelines:

- **Outside Border:** Write four of the most profound/significant quotes from the section.
- **Inside Border:** Write and/or draw the most important words (topics, themes, big ideas, images, symbols, etc.) from the section.
- **Upper Right Box:** In words and/or images, analyze one or more key characters from the section (characteristics, traits, conflicts, changes, etc.)
- **Upper Left Box:** In words and/or images, describe one or more of the major conflicts (internal and external) of the section.
- **Lower Right Box:** In words and/or images, analyze the specific setting of the novel.
- **Lower Left Box:** In words and/or images, highlight the author's writing style and use of figurative language.

There's no question that the three one-pagers deepened students' understanding of the novel. They also appreciated the opportunity to showcase their creativity and critical thinking. Here are a few final pieces of advice:

1. Give students time to work on their one-pagers in class (while also encouraging them to "perfect" them at home).
2. Art can be intimidating, so make sure it's possible for every student to achieve "success."

3. Share lots of student examples (from your own class or from the Internet) – along with your own (if you have time).

4. Build in time for students to share their finished products. They love inspiring and celebrating one another. (Students will literally clap and cheer when they see some of their classmates' artwork.)

NARRATIVE WRITING

Overview: One of the best ways to improve our own writing, particularly narrative writing, is to study and emulate authors we admire. (It's the same way that we sports fans watch clips of our favorite basketball players and try to mimic their moves in the driveway.) In Option A, students take a noteworthy scene from their book, determine what makes the scene effective (compelling characters, witty dialogue, quick pacing, descriptive writing, etc.), and then rewrite it from a different point of view or perspective. Depending on the length of the scene, this task can be completed in one to two class periods, and you can check out a student example below. Meanwhile, Option B is a longer, more rigorous task. Students spend one to two weeks writing a narrative continuation of one of their recent reads (or our whole-class novel). Not only do students need to have a strong understanding of the original text (themes, conflicts, characters, setting, etc.), they also need to know how to punctuate dialogue, write in a consistent point of view of view and verb tense, incorporate imagery and allusion, and so much more. Students can write their narrative in the author's style (for example, I've had students write incredible continuations of *Long Way Down* and *Fahrenheit 451* that would make Jason Reynolds and Ray Bradbury proud) or in a format of their choosing (verse, prose, script/screenplay, etc.). A downloadable of the Self-Assessment Rubric below can be found on the online companion, resources.corwin.com/justreadit, for students to use as they plan and fine-tune their writing.

> The easier option is for students to simply switch the writing from first to third person PoV or vice versa. Meanwhile, the more challenging option is to rewrite the scene from a different character's perspective, which is what you see in the example.

online resources

OPTION A: SCENE ANALYSIS AND REWRITE

Prompt: Select a noteworthy scene from your current book. Read the excerpt aloud to your partner(s) and discuss.

—What do you notice?

—What point of view is the scene written from? (first, third limited, third omniscient, etc.) How do you know?

—What are the strengths and limitations of this point of view?

—How would the book be different if it was written from a different point of view?

—What makes it an effective scene?

—What does the author do well? What can you apply to your own writing?

Repeat the process with the remaining group member(s). Then, on your own, rewrite a portion of the selected scene from a different point of view.

Students can use the graphic organizer available on the companion website, resources.corwin.com/justreadit.

Book Title	*Thunderhead*
Author	Neal Shusterman
Brief Summary of Scene	Citra (Scythe Anastasia) is talking to her parents who mention Rowan, and Citra releases her anger on them.
Page Number(s) of Scene	80-81
What point of view is the scene written from?	Third person limited (in this chapter, limited to Citra's perspective)
What verb tense is the scene written in? How do you know?	Past
Type Narrative Excerpt Below (exactly how it appears in the book)	*Student typed the scene here.
Try rewriting a portion of the scene from a different point of view.	I always knew that Citra and that boy had a special relationship, and right after I advised her to distance herself from him, I knew that she would rebel. "I am a scythe," she began. "I might be your daughter, but you should show me the respect that my position deserves." The hurt look in Ben's eyes was that of which I've never seen. My daughter was gone. Citra Terranova was dead, and Scythe Anastasia, a total stranger, was sitting with my family at our dinner table. "So do we all have to call you Scythe Anastasia now?" Ben trembled. My heart sank at his innocence; I was scared for what Anastasia's response would be. "Of course not," Anastasia responded. My blood boiled; she sounded so irrational and careless. Robotic even.

Prompt: What are some of the most memorable and thought-provoking books you've read this school year? What books had an unforgettable ending? What books set readers up for a sequel? Your task here is to select one book and write a narrative continuation. How do you see things unfolding after the final page? What would you like to see in a sequel? You have the freedom to be creative in your continuation but be sure to demonstrate a clear understanding of the characters, setting, conflicts, and themes of the original version. Additionally, be sure to include narrative elements, such as dialogue, imagery, figurative language, and so forth. (Students can use the downloadable Narrative Continuation Self-Assessment and Reflection organizer found on the online companion, resources.corwin.com/justreadit.)

NARRATIVE CONTINUATION –
SELF-ASSESSMENT AND REFLECTION

CHARACTERS – Who are the central characters in your story? Does the reader get a strong sense of who they are? (Thoughts, appearance, motivation, etc.)	
SETTING (Time) – When does your story take place?	
SETTING (Place) – Where does your story place? Do you include imagery to help the reader visualize the setting?	
CONFLICT(S) – What is the core/driving conflict in your story?	
POINT OF VIEW – What point of view is your narrative written from?	
VERB TENSE – What verb tense did you write in? Does it stay consistent throughout?	
TONE – How would you describe the overall tone of your continuation?	
PLOT – How does your story begin? How do you draw readers in?	
PLOT – What is the tension/suspense in the rising action? What is the story building toward?	
PLOT – What is the climax or big moment in your continuation?	
PLOT – How does your narrative conclude? How do you want the reader to feel at the end of the story?	

THEMES – What theme(s) does your continuation explore? What is the big idea or message your story is trying to convey?	
DIALOGUE – Does your narrative include realistic dialogue? Does it reveal character and/or advance the plot? Is it formatted correctly?	
MONOLOGUE – Who delivers the monologue in your narrative? What purpose does it serve in the story?	
ALLUSION – What allusion did you include in your narrative?	
NARRATIVE TECHNIQUE – What narrative techniques did you include? (Flashback, foreshadowing, symbolism, imagery, figurative language, etc.) Share an example and name the technique here.	
+ What are two things you are most proud of in your narrative?	
– What is one area you'd like to improve or work on in the future?	

BOOK REVIEW

Overview: While the three book review options here vary in time and difficulty, they all have a place in our classroom. While the "poster" (Option A) is especially helpful for students new to the book review process, it's also a valuable exercise for our strongest readers and writers. The official review (Option B) is the culminating task in our mini unit, and my goal is for students to write at least one, if not two, of these per year. The book talk (Option C), whether formal or informal, encourages students to hone their communication skills and engage authentically with their classmates.

OPTION A – BOOK REVIEW "POSTER"

Overview: Our students need continuous practice distinguishing between summary and critique, and this assignment is an effective way to do so. The book "poster," which I created in Microsoft Word years ago, helps students of all ability levels learn how to write an effective book review. The first section includes a line for students to write an original headline (for example: "*The Crossover* Is a Slam Dunk") along with a clear, concise, objective summary. The second section invites students to come up with three strong adjectives to describe the novel ("*The Crossover* is fast-paced, heartfelt, and unforgettable!") and then write four original "blurbs" or "short critiques". (Note: You can also have students include excerpts from actual reviews that they find online.) At the bottom of the posters, students will give the book an overall rating, coloring in up to five stars. (Bonus: The finished posters look great on a classroom or hallway bulletin board!) You can download a poster template from the online companion site, resources.corwin.com/justreadit.

OPTION B – TRADITIONAL BOOK REVIEW

Overview: While many of our WRAP tasks are completed in one class period (including Option A), others, like this one, require dedicated time over several class periods. Here's an overview of our book review unit.

Step 1: Here are several potential questions to "launch" our unit:

- What is a review/critique (noun)?

- What does it mean to review or critique (verb)?

- Why are reviews/critiques important? What purpose do they serve?

- What are the key elements of an effective review?

- What are some examples in society and in our own lives?

- Where do you go to find reviews? What are some of your favorite websites and apps? (IMDB, YouTube, Yelp, Instagram, TikTok, etc.)

- How do you determine what's worth reading, watching, buying, and consuming?

- In general, what specific topics/categories are you most interested in reviewing? (food, TV, movies, music, products, games, books, etc.)

- Have you ever reviewed something before? (Posting on social media counts!)

Access the contest-winning reviews.

Step 2: Analyze Exemplar Book Reviews

We analyze two exemplary book reviews, one positive and one negative, from the *New York Times* Learning Network national student writing contest. The goal is for students to write an all-star review of a book they have read and loved (or perhaps hated) this year.

> - What are five things that the author did well in their review, "*Diary of a Wimpy Kid*: A Perpetual Nightmare"? What impressed you? What stood out? What can you emulate in your review? *Note: You do not need to write in complete sentences, but your list should be thorough and insightful.
>
> - What are five things that the author did well in their review, "*All The Light We Cannot See*: A Story of Friendship"? What impressed you? What stood out? What can you emulate in your review? *Note: You do not need to write in complete sentences, but your list should be thorough and insightful.

Step 3: Read Book Review Tips

We read advice and inspiration from literary experts, including the Grammarly team in the article "How to Write a Book Review," and three *New York Times* critics, in the article "Advice on How to Write a Review by Three New York Times Critics."

Read the Grammarly article.

Step 4: Develop a Rubric

Students work in groups to develop a rubric for the review. Specifically, they answer the question, What made the two exemplars "A" quality? They brainstorm categories and assign point totals (adding up to one hundred) for each. You can see one student-generated rubric on the next page.

Read the NYT piece.

Step 5: Write First Draft

Students write the first draft of their book review, using the two exemplars as a guide.

Questions after reading Grammarly's "How to Write a Book Review"

- What is the definition of *avid*?

- Use *avid* in an original sentence.

- When writing a book review, what is the goal of a "hook"?

- When writing your review, what kind of "book information" do you plan to share?

- What tips does the Grammarly team recommend when writing a summary?

- What section is the "most important part" of the book review according to Grammarly, and why?

Questions after reading the third section of the piece, "Advice on How to Write a Book Review by Three New York Times Critics"

- According to Maria Russo, what is the "first job" when writing a review?

- What is Russo's advice when it comes to spoilers?

- What is the "second task—and privilege" of a book reviewer?

- True or false: It is okay to be creative with this assignment.

- What is your favorite line/sentence/piece of advice from this article?

- Do you feel prepared to write your first book review this week? Any questions for Dr. A?

STUDENT-GENERATED RUBRIC

- Hook/Intro (15 points)

- Book Knowledge/Context (5 points)

- Plot Summary (15 points)

- Your Critique/Opinion (counterclaim) (25 points)

- Recommendation/Rating (5 points)

- Clincher/Conclusion (15 points)

- Sophisticated Syntax and Vocabulary (10 points)

- Word Count (400–500) (5 points)

- Original Title (5 points)

Step 6: Revise

Students engage in the peer review process and confer with the teacher to improve their initial drafts. You can use the steps outlined below.

A. Review the Rubric

B. Background

- What is the title of your book review?

- Where are you in the writing process?

C. Glows

- What aspects of your review are you most pleased with thus far? List at least three.

D. Grows

- What aspects of your review would you like to improve this week? Ask up to three questions or identify three areas of focus for Dr. Amato and your writing group.

E. Peer Revision

- Partner A shares their notes from steps 2–4 above, giving Partner B a chance to ask any clarifying questions.

- Partner A reads aloud their review. Partner B takes notes.

- Brief discussion. Goal: Help identify possible changes/tweaks/improvements.

- Repeat with Partner B's review.

- Partners A and B swap reviews/laptops for a "second read." Offer feedback via sticky notes or Google Doc "comments."

- Brief conversation and debrief. Thank partner and identify next steps in the process.

F. Reflection (To be completed after our peer review protocol.)

- Who was your partner?

- What feedback and advice did you offer your partner?

- What feedback and advice did you receive from your partner?

- Overall, how would you describe the peer review process for you and your group? How did it go? Any changes or recommendations for the future?

Step 7: Write Final Draft

Step 8: Complete Reflection and Self-Assessment

You can create your own, or download the Self-Assessment/Relection and Teacher Rubric from the online companion: resources.corwin.com/justreadit.

Step 9: Publish and Celebrate

Share final drafts by printing and displaying prominently in your classroom and celebrating and highlighting "impressive lines" from each review.

OPTION C – BOOK TALK

Overview: Along with traditional book review writing, we can also encourage our students to create "book talk" videos. Some teachers and students prefer to write the book talk out beforehand, while others may choose to record it extemporaneously. Either is a great opportunity to help students develop public speaking and communication skills and connect with their classmates (and possibly others in the literary community). You can provide students with a graphic organizer to help them jot their key points: hook, introduction, main points one-two-three, conclusion, and call to action.

Prompt: In a two-to-three-minute presentation, deliver a "Book Talk" video about the independent book you are currently reading (as long as you are nearly finished) or one you have read recently. The goal is to convince the audience to read your book—the more persuasive the better. You are encouraged to be creative, but here are a few guidelines:

- **Introduction:** Grab the viewer's attention with a hook, such as an intriguing quote from the book or a personal anecdote, and be sure to introduce yourself, your book, and the author.

- **Body:** Share what you specifically enjoy about the book—try to come up with two to three compelling reasons. Is it the fast-paced and unpredictable plot? The compelling characters? The author's poetic prose? The jaw-dropping ending? (Remember: no spoilers!)

- **Conclusion:** Be specific about the target audience for the book. What type of readers will particularly enjoy this book? Try to leave your viewers with some sort of "clincher" or "mic drop."

CHAPTER 6

. . . .

Finishing With Finesse

Celebratory End-of-Year Activities

Growing up in Massachusetts, one of my favorite days of the year was "Marathon Monday." And not just because we had the day off from school. The entire community comes together on the third Monday in April to celebrate the incredible feats of strength and endurance. I remember, as a nine-year-old, standing on the side of Commonwealth Avenue, passing out water to runners as they trekked up "Heartbreak Hill," arguably the most grueling stretch of the 26.2-mile Boston Marathon. We were in awe as the professionals sprinted by us first, but for the rest of the day we were cheering on the amateur runners—moms and dads, friends and neighbors. As Adrian Hanft wrote in a 2019 blog post, "Every time I line up at the start of a marathon I am amazed by the diversity of humans I see. Running is truly a sport for all shapes, sizes, and varieties of people. While the top finishers steal the headlines, the real story to me is the thousands of runners who finish behind the winners" (Hanft, 2019).

For these individuals, it didn't matter what time they crossed the finish line; it just mattered that they finished. And we were there, lined up near Mile 20, ready to do our small part to ensure that they did. *Way to go! You're almost there! Great job! Keep it up! We see you! Wooooo!*

In many ways, the school year feels like a marathon. That's why, in May or June, as we near the finish line and prepare for a summer of well-deserved rest and recovery, we owe it to ourselves to appreciate the journey and acknowledge our students' accomplishments (along with our own). *Think about where all of you were in the fall. Look at where y'all are now. How much you've read.*

How much you've written. How much you've learned. How much you've grown. Look at how many PRs (personal records) were set.

At the same time, as my middle or high school students grind their way through one state test after another—most recently, ninety minutes a day for eight days over a three-week period—there's inevitably a moment of doubt. *Are my students prepared? How could I have been better? My goodness, there are so many things I want to do differently next year.* This ability to self-reflect is an important attribute. However, our desire for perfection cannot prevent us from celebrating or appreciating the solid work we are already doing. Yes, there's always room for improvement. Yes, our students are prepared.

Because our "testing season" is so long and draining, it's easy to lose momentum for the home stretch. (Which is another reason why I find high-stakes testing so frustrating.) However, it doesn't have to be this way. In chapter 4, we looked at how to start the school year strong. Why not end it even stronger? While the year is inevitably full of ups and downs, I believe wholeheartedly that the final days and weeks should be some of our most enjoyable. For me and my students, they often are. That's not an accident; it's by design.

Therefore, the goal for this chapter is straightforward: to show how ELA teachers can make the most of the home stretch and ensure that we end the school year, or "season," on a high note. Specifically, I share several joyful and challenging activities that encourage reflection, promote creativity and critical thinking, and push students to apply some of the skills they developed during our Read and WRAP time over the previous 8-9 months.

The **"For Every One"** activity ensures that our ELA classroom comes full circle. In **"Lit Awards,"** students take time to celebrate their favorite books, authors, and characters from the past year. The **Independent Reading Project** can be scaled up or down, depending on time and objectives, and we've included several quality options for students to choose from, including a **Culminating One-Pager, Book Talk,** and **Character Graduation Speech** (which also work well as standalone assignments). Students also can write **one final letter**, whether it's to their ELA teacher, next year's students, or someone they're grateful for. The **ELA Portfolio and Reflection** and third and final **Reading Attitude Survey** help students (and their teachers) document the incredible year of reading and writing and look ahead to the future.

The chapter closes with two teacher "assignments"—updating our Literacy Dashboard and developing our Summer Reading game plan.

END-OF-YEAR ELA ACTIVITIES: AT-A-GLANCE

ACTIVITY	PAGE NUMBERS
"For Every One" Reflection	180
Annual "Lit Awards"	182
Sample Independent Reading Project	185
Culminating Letter	187
ABCs of ELA Project	190
"My Ten" Column	192
ELA Portfolio and Reflection	193
Third and Final Reading Attitude Survey	195
Updating Our Literacy Dashboard	196
Summer Reading Game Plan	199

First impressions matter a great deal, and so do our final ones. What do we want students to remember about our classroom? What should their lasting impression be? If the school year is indeed a marathon, let's try our best to enjoy the finish, no matter how difficult some of those "middle miles" may have been. Let's strive to come down Boylston Street (that's where the Boston Marathon ends) in a comfortable jog with our arms raised triumphantly in the air. We made it. And we all have so much to be proud of.

> *What do we want students to remember about our classroom? What should their lasting impression be?*

"FOR EVERY ONE" REFLECTION

Watch "For Every One" **here**

Overview: In our classroom, we start and end the year with Jason Reynolds. As you may recall, one of the first Intro to Lit activities is our "Ten Things I've Been Meaning to Say to You" letter. One of our final tasks is a "For Every One" reflection. First, we read the text, which is an extended letter/long-form poem full of reflection and inspiration, aloud as a group. Years ago, I purchased a class set so that every student can follow along during the read aloud. (However, if you only have one copy, you can have each person read one page and then pass it to the next reader.) Then, we watch and discuss Reynolds's video performance of his text, which is produced by 826 Digital (and available online), before completing the following task. I've included here the wording I and my colleague, Mrs. G, have used in past years:

Dear Dreamers,

Thank you for an unforgettable year. We are so grateful for all of you. Continue to be you. Continue to follow your dreams. Continue to jump anyway. We love you.

– Dr. Amato and Mrs. G

After watching Jason Reynolds perform "For Every One," submit a reflection in paragraph form or as a series of bullet points. Feel free to use some of the prompts below:

- Discuss some of your favorite quotes and lines from the poem. What made them stand out? Why did you find them profound or powerful?

- Share your interpretation of the poem and performance. What do you think Jason is trying to say about dreams? About life?

- How did the poem and performance make you feel? How did it change or challenge your thinking/perspective? What are your main takeaways?

- As Jason mentions, would you burn this poem or keep it? Why? (Essentially, what's your overall critique?)

- If we look at the credits, we notice that a lot of people worked on the video (director, cinematographer, sound mixer, animators, original score, etc.) What are your thoughts on how the video was produced? How did the video help bring the poem to life and enhance the experience?

Following the reflection and discussion, students are encouraged to write or create something from the heart:

1. At one point in the poem, Jason encourages the audience to write a letter back to him, so feel free to do that here! What would you like to say to Jason? Thoughts on his poem? Your own take on dreams and life? Or feel free to start your letter like this: "Dear Dreamer" and go from there...

2. As Jason mentioned, this poem is for dancers, musicians, painters, actors, photographs, writers, athletes . . . for EVERYONE! What are some of your dreams?! Using "For Every One" as inspiration, create a poem, letter, song, piece of art, video, speech, or TED Talk.

ANNUAL "LIT AWARDS"

Overview: The "Lit Awards" were a recent addition to our classroom, and I have a feeling they're going to become a yearly staple. They were hit with my tenth graders in Nashville and eighth graders in New Jersey. The goal, of course, is to celebrate an incredible year of reading both individually and collectively. First, students create a slideshow recognizing their personal favorites from the year. To keep things simple, everyone followed a similar template, which you can download from resources. corwin.com/justreadit.

Slide 1: Cover Slide. Include title, your name, appropriate photos/images, background music, etc.

Slide 2: Share two to three of your **favorite quotes** from books you have read this year.

Slide 3: List the number of books you read this year—feel free to include some/all the book covers, too.

Slide 4: Introduce your **five "Lit Awards" categories**.

(Note: Most students start with **Best Book**, **Best Author**, and **Best Character** before coming up two of their own categories, including but not limited to Best Book Cover, Best Storyline, Best Setting, Best Plot Twist, Best Scene, Best Series, Best Ending, Best Villain, Most Creative, Best Theme, Most Unique, Best Supporting Character, Best Duo, Best Relationship, Best Ending, Most Memorable, Most Meaningful, etc.)

Slide 5: Share your **complete list of nominees** (see sample template below). Five categories, four nominees per category.

Best Book	Nominee A	Nominee B	Nominee C	Nominee D
Best Author	Nominee A	Nominee B	Nominee C	Nominee D
Best Character	Nominee A	Nominee B	Nominee C	Nominee D
Own Category	Nominee A	Nominee B	Nominee C	Nominee D
Own Category	Nominee A	Nominee B	Nominee C	Nominee D

Slide 6: Best Book Nominees. Be sure to include all four book covers.

Slide 7: Best Book Winner and Why It Won. Share your rationale/why you loved the book. For example:

WHY _____ WON

- Checked all the boxes I'm looking for in a book
- Exceptional writing style
- Unforgettable characters
- Powerful themes
- Masterful storytelling
- Gave me all the feels

Slide 8: Best Author Nominees. Include a photo/headshot of each author.

Slide 9: Best Author Winner and Bio. Provide a brief "biography" of the winning author (start by checking their website). For example:

BEST AUTHOR WINNER—
Tiffany D. Jackson

- NYT bestselling author
- Brooklyn raised, Howard made
- *Monday's Not Coming, Allegedly, Let Me Hear a Rhyme, Grown, White Smoke, Santa in the City, The Weight of Blood, Blackout, Whiteout*
- TV/film background
- Known for her twisty, suspenseful endings

Slide 10: Best Character Nominees

Slide 11: Best Character Winner and Why They Won.

Slide 12: Own Category Nominees

Slide 13: Own Category Winner and Why It Won

Slide 14: Own Category Nominees

Slide 15: Own Category Winner and Why It Won

Slide 16: Reflection. Write one paragraph reflecting on your voting process. What categories were the easiest and hardest for you to pick a winner? What criteria did you use? How would you describe your year of reading overall?

Slide 17: Closing Slide

Students then present their awards, either in small groups or to the entire class. We can even coordinate an actual "Lit Awards" ceremony, where everyone dresses to impress (or dresses as a character from one of their favorite books) and enjoys snacks and refreshments while celebrating a great year of reading. Students can sign up for one of three possible roles—two to three students will host the awards, several will serve as presenters (reading the nominees and announcing the winners), and others will come to the stage (ideally dressed in character) and deliver acceptance speeches. The teacher can also use this opportunity to hand out "Class Superlatives" and/or to recognize readers for their progress and accomplishments. At a minimum, this event helps students strengthen their public speaking skills in an authentic environment and ensures that we all end the year with one final positive literacy experience.

INDEPENDENT READING PROJECT

Overview: Here's a sample end-of-year Independent Reading Project where students choose three of nine possible "menu items" to complete. Remember that each of the nine tasks also work well as standalone assignments, and as always, be sure to design a choice board that meets the specific needs of your students. You will also find full descriptions of the book talk and graduation speech tasks in the ensuing pages.

SAMPLE INDEPENDENT READING PROJECT		
POETRY Write a poem (perhaps a sonnet) that successfully captures your year of reading or celebrates one book in particular.	**ARTWORK** Create a piece of art of your choice (collage, painting, character sketch, cartoon, etc.) that honors the books that you'll remember most from the past year.	**BOOK TALK** Deliver a book talk to document your year of reading. For example, feel free to discuss your "Lit Awards" winners. Other possibilities include "The Top _____ Books I Read This Year"; "_____ Reasons Why _____ is the Best Book of the Year"; " _____ Reasons to Read _____ "; " ____ Authors You Need to Check Out."
AUTHOR EMAIL Write a thoughtful email to the author of the most meaningful, memorable, unforgettable, unputdownable, etc. book you read this year.	**LIT AWARDS (*Required)** Create a "Lit Awards" slideshow that includes the Best Book, Best Author, Best Character, and at least two categories of your choosing.	**PLAYLIST** Create a playlist (minimum of ten songs) inspired by your reading from the past year. In your interactive slideshow, be sure to share your rationale for each selection.
CULMINATING ONE-PAGER Create a one-pager that captures your entire year of reading. As always, be creative, but here are some suggestions: —Display the number of books you read this year (possibly as big block letters with the book titles written inside)	**GRADUATION SPEECH** Craft a graduation speech from the point of a view of a character from a book you've read this year. What message would they want to leave with their audience? What personal stories would they share? What style, structure, tone, etc.? What allusions would they make?	**GROUP CHAT** Set up a group chat between three or more characters. Try to set up the text message conversation with characters from different books (as opposed to three from the same book). What could you see them talking about? (Perhaps they're discussing the end of the school year and their summer plans?)

(Continued)

(Continued)

SAMPLE INDEPENDENT READING PROJECT		
—List the genres you explored (possibly with the most frequently read genres written in a larger size) —Include your favorite quotes from your favorite books —Draw/display some of the key images, scenes, characters, symbols, themes, etc. —Share how have you grown as a reader and what you've learned from your books —"Honor" your favorite books, characters, authors, etc. (for example: you could draw a "podium" with your top three)	Before writing, feel free to complete a graphic organize with the following: speaker (character name), book title, author, occasion, audience, purpose, hook/opening, acknowledgements, main points, quotes to include (powerful lines from the book itself or from songs, poems, famous people, etc.), clincher/closing, etc.	

CULMINATING LETTER

Overview: Letter writing is powerful, especially at the start and close of a school year. Along with the aforementioned "For Every One" activity, here are four additional options to consider:

OPTION A: TRADITIONAL LETTER TO TEACHER

- Discuss your ____ (seventh, eighth, ninth, etc.)-grade year. What were your highs/lows, ups/downs? What went well? What didn't? What are you most/least proud of?

- How did this year compare to your expectations? Easier, harder? Similar, different? How so?

- What's changed from the beginning of the year to now (personally, academically, socially, etc.)? How have you grown?

- What did you enjoy most about your ____ -grade experience? Do you feel prepared for ____ grade? Why, or why not?

- What lessons have you learned? About school? Yourself? Life?

- Moving forward, how do you plan to continue improving as a reader and writer?

- What books remain on your TBR for the summer (and beyond)?

- What suggestions/ideas do you have to help Dr. A improve this class in the years ahead?

OPTION B: ADVICE FOR NEXT YEAR'S STUDENTS

What advice, suggestions, tips, etc. would you give next year's ____ -graders? (Think about teachers, classes, schedule, lunch, bus, HW, friends, sports, etc.) Feel free to frame this as a "Top 10" list. The tone can be serious or silly or somewhere in between, for example, "8 Lessons I've Learned as an 8th Grader," "How to Get an A in Honors English," "10 Tips for the Current 7th Graders," "High School Survival Strategies," "Parting Wisdom from a High School Senior," "What You Should Know About Dr. Amato's English Class," and so forth.

Student Example (option B)

Ten Things I've Learned Through Reading and Project LIT

1. Picking up a book is one of the best things you can do.

2. Book clubs are nothing like the boring ones I see on TV.

3. Finding a book that you can relate to means everything.

4. Project LIT gives you something to be excited about when coming to school.

5. Never really judge a book by its cover.

6. Project LIT is like a second family. There is a deep bond, and we all care about each other.

7. People who don't know each other can come together over a book.

8. Reading helps my mind find peace.

9. Reading shapes how I think about others, the world, and life as a whole.

10. Reading set me up for my future.

OPTION C: BOOK RECOMMENDATIONS FOR NEXT YEAR'S STUDENTS

- What books would you recommend for next year's _____-graders, and why? Write a brief introduction and conclusion along with three to five "bite-sized" reviews.

Student Example (option C)

Dear incoming 9th graders,

Get ready for a great year of reading. Hopefully you've had an awesome middle school experience, but even if you haven't been reading much lately, don't worry. Personally, I never considered myself a reader until this year when I got into a routine and found books that I actually enjoyed. I've read twelve books since the start of the school year, and here are three that I think you should check out in the fall:

> *Book 1: Title and Author*
>
> *Brief Review*
>
> *Book 2: Title and Author*
>
> *Brief Review*
>
> *Book 3: Title and Author*
>
> *Brief Review*

I hope that you enjoy your final days of middle school and have a wonderful summer break full of lots of fun (and maybe even a few books). High school will be different, but it's not as scary as you think. Happy reading!

OPTION D: THANK YOU LETTER

- None of us succeed on our own. Write a thank-you letter to a teacher, friend, classmate, coach, family member, or other individual who has helped you this year or over the course of your middle/high school career. What do they mean to you? How have they shaped you? What would you like to say to them?

ABCs of ELA PROJECT

Overview: I've seen lots of variations of the "ABC Project" over the years but none that encourage students to reflect on their independent reading. In this assignment, students select one word or phrase for each letter of the alphabet that connects to their reading: character names, book titles, setting, theme, author's craft, literary devices, vocabulary words, and so forth. Students can also work in groups to complete this project, ultimately creating and presenting an interactive slideshow/digital book (or perhaps even a print book with original artwork).

Interactive Slideshow Outline:

Slide 1: Title Slide

Slide 2: Dedication Slide

Slides 3–28: A through Z (each slide, or page, is visually appealing and includes both text and images)

Slide 29: Reflection Slide (briefly reflect on your year of reading and discuss how the project came together)

Slide 30: About the Author(s) Slide

Here is a partial example of a handout I created for this one.

Partial Sample ABC Outline Handout

	EXAMPLE	WRITE YOUR OWN
A	A is for **Adam** Silvera, **all-star author** of *They Both Die at the End*.	
B	B is **book burning** and **banning**, which is explored in Ray Bradbury's *Fahrenheit 451* and unfortunately remains relevant today.	
C	C is for **cooking**, a **central component** of *With the Fire on High* by Elizabeth Acevedo.	
D	D is for the **Defenders**, the track team that Ghost ends up joining.	
E	E is for ***Everything, Everything*** by Nicola Yoon.	
F	F is for **Filthy** McNasty, the nickname of Josh Bell, the star of Kwame Alexander's *The Crossover* (now streaming on Disney+).	

	EXAMPLE	WRITE YOUR OWN
G	G is for **Garden Heights**, the fictional neighborhood in *The Hate U Give* and *Concrete Rose*.	
H	H is for **hockey**, a sport I never played but one I grew to love thanks to Fredrik Backman's *Beartown*.	
I	I is for the **incredible** plot twists in all of Tiffany D. Jackson's **insanely** gripping books.	
J	J is for ***Just*** *Mercy*, for **Justyce** McCalister, and for liberty and **justice** for all.	

"MY TEN"

Overview: I love teaching the "art of the review," especially in the final quarter when we're incorporating multiple skills and writing for a variety of purposes within one piece. If time allows, I may have students submit two reviews—one book review and one of their choice (music, food, technology, fashion, TV, etc.). However, if we're running out of days, I may turn to the "My Ten" assignment instead, which has a similar feel to our "Ten Things . . ." assignment in the beginning of the year (another opportunity for our classroom to come full circle). Inspired by the *New York Times* Learning Network (an outstanding resource for educators), students essentially write ten mini reviews of the "books, movies, songs, hobbies, clothes, art, people, places or cherished objects that they can't live without" (Proulx, 2021).

As I tell my students, "treat your list like a time capsule." When you look back on this year in your life (eighth grade, ninth grade, twelfth grade, etc.), what do you hope to remember? What people and places and products are you most grateful for? How have you spent your time over the past year? What has brought you joy? What has brought you comfort? What has entertained you? What has made you laugh? What has made you think? What have you consumed (both literally and figuratively)? What has made you a better person? After reading examples from *The Times* (and from previous groups of students), students begin writing their own "My Ten" column that includes a list of their ten favorite "things" along with an explanation for each selection (pictures and videos are optional). They will also write a brief introduction and conclusion.

END-OF-YEAR PORTFOLIO AND REFLECTION

Overview: While I managed to save a few essays from my K–12 and undergraduate days, I wish I could go back and review all of them. I'd do anything to have a list of every book I've ever read. This task ensures that our students will be able to do both—at least for one year (and even more if we get our colleagues on board with this assignment, too). The steps below show how you might help students put together their ELA Portfolio.

HOW TO CREATE YOUR END-OF-YEAR PORTFOLIO

Step 1: Review the incredible reading and writing you have completed over the course of the year (in your composition notebook, ELA folder, Google Classroom page, etc.)

Step 2: Begin your digital portfolio. On page one, "Books Read during School Year," list both the title and author of every book they read, and on page 2, complete your "Reading Reflection," or "My Year of Reading in 100 Words." Possible prompts include the following:

- How have you grown as a reader over the course of the year?

- How would you describe your reading identity, habits, routines, etc.?

- How would you assess/evaluate your reading this year? In what areas have you seen the most growth?

- What books, authors, and genres stand out the most from the year, and why?

- What trends did you notice in your reading?

- What reading challenges did you face?

- Did you accomplish your reading goals? Why, or why not?

- When did you do your best reading?

(Continued)

(Continued)

Step 3: Copy and paste your best/favorite pieces of writing from the year into the portfolio, starting on page 3. From there, write your "Writing Reflection," or "My Year of Writing in 100 Words." Possible prompts include the following:

- How have you grown as a writer over the course of the year?

- What were your favorite writing assignments from the year, and why?

- What writing assignments did you least enjoy and/or struggle with, and why?

- What writing are you most proud of, and why?

- What trends did you notice in your writing?

- How would you assess/evaluate your writing this year? In what areas have you seen the most growth?

- When did you do your best writing?

We can also ask students to evaluate their performance in specific areas. For example, I may have students score themselves (1 to 5) in each of the following categories:

- Writer's Notebook/WRAP Responses

- Article of the Week

- Poetry Analysis

- Original Poetry

- Personal Narrative

- Narrative Writing (such as original short stories and narrative continuations)

- Digital Storytelling (Interview Project)

- Literary Analysis

- Argumentative Writing

- Explanatory Writing

- Review Writing

- Research Project

READING ATTITUDE SURVEY

Overview: During the final week, I set aside time for students to complete their third and final formal reading survey. You can find examples of the survey in the online companion, resources.corwin.com/justreadit.

By administering via Google Forms, I'm able to share the results with students immediately: *On average, guess how many books y'all read last year? What about this year? Who wants to guess how many books we read collectively? What do you notice in these graphs?* I'm also able to include the data in an "Annual Literacy Report" that I share with colleagues, families, community members, school and district leaders, potential grant reviewers, etc. (See appendix for an example of the full report from Spring 2022.)

I've been creating a version of this report for the better part of the past decade. The goal is to help us tell the story of our classroom and to garner additional support for our literacy efforts. *What's going well? Where can we continue to improve? What's worth celebrating? What's worth replicating or investing in?* To that end, feel free to share the data from your class surveys with your colleagues and school/district leaders as you make the case for daily independent reading.

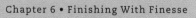

UPDATING OUR LITERACY DASHBOARD

As we close out the year, I also take time to update our **Literacy Dashboard**, which helps us capture a more complete picture of each student's progress. Possible columns in our Excel document or Google Sheets include the following:

- **Attendance:** List the total number of absences for each student, making note of those who are considered "chronically absent" (missing more than 10 percent of the school year).

- **Behavior:** As an ELA team, determine how you want to define and measure student behavior, whether it's specific to their ELA class (perhaps ELA teachers score students on a 1–5 scale based upon observable, agreed-upon criteria) or their behavior more broadly (for example, the total number of office referrals).

- **Grades:** Enter students' grades for each quarter/trimester along with their overall GPA.

- **NWEA/MAP Scores:** Enter students' NWEA/MAP RIT scores and percentile rankings from the fall, winter, and spring assessments. How much did they improve from Test 1 to Test 2, Test 2 to Test 3, and Test 1 to Test 3? Did students meet their annual growth projection (yes or no)?

- **ACT/SAT:** For high school students, enter students' ACT/SAT (or Pre-ACT/PSAT) scores.

- **Number of Books Read:** Record the number of books each student read during the year, especially in comparison to the previous year(s).

- **Overall Reading Attitude Score:** Use the results from the third formal reading survey to update our students' "Overall Reading Attitude Score." (Reminder: A score of 1 reflects a negative reading attitude/identity while a score of 5 is for the "book worms" and avid readers.)

- **Overall Writing and Speaking and Listening Scores:** As an ELA team, determine how you want to assess students' writing and communication skills. In the past, we've scored students on a 1–4 scale (1 below expectation, 2 approaching expectation, 3 at expectation, and 4 exceeding expectation).

The following thumbnails are of two "Literacy Dashboard" examples— one for a middle school classroom along with additions for a high school classroom (where students are expected to meet "college readiness" benchmarks on the ACT). Of course, the hope is that you tweak the dashboard to reflect the specific needs and goals of your classroom, school, district, and state. You can download a reproducible Literacy Dashboard from the online companion, resources.corwin.com/justreadit.

Literacy Dashboard Templates

MIDDLE SCHOOL

	ATTENDANCE	BEHAVIOR	BOOKS READ (PREVIOUS YEAR)	BOOKS READ (CURRENT YEAR)	READING ATTITUDE PRE-SCORE (FALL)	READING ATTITUDE POST-SCORE (SPRING)	STATE ASSESSMENT (PREVIOUS YEAR)	STATE ASSESSMENT (CURRENT YEAR)
Student A								
Student B								
Student C								

	NWEA/ MAP FALL RIT SCORE	NWEA/ MAP FALL PERCENTILE	NWEA/MAP WINTER RIT SCORE	NWEA/MAP WINTER PERCENTILE	NWEA/ MAP GROWTH (FALL TO WINTER)	NWEA/ MAP SPRING RIT SCORE	NWEA/MAP SPRING PERCENTILE	NWEA/MAP GROWTH (FALL TO SPRING)
Student A								
Student B								
Student C								

	MET ANNUAL NWEA/MAP GROWTH PROJECTION (Y/N?)	ELA GRADE TRIMESTER 1	OVERALL GPA TRIMESTER 1	ELA GRADE TRIMESTER 2	OVERALL GPA TRIMESTER 2	ELA GRADE TRIMESTER 3	OVERALL GPA TRIMESTER 3	OVERALL WRITING SCORE (1–4)	OVERALL SPEAKING & LISTENING SCORE (1–4)
Student A									
Student B									
Student C									

HIGH SCHOOL ADDITIONS

	ACT COMPOSITE SCORE	ACT ENGLISH SCORE	MET ENGLISH BENCHMARK (Y/N?)	ACT READING SCORE	MET READING BENCHMARK (Y/N?)	ACT MATH SCORE	MET MATH BENCHMARK (Y/N?)	ACT SCIENCE SCORE
Student A								
Student B								
Student C								

SUMMER READING GAME PLAN

Overview: When it comes to summer reading programs, context matters a great deal. What works for one student or one school may not work for another. However, on a broad level, here's what I am for and against: I am *for* encouraging students to read widely and read often over the summer. I am *against* summer reading lists that haven't been updated in decades. I am *for* sending students home with stacks of great books and making sure they're aware of all the resources their public library has to offer. I am *against* assignments that students can "cheat" or "ChatGPT their way" through. I am *for* offering students choice—beach reads and biographies, novels in verse and graphic novels, romance and realistic fiction, heavy and lighthearted. I am *against* forcing students to complete tedious tasks that ruin the experience of reading an otherwise wonderful novel. I am *for* ELA teams coming together to discuss their approach: *What's been done in the past? Is it working? How do we know? What are our goals for summer reading? What do we want students to "do" with their reading? Are we meeting them? How do students and staff members feel about our summer reading? What ideas or recommendations do they have?*

For me, the specific books students are reading over the summer isn't nearly as important as the fact that they're reading. My general approach is to keep it simple and make it meaningful. There's no reason to overcomplicate things. For example, here's an easy but effective reflection we can share with students before they depart for the summer:

---

1. What is your reading goal for the summer?

2. During the summer, keep track of the following:

TITLE	AUTHOR	GENRE	RATING (1–5 STARS)	BRIEF EXPLANATION

Before returning in the fall, answer the following questions:

3. What was the best book you read this summer and why?

(Continued)

(Continued)

4. Who was the most interesting character you "met" this summer and why?

5. Where was your favorite place to read this summer?

6. Overall, how would you evaluate your summer reading experience/performance?

7. What did you learn this summer—about yourself, the world, specific things? Along with books, what else did you read, watch, or listen to this summer? (Podcasts, documentaries, songs/albums, etc.)

We can also modify our Independent Reading Project (outlined earlier in the chapter) and create a Summer Reading Edition.

SAMPLE SUMMER INDEPENDENT READING PROJECT		
POETRY Write a poem (perhaps a sonnet) that successfully captures your summer of reading or celebrates one book in particular.	**ARTWORK** Create a piece of art of your choice (collage, painting, one-pager, character sketch, cartoon, etc.) that honors the book(s) that you'll remember most from the summer.	**BOOK TALK** Deliver a book talk where you provide a recap of your summer reads and/or rank some of your favorite books, characters, authors, etc. from the summer.
AUTHOR EMAIL Write a thoughtful email to the author of the most meaningful, memorable, unforgettable, and/or unputdownable book you read this summer.	**"MY SUMMER TEN"** Write about ten books, movies, shows, places, people, songs, hobbies, clothes, cherished objects, products, etc. that you'll remember most from the summer.	**PLAYLIST** Create a playlist (minimum of ten songs) inspired by your reading from the summer. In your interactive slideshow, be sure to share your rationale for each selection.
BOOK REVIEW Pick one book you read this summer and write a concise and compelling book review.	**JOURNAL** Keep a journal/notebook and jot down your thoughts, questions, connections, favorite quotes, etc. as you read throughout the summer.	**GROUP CHAT** Set up a group chat between three or more characters. Try to set up the text message conversation with characters from different books (as opposed to three from the same book). What could you see them talking about? (Perhaps they're discussing the end of the school year and their summer plans?)

PART 3

Leveling Up and Maximizing the Impact of Independent Reading

CHAPTER 7

Leveraging Student Feedback to Strengthen Read and WRAP Routines

Over the course of the year, every student will have their ups and downs as a reader. Even you and I go through reading "slumps" from time to time. Progress is not always linear, and not every student will grow to "love" reading over the course of a quarter or two, even if our "Intro to Lit" unit is a smashing success and our WRAP prompts are engaging and effective. That's okay! Our focus is supporting all students so that they continue to have agency in their reading lives and end the year a stronger reader and writer than they started. We must be willing to adjust and adapt as needed. To remain passionate and patient. (And to be clear, many students *will* test our patience.) To celebrate our young people for their steady (and occasionally uneven) progress. To build them up.

And by committing to the Read and WRAP routine from day one, beginning the year with the "Intro to Lit" unit, being intentional with our prompts, and remaining consistent in our care and approach, we find that many of our students' reading attitudes and identities gradually begin to shift. How can we tell? Often, it's through the casual conversations and comments we overhear as the timer goes off and notebooks come out:

- "I've already read more books this year than I did all of middle school."
- "This is the first year I've ever read a book on my own. Like where I actually liked and finished it."
- "This book is so good I don't want to stop reading."
- "Amato, I finished it!"
- "We should read for the whole period today."
- "This book is so deep that I just wanna take my time with each page."
- "I finished my book just as the timer went off. It's like a buzzer beater."
- "I am low key beginning to like reading."

Along with the "overheard" feedback, it is important that we provide students with more structured opportunities to reflect on their reading progress. We need to "hear" from every reader on an ongoing basis. These reading check-ins, whether written or verbal, help us (a) recognize and reward student growth and (b) identify when students are not meeting expectations (ours and/ or their own). Check-ins can help us to keep nudging students forward when they're succeeding or develop a plan for improvement when they're struggling. We never want readers to feel like they're on their own, especially when they're in the process of forming their reading identity. Without accountability and support, some readers begin to slip through the cracks and "go through the motions"—the pages may be turning but they're not getting much value from the reading experience. It's easier to confer with students regularly when class sizes are smaller, but regardless of class size, there are several ways we can check in with every reader on an ongoing basis and provide them with the resources and support needed to thrive. In this chapter, we will highlight four of them:

1. WRAP prompts that encourage reflection and refinement
2. Student-teacher reading conferences
3. Quarterly reading reflections
4. Formal reading surveys (beginning, middle, and end of year)

We never want readers to feel like they're on their own, especially when they're in the process of forming their reading identity.

Even when things are running smoothly and students are progressing nicely, we know there is always room for improvement.

Therefore, this chapter focuses on ten strategies to strengthen our Read and WRAP routines.

WRAP PROMPTS FOR REFLECTION AND REFINEMENT

While many of our prompts promote literary analysis and skill building, others encourage students to reflect on their reading and share a "status update." For example, here's a question I may pose on the board following (or perhaps right before) our independent reading time: *What should Dr. Amato know about your reading lately? What would you like to share? What support do you need this week?* To make it easier for me to review and sort responses quickly, students complete their reflections on sticky notes or index cards (as opposed to their writer's notebooks, which take longer to flip through). As I read through the responses, I'm able to identify the students most in need of my attention.

For example, in just a minute or two, I learn that Student A wants help finding a new mystery book to read, Student B needs a quick pep talk (life stuff is understandably getting in the way of their reading), and Student C would benefit from listening to an audiobook. Once students are reading or working independently, I'll grab three mystery books from our shelf for Student A to consider (another reason why access is so critical), tell Student B to stop by my room during lunch, and send Student C to the media center to talk to our librarian about audiobook options. Scenes like this one play out in our classroom all the time.

It's remarkable how much we learn about our students if we simply take the time to ask. To that end, the fourth WRAP collection in Chapter 5 (pages 125–126) includes a dozen questions that help us fine-tune our routine and differentiate our support. We want students to be mindful of their reading "pace" (how long it's taking them to finish books). We want students to provide feedback on the length of our reading time—especially if they're struggling to remain focused for the ten or fifteen or twenty minutes we're allotting. (If our entire class is advocating for more time to read, we know things are going well.) We want students to get better at abandoning books when they're too easy or too difficult—or just not the right fit. We want students to be invested in their own reading goals. For example, here is how our students responded to the following sticky-note prompt: *What is your reading goal or mindset heading into the next trimester?*

- Read two books of different genres
- I hope to finish at least five books this trimester

- Read ten books this trimester, including a horror novel
- Read fifteen to twenty minutes a day
- I want to read more on the weekends
- My goal is to read as many books as I can of all types
- Just Read!
- Read diversely
- My goal is to find more books that I like and will actually read

I don't require students to read X number of books or pages per week, quarter, trimester, or any specific period of time. In my experience, doing so only increases the likelihood that students will cheat, "fake read" (via SparkNotes or ChatGPT), or select "easier" books to simply meet the requirement. Some students will even stop reading once they've reached the "number" needed to get the desired grade. I also don't want to be in the position of policing our students' reading or punishing them for taking their time with a book or going through an occasional slump.

STUDENT-TEACHER READING CONFERENCES

As we discussed earlier, when class sizes are manageable, I can touch base with every reader, every week. For instance, I can usually check in with at least three or four students per day (while we're responding to our WRAP prompt). However, with larger class sizes, it's more likely that I get to every reader, every other week. To overcome that challenge, I try to zip around the room and get a "pulse check" from everybody in a matter of minutes.

What genre is everyone reading right now? And I move from desk to desk, getting an answer from each student. *Realistic fiction. Fantasy. Memoir. Graphic novel. Fantasy. Umm, I'm not sure? Oh, let's take a look . . .*

How are we feeling about our books? Everyone, I want you to hold up one to five fingers. One . . . you're ready to abandon it. Three . . . it's good but not your favorite. Five . . . you don't want to put it down. And I'm able to scan the room and narrate. It looks like a lot of us are putting up four or five fingers, which is great to see. For those with a one or two, let me know if you'd like to go to the library or need a recommendation from a classmate.

While these "speed rounds" are helpful, they don't replace the one-on-one conversations.

Along with the reflection prompts in Chapter 5, here are several questions to help ELA teachers facilitate authentic reading conferences (they can be as formal or informal as you'd like) with students. Students can also use these questions to guide their own peer "lit chats." (We can even call it "Group Chat," where students take turns discussing their current books and overall reading lives.) Part A includes prompts that are specific to the book students are currently reading, while Part B encourages students to discuss their reading life more generally.

QUESTIONS TO GUIDE CLASSROOM READING CONFERENCES AND CONVERSATIONS (PART A)

- What book are you reading? How and why did you select it?

- What genre are you reading currently? Is this book in your wheelhouse or are you trying something different?

- How would you summarize the book in one sentence? How would you critique the book in one sentence?

- On a scale of one to five, what would you rate your current read, and why?

- On a scale of one to five, how likely are you to recommend this book to friends, and why?

- Who is the recommended audience for this book, and why?

- Who is the narrator? What effect does this have on how the story is told?

- What should I know about the characters in your current read? What do you find most interesting about them?

- What is the main conflict that the protagonist is facing? Is it compelling? In what ways can you relate? How do you anticipate it will get resolved?

- What specific scenes or moments stand out so far?

- What can you tell me about the book's setting in terms of both time and place?

- Make a prediction. What do you think will happen next? How do you see things unfolding?

- What parts of the book do you find particularly interesting, confusing, thought-provoking, etc.?

- What questions, thoughts, and emotions does this book bring about?

- Why do you think the author wrote this book? What do you think they wanted you to take from it? What lessons did they want to leave you with?

- Who is the author? What do you know about them? What do you appreciate about their craft and writing style?

QUARTERLY READING REFLECTIONS

Along with our WRAP prompts and reading conferences, I also encourage students to submit a written reflection upon the conclusion of every quarter (or in my new school, at the end of each trimester). Because I am constantly tweaking and refining the assignment, you will notice that I've included a few versions (Version A, B, and C) of it in this section. Go with your favorite one, or as always, modify as you see fit.

QUARTERLY REFLECTION, VERSION A

In "Version A," which I first assigned in the fall of 2019, students assessed their performance, wrote an objective summary, critique, and character analysis, shared teacher feedback, and showcased their creativity via poetry or artwork.

QUARTERLY REFLECTION (VERSION A)

1. **LIST** all the books you read this quarter. Include both title and author.

2. **PERSONAL REFLECTION:** How would you evaluate your performance as a reader this quarter? (Enjoyment, improvement, strengths/weaknesses, habit/routine, focus, genres, etc.) *Approximately 150 words*

3. **PERSONAL REFLECTION:** How would you evaluate your performance as a writer this quarter? Did you notice improvement? Strengths and weaknesses? *Approximately 100–150 words.*

4. **SUMMARY:** What was one of the best books you read this quarter? Write an objective summary. *Approximately 75–100 words.*

5. **CRITIQUE:** What was one of the best books you read this quarter? Write a critique sharing why you enjoyed it, favorite aspects, recommended audience, etc. *Approximately 75–100 words.*

6. **CHARACTER ANALYSIS:** Who was the most memorable character you "met" this quarter? What made this character stand out? What qualities did they possess? What conflict(s) did they overcome, and how? In what ways are you similar and/or different? *Approximately 100 words.*

7. **FEEDBACK:** What did you enjoy about our class this quarter? How can Dr. Amato make this class better moving forward? What ideas or suggestions do you have? (Be specific!)

8. **CHOOSE ONE** (Goal: create something you'd be proud to display in our classroom!)

    A. Write a **POEM** that focuses on one book/character or makes connections between several you've read.

    B. Create a **ONE-PAGER** for one or all the books you read this quarter.

    C. Create a **VISUAL** of your choice (book cover, scene, comic, collage, painting, etc.).

    D. Other idea? Just be sure to run it by Dr. A first! The goal is to create something meaningful that we can display in our classroom.

Assignments like this one help us assess student performance—and our own. For example, here's what one ninth grader (who is preparing to head off to college as I type this paragraph) wrote about our English classroom in response to question number seven:

> This class has definitely been one of my favorite English classes. There's something about your room that's just so calming and relaxing. It could be the lighting or the fact that a whole fifteen minutes of the class are dedicated to complete silence and solemnity. While I do hold your class in high regard, I still believe that improvements may be needed, as is the same for all aspects of life. As for what those improvements are, I'm not sure of that quite yet. A possibility could be to make reading time a permanent grade. Another suggestion I have is to give more writing opportunities to people, more particularly narrative stories. I really enjoyed writing my first narrative, and I'd love to have another opportunity to display my storytelling skills.

His feedback was super helpful for a few reasons. One, the praise was specific and let me know that students valued our reading ritual. Two, the feedback was equally precise. In full transparency, I still struggle with how to grade our independent reading time and hold students "accountable." Here's where I've ultimately landed:

- While I do not grade every WRAP prompt (such as our notebook quick writes), I do grade the "formal" WRAP tasks, such as character analyses, book reviews, author letters, and one-pagers.

- Students also receive an "Independent Reading" grade for the quarter, which is based on several factors—their notebook responses (I conduct periodic "notebook checks"), teacher observation (monitoring student behavior during our reading time), and student self-assessment (they have an opportunity to explain what they believe their reading grade should be and why).

Three, I appreciated the student's request for more narrative opportunities. As Pam Allyn says, "Reading is like breathing in, and writing is like breathing out." I am constantly trying to find more time for students to dream up characters and worlds as they craft stories of their own.

Here's another beautiful reflection, specifically the response to question number two, from a student who read *Scythe*, *Thunderhead*, *The Hate U Give*, *We Contain Multitudes*, *Simon and the Homosapien Agenda*, *Speak*, *Shout*, *Born a Crime*, and *Goodbye Days* during the first quarter:

This quarter, as a reader, I feel like I have grown a lot. I have read many interesting and enriching books. You have created a space where reading is not only enriching; it is truly entertaining and relaxing. I feel like I have discovered new genres and expanded my reading selection exponentially. I read about joy and grief and love and hate. I read about the distant future, I read about the recent past, and I read about the present. For the first time, I read and truly enjoyed nonfiction, finding it just as engaging as fiction would have been. I read poetry that spoke to my soul and narratives that made me really think. I hope next quarter will be as fun and engaging as this one was.

Many of our students are already wonderful chefs. If we provide a safe, inviting kitchen (in this case, classroom) that is stocked with ingredients (books), they're ready to prepare a variety of delicious meals. Let's encourage that! At the same time, some students need more support to get there. For example, here's another response to question number two:

My performance as a reader has improved. I can easily say this because my mentality as reader has changed. How, at the beginning of the year I was hoping I wouldn't have to read at all because I never liked to read. Why, I have always been told reading helps, it's important, and I must do it, but I never felt that (this was actually true). Therefore, I thought of it as a chore but since I came to this school, I think different. Reading has been interesting because I'm a person who can read non picture books but graphic novels appeal more to me. Furthermore, I've felt connected to the books I've been reading and think I've improved my writing too. Overall though I'm glad that I like to read now and my love for books continues to grow with every book I read.

Graphic novels were the entry point for this student. I didn't judge him or shame him for that. Instead, I encouraged him to read as many as he could, including *Hey Kiddo* by Jarrett Krosoczka, which resonated with him on a deeply personal level. Over the first quarter, this student devoured one graphic novel after another, building his confidence and shifting his reading mentality. By giving him permission to read freely, I also gained this student's trust, and over time, the student felt comfortable branching out and exploring other genres.

Finally, here's one more reflection from a student who read *The Poet X, They Both Die at the End, Long Way Down, The 57 Bus,* and *Towers Falling* during the first nine weeks:

> In general, I've really enjoyed reading so many books. The books I've read are REALLY good reads. They're deep and fun to explore. I've read more books this quarter than I did in Battle of the Books. I haven't read as many "for fun" books; all the books have an underlying message that correlates with my life in some way or another.

Feel free to share this one with any adult who claims that students will only read "easy" or "fun" or "less rigorous" books when given choice. To those who believe that our students will only read "hard" or "challenging" books if we assign them, I say this: you are not giving our young people nearly enough credit. And respectfully, as someone who has read alongside adolescent readers in a variety of settings over of the past fourteen years, you would be wrong.

QUARTERLY REFLECTION, VERSION B – NEW STUDENTS, SIMILAR RESULTS

I tweaked the assignment slightly in October 2021, but the results—with a new group of students in year two of a pandemic—were nearly identical to 2019. Students reflected on their performance, wrote a brief author letter, set goals and provided teacher feedback, and created a poem or visual to celebrate their reading.

QUARTERLY REFLECTION (VERSION B)

1. **LIST** all the books you read this quarter (title in italics and author). (5 pts)

2. **PERSONAL REFLECTION:** How would you evaluate your performance as a reader this quarter? (Enjoyment, improvement, strengths/weaknesses, habit/routine, focus, genres, etc.) *Approximately 150 words.* (20 pts)

3. **PERSONAL REFLECTION:** How would you evaluate your performance as a writer this quarter? Did you notice improvement? In what areas? Strengths and weaknesses? Goals for the next quarter? *Approximately 150 words.* (20 pts)

---

4. **LETTER TO AUTHOR:** What was one of the most memorable books you read this quarter? Write a brief letter to the author of that book. What would you like to share with them? For example: what you appreciated and enjoyed, favorite characters and/or scenes, lessons and takeaways, personal connections and questions, and the like. *Approximately 150 words.* (20 pts)

5. **GOALS AND FEEDBACK:** Thank you for making the start of this school year so enjoyable. I know it's been a hard adjustment for many of us, but you should be very proud of yourself. What did you learn this quarter (about reading/writing, topics/themes, and/or yourself)? Do you have any goals for the next quarter? Anything Dr. Amato can do to better support and teach you? *Approximately 150 words.* (20 pts)

6. **CHOOSE ONE** (Feel free to submit/turn in separately. The goal is to create something you'd be proud to display in our classroom!) (15 pts)

   A. Write a **POEM** inspired by a book and/or character (or write one that makes connections between several).

   B. Create a **VISUAL** (book cover, scene, comic, collage, painting, portrait, graphic design, sketch, etc.) inspired by your reading!

   C. Other idea? Just be sure to run it by Dr. A first!

Again, there's so much value in assignments like this one. For instance, in the quote below, we're reminded of the fact that our students lead busy lives outside of school. If we don't give them time to read in school, many of them will simply not read at all. We're also reminded that our students, like us, appreciate time to read without having to annotate or analyze every piece of figurative language.

> I only read one book this quarter. I only read during the 15 minutes in class because I was so busy outside of school. I want to try and make more time for reading outside of school. Nonetheless, I still enjoyed taking my time to just read without an assignment attached. Being able to imagine the picture the words on the paper create without feeling the need to recognize every simile and metaphor I come across was very refreshing. The only genre I read this quarter was drama, but that's always been my favorite genre to read. Next quarter, I'll definitely want to read more genres too. I've always

liked poetry, but *The Poet X* made me fall in love with it even more. The way the author took poems and turned them into a chronological story was amazing to read, and I can't wait to read more of her (Elizabeth Acevedo) works.

It would have been easy to "penalize" this student for only reading one book during the first quarter. However, doing so would have been counterproductive. Instead, we worked together to set a more ambitious goal for quarter two. Similarly, the next reflection highlights the importance of "quality over quantity." Yes, volume matters, but let's not stress over the number of books read. For example, this student clearly had a successful quarter of reading:

I would evaluate my performance as adequate. I went at a slower pace than expected but got to dive deep into the books I've read and enjoyed each one. My reading routine was reading 15 minutes in the morning (during English class) and if I had time at home, I would pick up my book. Although this is a decent schedule, I want to read more, so one way I could improve this is allocating time when I'm going to bed or instead of going on my phone picking up a book. When reading this quarter, I was introduced to thrillers. Typically, I don't like scary things, but the writing style and storyline kept me reading more. I also fell back in love with romance novels and teen dramas this quarter. Next quarter I want to focus on reading more books and finding genres I'm not usually drawn to.

Here's another reflection that captures the heart of this work and importance of our Read and WRAP routine:

I've read more books than I have ever read in one year. Usually I don't read any books because I'm on my phone the majority of the day but in English class I have time to get into the reading zone. I think I've been able to read faster and comprehend even when things are going on around me. The genre I have explored in all three of my books was realistic fiction. Realistic fiction helps the reader step into the main characters shoes and learn about what is going on around the world. It helps raise awareness to things like racism and that's why I've been so into this genre. A weakness I have when reading is the only time I feel like reading is in English. It's like as soon as I get home, I don't have the energy to read anymore. I'm going to learn how to overcome this weakness so I can read more books.

QUARTERLY REFLECTION (VERSION C)— NEW STATE, NEW GRADE LEVEL

In March of 2023, my eighth grade students completed a slightly condensed reflection as we wrapped up our second trimester. I wanted us to maximize our final sixty days together, so students reflected on their ELA performance, set goals for the home stretch, shared their TBR (to be read) lists, and offered feedback for our upcoming unit. Teaching in a new school in a new state, I found that my students were generally "quieter" about their reading, and because I wasn't getting as much real-time, "overheard" feedback, their written reflections were even more valuable.

TRIMESTER 2 REFLECTION (VERSION C)

1. **LIST** all the books you've read this year, including our required reads (italicized title, author, and genre).

2. **OVERALL REFLECTION:** How would you evaluate your performance in ELA thus far? Feel free to consider reading, writing, communication, critical thinking, creativity, effort, and participation. In what areas do you think you've shined and/or improved? What essays, assignments, projects, or work are you most proud of? Approximately 100–150 words.

3. **GOAL-SETTING:** What specific reading and/or writing goals do you have for the third and final trimester? What will you need to do in order to achieve those goals? How prepared do you feel for high school English? Is there anything you'd like for Dr. Amato to teach or review over the final three months? Approximately 100 words.

4. **TBR:** What books do you have on your TBR (to be read) List? What genres would you like to try? Do you have any books that you'd recommend to others? Are you in need of any recommendations—if so, what are you interested in reading?

5. **UPCOMING UNIT:** As we begin our argumentative unit, what are some potential topics you'd like for us to discuss and/or research? What ideas or suggestions do you have?

FORMAL READING SURVEYS

Along with our quarterly reflections, I also administer a formal reading survey three times during the school year. The Reading Attitude Survey is given to students during the first week of school (see Chapter 4) and during the final week (see Chapter 6). Midyear I give a slightly different version. You can download each survey from the online companion, resources.corwin.com/justreadit.

You will notice that the first part of the midyear survey encourages students to reflect on their reading performance—number of books, genres read, enjoyment, and improvement. The second part—the Likert Scale statements—helps us quantify students' reading attitude and identity changes (hopefully positive) over the course of the year. In the third part, students have a chance to reflect on the positive literacy experiences from the first semester and provide feedback for the second semester. Finally, there's an opportunity for interested students to get more involved in our school-wide book club, which is discussed in more detail in Chapter 8.

Our goal with the second survey is to identify individual and class-wide trends. *When looking at the results, especially in comparison to the first survey (and when we look at it in conjunction with other data in our Literacy Dashboard), what stands out? How has each student and each class progressed (or possibly regressed)? What adjustments do we need to make as we prepare for the second half of the "season"?*

The surveys not only help us make adjustments in our day-to-day; they also provide us with data to show our colleagues, administrators, and families if ever there's a question about the independent reading practice in our classroom. Year after year, my colleagues and I have seen marked results when we're able to dedicate time

MIDYEAR READING SURVEY

Name _____

Grade Level _____

- This semester, I'd estimate that I read _____ books in total.
- Next semester, my goal is to read _____ books in total.
- What was your favorite book you read this semester, and why?
- How would you evaluate your performance as a reader this semester, and why?
- How would you evaluate your performance as a writer this semester, and why?
- What genre(s) did you read this semester?
- What genre(s) would you like to explore next semester?
- How do you feel about reading? (1-hate it, 2-don't like it, 3-okay, 4-like it, 5-love it)
- Explain why.

- Likert Scale Statements (1–5, strongly disagree to strongly agree)
  - I have become more interested in reading since coming to our school.
  - I enjoy talking about books with my peers and/or community.
  - Reading is cool.
  - I like that we have time to read in class every day.
  - I like that we have choice in what we read in class.
  - Reading is boring to me.
- What literary moment(s) or experience(s) stand out from the first semester? (Book clubs, author visits, book talks, projects, writing prompts, texts, etc.)
- What feedback do you have for next semester? How can make this class even better?
- What topics, books, or issues would you like to read and discuss in class? What writing ideas do you have?
- How many Project LIT Book Clubs did you attend this semester? (0–8)
- Are you interested in serving on the Project LIT Leadership Team?
- If yes, what areas are you most interested in?

  _____ Starring in videos and photos (in front of the camera)

  _____ Producing videos and photos (behind the camera)

  _____ Planning and leading book clubs

  _____ Reading to elementary students (LIT buddies)

  _____ Creating digital posters/infographics

  _____ Project LIT merchandise

  _____ Public speaking

  _____ Social media and marketing

  _____ *Other*

and space to independent reading. Specifically, in December 2019, my fellow English teacher, Nikki Healy (affectionately known as Mrs. G) and I administered the midyear survey featured here to our ninth and tenth grade students. In total, 120 students read a combined 1,417 books during the first semester, an average of nearly twelve books per student. As you can see in the table, students appreciated having choice and consistent time to read and reported an increasingly positive attitude toward reading.

SEMESTER 1 SURVEY RESULTS	1	2	3	4	5
I like that we have choice in what we read in class.	1 (0.8%)	0 (0%)	7 (5.7%)	16 (13.1%)	98 (80.3%)
I like that we have time to read in class every day.	4 (3.3%)	4 (3.3%)	17 (14.2%)	34 (28.3%)	61 (50.8%)
I have become more interested in reading since coming to MCHS.	2 (1.7%)	9 (7.4%)	21 (17.4%)	36 (29.8%)	53 (43.8%)
How do you feel about reading? (1-hate it, 2-don't like it, 3-okay, 4-like it, 5-love it)	0 (0%)	4 (3.3%)	29 (23.8%)	49 (40.2%)	40 (32.8%)

Did these results (number of books read, interest, attitude, etc.) also lead to improved literacy outcomes? They sure did. Our ninth graders' growth on the NWEA/MAP Assessment was literally off the charts (see below). On the fall assessment, my sixty-nine 9th grade students had a mean RIT score of 223.3 (good for 67th percentile nationally). On the winter assessment, their mean RIT score was 231.3 (good for 91st percent nationally). Their projected growth from the first to the second assessment was 1.3; in actuality, it was 8.0, placing our school in the 99th percentile nationally for growth. Moreover, fifty-seven of our sixty-nine students had already met their annual growth projection by the halfway point of the school year. Again, these results were a byproduct of a sound process and strong team. Everybody was aligned. Our principal. Our ELA department. Our students. Our families.

FIGURE 7.1 ● NWEA MAP Data

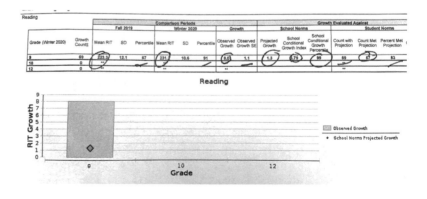

MAKING ADJUSTMENTS

While we may teach four or five sections of the same ELA course, we know that each class, like each individual reader, has a slightly different "personality." Some classes are "low maintenance," which means that once we set the timer, students are off for fifteen or twenty minutes with minimal distractions or disruptions. When the buzzer goes off, notebooks come out, and they are ready to WRAP—rinse and repeat. Meanwhile, other classes struggle to find their collective groove. Whether we're noticing resistance and/or apathy, our first job is to figure out why our Read and WRAP routine isn't working. *Is it them? Is it me? A mix of both? Why is this specific group of students struggling to buy in? What can we learn from the data in our literacy dashboard?*

Sometimes it's just the mix of personalities in the room. Peer pressure, both positive and negative, can be incredibly powerful. Sometimes it's our classroom arrangement—perhaps we've got to ditch the row or tables or shake up the seating chart. Sometimes it's our classroom management—perhaps there's been a culminative effect of letting too many "little" things slide. Sometimes it's the time of day. In my experience, the periods right after lunch and at the end of the day can be the toughest for everyone (teachers included). Sometimes it's an access issue — how can we expect students to get into a rhythm without quality book options?

Here are several questions to consider when determining where/why our independent reading routine is breaking down:

- Are students struggling to stay focused for the entire ____ minutes? Should we shorten our reading time for a bit?
- Are students attempting to talk and/or text during our reading time? Should we revisit and review expectations?
- Do students need more structure and "accountability" or less?
- Should we rearrange our classroom and/or update the seating chart?
- What's the status of our classroom and/or school libraries? Are students struggling to find "good" books? Is access an issue?
- Would students benefit from another "book tasting" day or "field trip" to the library?
- Have we tried introducing students to audiobooks?
- Have we tried reaching out to families for support?
- Do we think students would benefit from a whole-class reading experience?

As we all know, there's no "one-size-fits-all" solution. The strategies that work during first period may backfire during fifth. **Nonetheless, here are ten tips to consider when attempting to fine-tune our Read and WRAP routine:**

1. *Shorten our reading time to reestablish success and build confidence.* For example, if fifteen minutes of reading feels overwhelming and students are losing steam/focus, try setting the timer for ten minutes. *"Hey y'all, I've noticed that during the last five minutes, many of us start to fade. How do you feel if we shorten our reading to ten minutes this week? Then, as we develop our stamina, we can start to bump it back up."* Imagine if our students were struggling to run a mile. Instead of forcing them to "suck it up" or penalizing them for "walking," the right move would be to scale back and say, "Alright y'all, let's all run one good lap. Can we do that?" And then, once students accomplish this feat, we can celebrate it ("great work, everyone!") and eventually add a second lap, then a third. The same is true with reading.

2. *Be sure to "inspect what we expect."* We should have a clear vision of what success looks like with our Read and WRAP routine. Once we've set that bar high for everyone, it's up to us to hold students to it. My advice for new teachers is simple—don't let the "little" things slide. As soon as we notice that the "vibes are off" with our Read and WRAP routine, we should intervene. Don't hesitate to address minor misbehaviors. Don't hesitate to reestablish our expectations. For example, go over the following items with students as often as needed: *Our reading time should be* _____. *Our reading time should not be* _____. *Reading time is* _____. *Reading time is not* _____. *During reading time, I will* _____. *During reading time, I will not* _____.

On the flip side, be sure to bombard students with praise, especially early on. Acknowledge students for their effort and try to keep everyone invested in both their individual and collective success. *"Hey y'all, I love how focused and 'locked in' you were during our reading time today. At one point, I looked up from my book and saw everyone fully immersed in their books. It was awesome. That's exactly what our reading time should look and feel like."*

3. *Sometimes our classroom just needs a makeover.* If, for whatever reason, things feel "stale," try rearranging your classroom. You'd be surprised at the difference it makes. Move your desk to a different part of the room. Change the layout of student desks and tables. Reorganize the bookshelves. Declutter. Not only will you feel better afterward, students will, too.

4. *Increase or decrease the level of accountability.* This one is tricky but important. My personal preference is to trust and empower our students and to avoid "over-grading" their reading. For example, I do not assign reading logs, require X number of books per quarter or pages per week, or grade every quick write. While most students respond well to this "relaxed" approach, I recognize that it can be a bit jarring for those who are accustomed to accountability. In these situations, I may try to grade more of our WRAP prompts, so that students can see they're being recognized and "rewarded" for their reading. If you have a class that needs even more real-time feedback, you can also assign a daily reading "grade" to each student based on their effort and engagement; develop a check-mark rubric based on key criteria so students know what the expectations are. *Did you read the entire time? Did you remain silent and respectful of others in the room? Did you complete our WRAP prompt?*

On the other end, there are times when students feel like there's too much attached to their independent reading. *Why can't we just read?* They may have a point. As such, I'm always willing to scale back our WRAP time, opting to go with some of our shorter, less cumbersome prompts. (This also ensures students have enough energy and focus for the "second half" of the period.) Ultimately, I am constantly recalibrating our Read and WRAP routine.

5. *Schedule another "book tasting" or library visit.* Sometimes our students are just struggling to find the right books. I can certainly relate. There are still times where I have no earthly idea what I want to read. Whenever I'm in one of these ruts, I try to make a visit to the local bookstore or library. Within a half hour, I've found at least three or four books that I cannot wait to dive into. Let's provide our students with the same opportunity. We can easily carve out time for a class trip to the library (a real field trip to your city or town's public library would be awesome, too). If the library is off limits, we can easily plan another "book tasting" activity in our classroom to help students find their next read and/or add titles to their TBR list. For example, place a stack of books on each table and have students spend time browsing each "collection." You'll be amazed at the conversation and excitement.

6. *Reach out to families for their support.* This is a simple one, but it works. Positive phone calls home. Email updates. Monthly newsletters. When families hear our passion and know that we're committed to their child's success, it makes the world of difference. Here are a few things we should communicate early in the school year, whether it's in person, over the phone, or via email:

- Our reading philosophy and vision.
- Our excitement and expertise.
- Our gratitude and appreciation for our families.

Additionally, table below shows a back-to-school letter that I share with families. Feel free to modify!

Dear ECHS parents, families, and caregivers,

It is an honor and privilege to teach your student. This is my 13th year as an English teacher in MNPS and third here at ECHS. I am thrilled to be a part of this wonderful community, and I look forward to helping all of our students grow as readers and writers as we return to our classrooms this fall.

This form will help me get to know and teach your student the best way that I can. I want to thank you in advance for all that you do for your student. Please do not hesitate to contact me at any time with questions or concerns.

Your Student's Name:

Your Name:

Your Relation to Student:

Your Preferred Email Address:

Would you like to communicate through email? Yes _____ No _____

Your Preferred Phone Number(s):

What are the best days/times to contact you?

What would you like me to know about your student? (strengths, talents, hobbies, health concerns, etc.)

How would you describe your student as a reader and writer?

How can I best teach and support your student?

What questions do you have for me?

FAMILY INVOLVEMENT – Please indicate your preferences for the following items:

I would like to bake or provide food for special celebrations. YES _____ NO _____

I would like to attend ECHS community book clubs. YES _____ NO _____

I would like to attend ECHS field trips and community service events. YES _____ NO _____

7. *Lean on audiobooks.* Another simple but effective strategy. For many students, including but not limited to those with dyslexia, audiobooks are a game changer, and all educators would be wise to embrace them. A quick Google search and you will find several benefits to audiobooks, especially with narrative texts: vocabulary acquisition, fluency, comprehension, and engagement. You will also find that the common concerns (such as "audiobooks are cheating" or "audiobooks don't count as reading") are flat-out false. There's no reason to pit print books and audiobooks against each other; as professor and author Daniel Willingham writes in a 2018 column for *The New York Times*, "examining how we read and how we listen shows that each is best suited to different purposes, and neither is superior."

8. *Survey our students.* Looking to improve our Read and WRAP routine? Start by asking our students. We don't have to wait until the end of the quarter or a semester, either. Two simple questions go a long way. The first is, **"How can I make this class better?"** Our young people are refreshingly honest and incredibly insightful, and they know better than anyone what a classroom should look and feel like. Look at their feedback in the box below. While we don't have to honor every one of their requests (such as "less writing" and more "treats"), I routinely implement changes based on their feedback. For example, since a student suggested I "play thinking music," I have made a point to ask every class if they'd like for me to play light background music while we're reading. When my high schoolers requested more ACT prep, I found ways to incorporate grammar into our WRAP prompts.

HOW CAN DR. AMATO MAKE THIS CLASS BETTER NEXT QUARTER?

- "Play thinking music when we are reading."

- "A little more reading time."

- "Less writing."

- "He can bring us treats and play music as we read."

- "He can have us do more projects."

- "A little more reading time since I'm not able to at home."

- "Need more help with grammar, maybe we could work on activities like that."

- "I would like more ACT practice."

- "Go over more English ACT."

The second question is, **"What do you like about our class?"** As I tell our students, the more specific the praise, the better. With both questions, the goal is simple—to determine what practices to continue and what practices to tweak or abandon. For instance, in looking at student responses in the box that follows, we learned several things. Our students valued our Read and WRAP routine. They benefited from small class sizes and a safe, comfortable learning environment. They appreciated clear and consistent expectations and relevant and rigorous instruction.

WHAT DO YOU LIKE ABOUT OUR CLASS?

- It is very easy to do work in here and it has less people, which helps me be more focused.

- That it's a class with open discussion and where everyone's opinions matter.

- What I like is that he gives you time to chill when you read.

- I like the topics and the articles we read about because it relates to me.

- I like that Mr. Amato doesn't make me feel bad about how slow I read. He is more understanding than others when I'm behind on my homework. And he is very patient.

- That we read and we focus on real-life situations and work on ELA at the same time.

- Probably the way the teacher runs his class. First thing on the agenda is reading and afterward is work. I like order.

- How we get time to work on things.

- It's more peaceful.

- The kind of books we read.

Here's another example that highlights the power of simple student surveys. In this case, I posed three questions:

1. What challenges and obstacles do you face as a reader?

2. How do you plan to overcome these challenges?

3. How can I help you achieve your reading goals?

I compiled their responses and projected them onto the board to kick off our conversation: "Hey, I know it's not easy for some of us to get into a reading routine. I looked through your surveys and found that we have a lot in common. Take a look at the board. How many of you can find your answer on the slide? How many of the listed challenges can you relate to or identify with?"

WHAT CHALLENGES AND OBSTACLES DO YOU FACE AS A READER?

I'm on my phone too much . . . band until 6 . . . football practice . . . homework . . . honors classes . . . helping my family after school . . . babysitting . . . distractions in the house . . . people talking . . . I can't sit in one spot for too long . . . my time management skills . . . I don't feel like reading sometimes . . . not enough time in the day . . . loud siblings . . . I get tired from reading . . . I have to work right after school and don't get home till late . . . .playing sports . . . social media . . . video games . . . chores at home . . .

"At the same time, I've seen tremendous growth and improvement since the beginning of the school year. What are some ways that you have been able to overcome these challenges? Check out the next slide. What suggestions resonate most with you? Is there anything we can add to this list?"

HOW DO YOU PLAN TO OVERCOME THESE CHALLENGES?

Put phone away . . . turn off TV . . . read at lunch . . . read in car . . . find a little time each day . . . don't waste time in class . . . start using my time wisely . . . read outside or in a quiet place . . . ignore my phone b/c it's not important . . . read when I have spare time . . . find audio books . . . find at dinner . . . read to my siblings . . . go to library every two weeks . . . put my phone away and go to a peaceful, quiet place . . . stay focused . . .

"Whether you're an athlete or a reader, it's always helpful to have a coach who will help you achieve your goals. With that in mind, what can I do to support you? Moving forward, what can I do differently or better? How can I help hold you accountable or provide motivation? Here are a few suggestions—can we add anything else?"

HOW CAN I HELP YOU ACHIEVE YOUR READING GOALS?

Give us a little more time to read . . . recommend good books . . . give me books I'm interested in and that aren't too long . . . tell me to get on task when I'm distracted . . . continue to encourage us (verbal or prizes) . . . maybe read a book together as a class . . .

The final suggestion ("maybe read a book together as a class") deserves its own section, so let's jump right to number nine.

9. Incorporate a whole-class novel. Whole-class novels, when done well, have tremendous value. Whether they are selected by students and teachers or determined by the school/district, whole-class reads help us build community and help students gain the confidence and skills to read entire books on their own.

I recently moved to a new district in a new state, where our eighth-grade curriculum included *Night, Fahrenheit 451,* and *Romeo and Juliet.* However, instead of jumping straight into our first of three assigned reads, our students started the year by exploring self-selected books during our Read and WRAP time and completing many of our "Intro to Lit" activities. This also gave me time to build relationships and develop a game plan for the rest of year that made sense for as many of our readers as possible.

With *Night,* we came to this decision: To allow adequate time to process such a heavy text and to maintain momentum with our own books, we dedicated Tuesdays and Thursdays to the memoir and continued reading our self-selected books on Monday, Wednesday, and Friday. Read and WRAP, however, remained a constant. In other words, on Monday, Wednesday, and Friday, students read their own books, then on Tuesday and Thursday, some classes voted to read *Night* aloud together while others preferred to read the memoir silently on their own (or listen to the audiobook). Class began the same way every day—welcome/ check-in, timer set, into our books, timer off, and WRAP prompt.

Of course, there was no "perfect" solution, but this game plan worked well for us. Students gained a lot from discussing a powerful text with their peers, collaborating on projects that pushed them to think critically including a literary analysis essay, and reviewing important literacy skills and concepts that they could apply to other texts and classes in the years ahead. It was also an opportunity to expose many students to a new genre (and one they don't often choose to read on their own) and deepen their understanding of the Holocaust.

Meanwhile, we approached *Fahrenheit 451* differently, embracing the fact that the novel is written in three sections. Students read the dystopian novel at their own pace; some read it on their own, both in class and at home, while others chose to read *451* exclusively during our reading time. We dedicated roughly one week to each section (which was a bit fast for some), and at the end of section, students completed a one-pager along with three or four extended-response questions. Students had ongoing opportunities to make connections, ask questions, and support each other as they followed Montag's journey. We also watched the 2018 movie adaptation (all of us agreed the book was better) and wrote brilliant narrative continuations.

There are always tradeoffs, and in the future I will get better at scaffolding and supporting those who weren't quite ready for the accelerated pace, but by and large, the unit was successful. There was very little "fake reading," if any. There was joy. There were incredible conversations and opportunities for creativity and critical thinking. Many appreciated the "productive struggle," the challenge of reading a complex novel and one that was outside of their comfort zone.

When we returned from winter break, students set goals for the new year, visited the library, added books to their TBR, and jumped back into our Read and WRAP routine. In late January, we spent two or three weeks performing the abridged version of *Romeo and Juliet*. At the conclusion of the play, students participated in a mock trial ("Should Friar Lawrence be charged with involuntary manslaughter for his role in their deaths?"), which served as an awesome transition to our argumentative unit. (In hindsight, this was one of my proudest teacher moments of the year—watching every single student, across all three ELA sections, shine in their role, whether it was a member of the defense or prosecution teams, judge, bailiff, witness, or juror.)

All in all, I'd estimate that roughly three-fourths of the 180 school days were dedicated to self-selected books with the remaining quarter dedicated to our whole-class reads. While I don't know if there's a "perfect" ratio, I do know this: **by establishing our Read and WRAP routine from week one, our whole-class novels were far more successful**. The inverse was also true: reading a book together helped some students experience more success when we returned our self-selected books.

10. *Implement "partner reads" or in-class book clubs*. Whether you plan to roll out formal literature circles (with strict deadlines, roles, and responsibilities) or opt to go with a more casual approach to in-class book clubs (students read and discuss at their own pace), the first step is to make sure you have multiple copies of several high-quality titles.

Another option is to encourage everyone to read a title within a specific theme or genre. For example, in April (National Poetry Month), groups select one title from our "Novel in Verse" collection. Then, during our WRAP time, groups meet and engage in authentic conversation and complete some sort of "Book Club Project." (Reminder: many of the WRAP prompts outlined in Chapter 5 would work great here.)

SAMPLE "NOVEL IN VERSE" COLLECTION

- *Alone* by Megan Freeman
- *Booked, The Crossover, The Door of No Return*, and others by Kwame Alexander
- *Before the Ever After, Brown Girl Dreaming*, and others by Jacqueline Woodson
- *Home Is Not a Country* by Safia Elhillo
- *House Arrest* by K. A. Holt
- *Inside Out and Back Again* by Thanhhà Lai
- *Land of the Cranes* by Aida Salazar
- *Long Way Down* by Jason Reynolds
- *Me (Moth)* by Amber McBride
- *Other Words for Home* by Jasmine Warga
- *Punching the Air* by Ibi Zoboi and Yusef Salaam
- *Red, White, and Whole* by Rajani LaRocca
- *Starfish* by Lisa Fipps
- *The Canyon's Edge* by Dusti Bowling
- *The Magical Imperfect* by Chris Baron
- *The Poet X* by Elizabeth Acevedo
- *White Rose* by Kip Wilson

My hope is that you, like me, revisit this chapter whenever you find your Read and WRAP routine in need of maintenance. The longer we do this work, the easier it becomes to identify possible solutions. However, it remains more of an art than a science. I am constantly adjusting the number of minutes on our timer. I love rearranging our classroom, especially when I sense things are getting "stale." I make a point to coordinate a whole-group library visit at the start of every quarter, and I'm always looking to put together new book stacks and displays in our classroom. I don't hesitate to reset and reinforce expectations so that we can maximize our reading time.

I believe wholeheartedly that "it takes a village" and work to establish partnerships with our incredible parents and caregivers. I frequently poll and survey students to ensure their voices are heard and to best meet their academic and social emotional needs. I try to incorporate positive communal reading experiences, whether through our whole-class novels, partner/group reads, or our school-wide Project LIT Book Club, which is the focus of the next chapter.

CHAPTER 8

Launching and Leading a Project LIT Chapter

Once we've established our Read and WRAP routine, what's next? We know that many of our young people are ready and eager to become the "Lit Leaders" in our classroom, school, and community. What does that look like in action? What does it look like to empower our students as readers, writers, and leaders? How can we provide students with additional positive literacy experiences? What does it look like to lead a Project LIT "chapter"? How can we keep our most effective ELA teachers in the classroom? How can we make a difference in our school and community?

The easiest way to answer these questions is to tell you a story, to start way back in 2015 during our Project LIT founders' ninth-grade year and my first year at Maplewood High School. This was the year we abandoned the *Lord of the Flies* and embraced our Read and WRAP routine. This was the year we became *readers*. When our students returned for their sophomore year, we hit the ground running. Our focus was simple—to increase book access and to promote a love of reading in our community. To read and write alongside one another. To change the world— one step, one book, and one conversation at a time. For three years, from the fall of 2016 to the spring of 2019, we did just that.

This chapter is formatted differently than others because my hope is that this story will remind you and me what is possible and, considering the times in which we're living and teaching, what is needed from all of us. That it will reignite that spark or help keep that flame going. That it will leave you with a potential "blueprint" for your own literacy leadership and advocacy.

That it will help you and your ELA team plan successful book clubs, author visits, community events, and more in the months and years ahead. I haven't written this as a how-to but more as a what's-possible, so you can use this as a model for your own kids, classroom, and community. And you can find many more resources for ELA educators and Project LIT chapter leaders online at https://jarredamato.substack.com/.

Getting started with Project LIT Book Club in your classroom and community:

Step 1: Complete the Project LIT chapter leader application.

Step 2: Form your initial team of students and adults.

Step 3: As a group, decide on your first book club title.

Step 4: Secure copies.

Step 5: Set the date and spread the word.

Step 6: Read and celebrate the book (inside and/or outside the classroom).

Step 7: Prepare for your first community-wide event (i.e., "game day").

Step 8: Host your first Project LIT Book Club featuring discussion, trivia, and food.

Step 9: Take time to reflect and debrief.

Step 10: Continue to build and sustain momentum.

OUR INAUGURAL PROJECT LIT BOOK CLUB

After launching a book drive that saw us collect more than ten thousand books and setting up LIT libraries (converted *USA Today* newsstands) in several East Nashville YMCAs and community centers, we were ready for the next step. To this day, none of us can recall who threw out the suggestion, but someone asked, "Why don't we start a book club?" Immediately, we all loved the idea. "What book?" was the next obvious question. Somebody then nominated *The Crossover*, and it was quickly seconded. Many of our students had already enjoyed the novel in verse during our Read and WRAP time, so they were thrilled that the book would now be getting even more love.

There was only one small problem. We didn't have enough copies. Yet. Over the next few days, my students and I put together a Donors Choose fundraiser, and I also shared the link and graphic with family and friends on social media channels. In less than twenty-four hours, the project was fully funded (thanks to seven wonderful humans), and within a week, the books had arrived. *Boom!* We had our next "ask" ready. We encouraged community members to get involved in one of three ways: read *The Crossover* and then pass it on to someone else; join us in January for our inaugural book club; and continue to support our team's literacy efforts.

FIGURES 8.1.1 – 8.1.4 ● Publicizing Our Inaugural Project LIT Event

Project LIT Community
Book of the Month: JANUARY

Purpose: To bring the Nashville community together through reading.

How it works: We encourage **ALL** of you to join us in reading Kwame Alexander's *The Crossover* in January.

Then, everyone is invited to attend a **Breakfast Book Club on January 31** from **7:30-8:30 AM** where students, teachers, and community members will come together in the **Maplewood HS library** to discuss important themes and takeaways from the novel. We will also host a Twitter chat (Date TBD) for those who cannot attend.

We will continue with a different book every month. February's selection is John Lewis' graphic novel, *March*.

How you can help: 1) Buy a copy *Crossover*, order one from Limitless Libraries, or borrow one from Mr. Amato. 2) Read it and then pass it on to a friend or family member. 3) Join us on **1-31 in the MHS library** for our first book club. 4) Continue to support Project LIT Community!

PREPARING FOR OUR
FIRST BOOK CLUB EVENT

When we returned from winter break, we set the date. We spread the word: "Nashville friends, you're invited to attend our 1st book club on Jan 31! Grab a copy & spread the word!" We created flyers. We posted on social media. We sent emails to community members and local businesses and organizations. We even advertised on the school marquee.

Meanwhile, as our students read (or in some cases, reread) *The Crossover*, we took time to celebrate its brilliance. During our WRAP time, we shared our favorite lines and recited our favorite poems. We created mock character interviews with Josh Bell. We penned heartfelt letters (students had the option of writing an email to the author, a letter of encouragement to Josh and/or Jordan, a eulogy for their father Chuck Bell, or a letter from the future—written by Josh and/or Jordan). We wrote our own "Basketball Rules," "Play-by-Play," and vocabulary poems, using Kwame Alexander's poems as mentor texts.

On January 24, one week before the community event, students began to prepare even more diligently for "game day." We

---

CLASS POEMS INSPIRED BY
THE CROSSOVER'S "BASKETBALL RULES"

Basketball Rule #1

Be strong with the ball

Protect it with your life

Don't let anyone

Grab it from you

Basketball Rule #2

It doesn't matter

If you start

Or come off the bench

Just be ready

When you get your chance

Basketball Rule #3

When you step

To the foul line

Remember that

Every hoop

Is 10 feet high

FIGURE 8.2 ● Class vocabulary poems using The Crossover as a mentor

Gloat
glöt/
To contemplate or dwell on one's own success or another's misfortunate with smugness or malignant pleasure
As in: Usain Bolt loves to *gloat* as he's crossing the finish line
As in: Steph Curry *gloats* after hitting a clutch three-pointer
As in: I can't help but *gloat* when I get an "A" on my English paper
As in: My dad always tells me
Son, the best players don't need to gloat
Always act
Like you've been there before

Banish
ban-ish
To send away from a country or place as an official punishment
As in: Our parents *banished* my brother and me
to the bedroom
after we burped the ABCs in front of granny
at the dinner table
As in: The troublemakers in school are
banished to the dungeon that is I.S.S.
As in: Mr. Amato, please don't *banish* |
me from the classroom
because I didn't finish this poem

Confrontational
con-fron-ta-tion-al
Tending to deal with situations in an aggressive way; hostile, argumentative
        As in: Bruh, y r u always
        so *confrontational?*
Me?! What the *?#@ r u talking about? im not confrontational *at all.*
        LOL. R u serious rite now?
        U no ur always getting mad 2 quickly
Ya, ur rite. i guess i am pretty confrontational.

reached out to a local Krispy Kreme, and they agreed to donate several dozen donuts for the event. We brainstormed potential discussion questions. We hosted an in-class book club, which we considered a practice session for the upcoming performance. The following is the discussion protocol we created; feel free to tweak and share with your readers. You can download this from the companion website, too.

THE CROSSOVER – BOOK CLUB DISCUSSION PROTOCOL

Group Members: _____

STEP 1:   Determine who will be the group's **facilitator**:

STEP 2:   As a group, decide on three **rules or norms** that you will follow:

_____

_____

_____

STEP 3: Fill in your responses (left column) to the discussion questions below (notes/talking points are encouraged—complete sentences are not necessary).

	NOTES FOR YOUR RESPONSE (BEFORE DISCUSSION)	INTERESTING COMMENTS FROM GROUP MEMBERS (DURING DISCUSSION)
Q1: What's your **critique** of the book? How'd it compare to your expectations?		
Q2: How'd your **mood** change from the beginning of the book (warm-up) to the end (overtime)?		
Q3: What was your favorite **scene** or moment, and why?		
Q4: Who was your favorite **character, and why**? If you had the chance, what would you like to say to him/her?		
Q5: Consider the **ending**. Did you expect it or were you surprised? Was it an appropriate ending? If so, why? If you would change it, how?		
Q6: In what ways could you **relate** to the book and characters?		
Q7: If you were to talk with the author, Kwame Alexander, what would you want to know? What **questions** would you like to ask him?		
Q8: If the author were to write a **sequel** to this book, what do you think would happen? What's your **prediction**?		
Q9: What do you think about how the book was written? How does the **structure and style** affect the story and its readers?		
Q10: What lesson or **theme** did you take away from *The Crossover*?		

STEP 4: Facilitator begins the discussion (starting with question number one), making sure that *all* group members feel included and participate equally. Be sure to *add* notes in the right-hand column on page 1 as you hear interesting comments from your classmates.

STEP 5: Now that your discussion has ended, answer the following Reflection Questions.

REFLECTION QUESTIONS

1. **How much did you participate in the discussion about this book? (CHECK ONE)**

   about the right amount _____ too much _____ too little _____ not at all _____

2. **How did you perform in each of the following areas? (1 – poor, 2 – average, 3 – excellent)**

   - Staying on topic/Making relevant comments _____
   - Encouraging others to contribute _____
   - Listening carefully _____
   - Making good eye contact _____
   - Being considerate of others' opinions _____
   - Asking questions or responding to others _____
   - Using appropriate voice level _____

3. **Overall, how would you grade your individual performance during the discussion? (A–F) _____ Why?**

4. **Overall, what grade would you give your group (A–F) _____ ? Why?**

5. **What did you like about the book club discussion? What are you proud of?**

6. **What improvements or adjustments could be made for the next book club?**

7. **What were the three best questions that led to the most interesting discussion?**
   Question # _____ , Question # _____ , Question # _____

8. **Would you like to participate in another book club like this?** YES _____ NO _____

9. **Overall, this discussion made me appreciate *The Crossover* even more.**
   AGREE _____ DISAGREE _____

10. **What's one thing you'll remember from today's discussion?**

11. **What other feedback do you want to provide?**

online resources

The results from the survey were overwhelmingly positive, with all indicating they'd like to participate in another book club like this. One student wrote, "I like that we all came together and shared our opinions." Another wrote, "This book club was fun and I'd like to do more activities like this," adding that the one thing they'd remember from the discussion was "how we should appreciate everything more."

We went all out for our first game. Students worked in groups to create trifold posters promoting *The Crossover*. We revised our discussion questions. We finalized and printed our agenda. (See below for an example.) Inspired by *The Crossover*, we decided to structure the event like a basketball game with a "warm-up" (attendees sign in and fill out name tags, mingle while enjoying refreshments, and await the official welcome from one of our student leaders), "first half" (small-group discussions facilitated by our student leaders), "second half" (trivia competition to see who knows the book best), and "overtime" (a brief survey and group photo).

FIGURE 8.3 ● Inaugural Project LIT Book Club Agenda

WELCOME to Project LIT Community's

Inaugural Breakfast Book Club

January 31, 2017 (7:30–8:30 AM)

Maplewood High School Library

BOOK CLUB AGENDA

Warm up (7:30–7:45): Please be sure to sign in, enjoy breakfast, introduce yourself to guests, and share your thoughts on *The Crossover!*

First half (7:45–8:15): Students, staff, and community members will participate in small-group discussions about *The Crossover*, facilitated by Project LIT students.

Second half (8:15–8:30): Determine who knows the Bell family best with a *The Crossover* Trivia Game!

Overtime (8:30–8:35): Be sure to complete a brief survey and join us for a group photo!

Thank you for joining us!

We hope to see you again next month for our discussion of *MARCH: Book One* by John Lewis.

BOOK CLUB COMMUNITY
EVENT = GAME DAY

January 31, 2017. I woke up super early (it felt like Christmas morning) and rushed out of the house so that I could pick up the donuts and finish setting up the library before the bell rang at 7:05. (Side note: Can we please push back our high school start times?!)

As our students slowly trickled in, we went through our checklist. One group set up the snacks and refreshments. A second group stood at the library doors to greet community members who would soon be joining us. Another group passed out name tags at the front table. Two students snapped pictures and posted them to our social media accounts.

By 7:15, none of our guests had arrived. Panic set in momentarily. *What if no one showed up?* And then I looked around the room and took a deep breath. Even if no adults decided to join us, the morning was still going to be an overwhelming success. A group of teenagers had chosen to spend their morning in a library—eating breakfast, laughing, smiling, and discussing a book they had all read. The game had yet to start, but we had already won. This is an important point for you to remember, too, as you embark on your Project LIT journey—simply organizing, promoting, planning, practicing, reading the book, and discussing it is a successful learning experience for our students. These are important skills they'll take with them outside of school.

PHOTO 8.1 ● Signed Basketball

Of course, people did in fact show up. It wasn't long before our library was buzzing. The group devoured five dozen donuts within minutes. Students went on to facilitate heartfelt discussions with community members like Whitney Weeks, Julie Simone, and Matt Rubinstein, who, over the next two and a half years, would become their friends and mentors. We competed fiercely to see who knew the Bell brothers best. We posed for pictures and signed a basketball (a last-minute Walmart purchase on my food run the night before).

Before cleaning up and heading off to class (or work, for the adults in attendance), we also took time to reflect on the experience. *How did it go? What are you most proud of? What stands out? What will you remember from the book club?* One student wrote, "I think our first official book club went very well. I'm proud that I've met Whitney Weeks. I learned from different people's perspective and I'll remember that this was a really good book and is loved by many." Another wrote, "The book club was great! I'm proud of how everyone communicated. What stood out to me was the positivity. I'll remember our group member, Julie Simone." A third added, "The way I got out of my comfort zone, it was very awesome." Very awesome, indeed. The event had an equally profound impact on our community members. One attendee, educator Katye Russell, tweeted, "Tenth graders I met today at #MaplewoodHS make me proud to be a graduate of @MetroSchools."

FIGURE 8.4 ● The Crossover Graphs

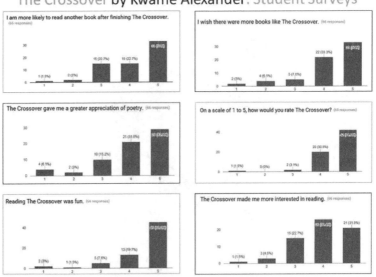

Over the next few days, we continued to reflect and debrief (check out our survey results and student reviews below) and soon shifted our focus to preparing for the next "game." Everyone returned to the library a month later to discuss *March: Book One* by John Lewis, Nate Powell, and Andrew Aydin. Students also presented their Civil Rights Movement research projects, inspired by the graphic memoir, in front of an authentic audience.

FIGURE 8.5 ● The Crossover Reviews 1

Maplewood H.S. Reviews of The Crossover

"The Crossover was different than most books I have read. I really liked all of the styles of poems and how just about every page was written differently. I'd like to tell him that he's a great writer and that it amazes me how creative someone can be."

"Overall, I think The Crossover was amazing! It was inspirational, mind-blowing, and emotional. I really wish he'd make more parts to it so I can enjoy him as an author more. Kwame Alexander, the GOAT of book writing, is now one of my favorite authors of all time! Keep writing!"

"Overall, The Crossover was a great way of using poetry to explain life events and feelings. I felt that I was a part of the family and could feel what they went through. It uniquely blended poetry into story form, making it memorable and added more meaning within the lines. I'd like to tell Kwame that more books should have as much creativity as this one."

"Thank you Mr. Alexander for a wonderful book. This book is for everybody, especially athletes. Mr. Alexander, thank you for such a good job. You make me feel better about reading. I feel like I want to read more books like The Crossover."

FIGURE 8.6 ● The Crossover Reviews 2

Maplewood H.S. Reviews of The Crossover

"The book was breathtaking and also unbelievably fun to read. The author did a fantastic job of keeping the reader hooked. I mean a lot of kids hate poetry and some (including me), find it hard to understand and read. This book is one of the greatest."

"I love the book. It's very different from other books and that's what makes me like it even more. I would read all your books if I had the time."

"The Crossover made me appreciate family more than ever. The Crossover made me feel the pain the twins and the mother was feeling. I would say to the author thanks for sharing a great book with me and I think you should make a part two. The Crossover had a lot of inspiring and motivational lines that I could use in the future."

"I think The Crossover was a very well written book. I enjoyed talking about it and making poems like the ones in the book. I think Kwame Alexander did a wonderful job at writing this book."

"I thought the Crossover was a really creative book and I enjoyed it a lot. I thought it was well written and was very relatable. I would like to thank Kwame Alexander for writing this book. I would definitely read more books by Alexander."

A SPECIAL BONUS

Later that spring, on a Wednesday afternoon in April, we got in the bus and drove across town to see Kwame Alexander lead a "Literacy Pep Rally" at Lipscomb University's Allen Arena. Before the event, we distributed books to local elementary and middle school students in attendance (titles that we had collected during our fall book drive), and afterward, we joined Kwame on stage for a group photo and presented him with our signed basketball from January's book club. It was the highlight of what was already an incredible first season.

BUILDING MOMENTUM

We spent the final month of the school year designing our Project LIT t-shirts, coordinating summer events and meet-ups, and planning for the following season. The whole team would be returning in the fall—in fact, I received permission from our principal to "loop" once again and teach two sections of English III (or Junior) Honors along with my four sections of English I. By early June, we tweeted a link to our Project LIT chapter leader application and encouraged educators across the country to join our community. Soon, there were chapters launching from the Bronx to Tacoma and everywhere in between, and within a few years, there were more than two thousand chapters nationwide, all led by passionate students, teachers, and librarians.

When our Project LIT founders returned in the fall of 2017, we got right back to work. We packed the library for two powerful book clubs to start the year—*All American Boys* by Brendan Kiely and Jason Reynolds and *The Hate U Give* by Angie Thomas. As one community member, Allison Buzard, so eloquently tweeted at the time,

> Some key takeaways for me are: 1. Students can love to read if they can see themselves in the literature, if they can find their story in the plot line, if they have choice in the literature, and if they are engaged in discussion around the text. 2. Adults can love to read, too, if they are challenged to do so, if they can see themselves in the book, and if they can find their story in the story. The adults at my table discussion were as eager to discuss the book as the students. 3. Students are brilliant. I observed students leading peers and adults in discussions about racism and civil rights this morning. 4. Teachers, school and district staff, and community partners can and want to be engaged in schools. And they will engage if given opportunities.

5. We have some amazingly passionate, creative teachers in our district. We need to value and listen to them. They get it!

The rest of the year flew by. There were so many wonderful moments; there's not enough space to recount them all here. Best-selling author Nic Stone drove from Atlanta, Georgia, to join us for our celebration of her debut novel, *Dear Martin*. We continued the *March* trilogy. We even brought our book club on the road, discussing *Long Way Down* with college students on three campuses—Lipscomb University, Tennessee State University, and Vanderbilt University. The pinnacle, though, was our inaugural Project LIT Summit, which saw two hundred Project LIT teachers and students across twenty-seven states descend on Nashville for the weekend to learn and celebrate together alongside bestselling authors Nic Stone, Tiffany D. Jackson, Jeff Zentner, and yes, Kwame Alexander.

And just like that, our Project LIT founders were seniors. David Briley, Nashville's mayor at the time, joined us for our powerful discussion of Trevor Noah's *Born a Crime*, and applauded our students for their leadership and advocacy. We also took a few field trips inspired by our reading. I'll never forget the experience of watching *The Hate U Give* together in the movie theater. Or seeing *Ghost* brought to life on stage at the Nashville Children's Theatre. Or taking the city bus downtown as part of our study of Dashka Slater's *The 57 Bus*.

Another special moment came on Valentine's Day when thirteen of our students were called down to the office. No, they were not in trouble—quite the opposite. Our principal was there to deliver the news: they had just received a full scholarship to attend Belmont University. When I got home from school that afternoon, I posted a full Twitter thread (now X) with pictures and shout-outs for each student, nearly all of whom I had taught since ninth grade: Angel, Adrian, Cerica, CJ, David, De'Montre. Jakaylia, Lauren, Kiara, Olivia, Paisley, Mi'Keria, and Toniya. I still get emotional every time I revisit the thread.

X thread about student scholarships

SENIOR SENDOFF

In May, we came together for one final book club and celebration—our "Senior Sendoff" (which we modeled after the "Signing Day" event that many high schools host for their student-athletes). Years later, I still beam with pride when I think about this day. CJ and David performed original poems reflecting on our journey and celebrating our accomplishments. We watched a slideshow full of pictures and videos from the past three years. We laughed. We cried. We played trivia. We ate. We handed out awards. (You can see our full agenda below.)

What stands out the most in my memory, however, was our group read-aloud. As our friend Vesia Hawkins tweeted that afternoon: "I will never forget being part of 50-person read aloud of @JasonReynolds83's book For Everyone. Standing shoulder-to-shoulder with students who founded @ProjectLITComm 3 years ago and most of whom are now headed to the college of their choice. Amazing." I will never forget it, either.

FIGURE 8.7 ● Senior Sendoff Agenda

**PROJECT LIT
SENIOR SENDOFF
AGENDA**
May 15, 2019

I. Student Welcome
II. Project LIT Slideshow
III. Small-group Discussion
  A. Favorite books you have read, and why?
  B. What characters stand out?
  C. What does Project LIT mean to you?
  D. What are some of your favorite Project LIT moments/memories?
  E. What have you learned through Project LIT?
  F. What will you miss most about Project LIT?
IV. Project LIT Circle
V. Group reading of *For Every One*
VI. Ultimate Project LIT Competition
  A. Kahoot
  B. Anagram Challenge
  C. Author/Title Scramble
  D. Name That Quote
VII. Closing Message
VIII. Presentation of Awards
IX. Group Picture

After our "Senior Sendoff," it was time for graduation, where I clapped loudly (and perhaps shed a few tears) as our students walked proudly across the stage to receive their diplomas. And just like that, it was over. The end of an unforgettable chapter.

THE NEXT CHAPTER

As the 2018–2019 school year ended, I took a position at a different high school in our district for the following year. I felt reenergized working alongside the incredible Mrs. G (it's so hard to sustain this work on our own) and knowing we had full support of our principal to do what we knew was best for our students, regardless of our district's mandates. That meant, as the two English teachers at our small high school, we were 100 percent committed to Read and WRAP and building a

What does Project LIT Community mean to you? These are responses from that initial group of students.

- Project LIT has become a big part of my life. I love representing Project LIT and doing everything I can to help.

- Project LIT means I'm making a difference in other people's lives and helping others come together through the power of literature.

- Project LIT means a lot to me. It's a place where someone who feels alone can fit right in.

- Project LIT to me means raising awareness to reading and literacy. Showing that reading can be fun along with the benefits that come with it.

- Project LIT means a lot to me because we are really making a huge difference little by little. I like how we got different schools to create their own chapters.

- A worldwide book club to help kids in need receive and love books.

- We are making a change and it is special to know I'm helping do that.

- Project LIT gives us a chance to give back and I've always wanted to get into the community to see what I could do for them. I know I'm very fortunate to have things, so I would like for others to have the same opportunities I've had. This project is one of my proudest accomplishments and I'm grateful I got to be a part of this.

- Project LIT is everything to me. I am always bringing up the project and activities that we have coming up because it's a really great program that is 100% student led and planned. Of course I love Amato and many others that have helped it take off. It's not just about reading, either. We have athletes who read to children proudly and deliver books to (community) centers without hesitation. The stereotype is that athletes are dumb and can't read and that all they can do is hold a ball or run when that isn't the case. We have a mother in the program. She might be young, but she's super bright and intelligent and once again not the typical stereotype. In this program, you have the quietest students bouncing around, laughing and smiling and being themselves because they are in an environment where NOBODY JUDGES ANYBODY! That's why Project LIT is everything to me and more. I could honestly go on forever.

- Everything.

schoolwide literacy culture. We routinely brought our classes together for read aloud, book talks, and author events. We wrote grants (shout-out to First Book!) to ensure that our students had access to great books even though our school did not have a library or librarian. We encouraged students to join our Project LIT Leadership Team. An example of the application we created is shown in the box on the next page, and you can download a copy from the companion website.

PROJECT LIT COMMUNITY STUDENT LEADERSHIP TEAM APPLICATION

DESCRIPTION: Your teachers are looking for a team of dedicated students to lead our Project LIT chapter. This group will work to plan events (book clubs, field trips, service days, etc.), promote our organization, and engage our school and community.

COMPENSATION: We cannot pay you a salary for your time, but this will, however, be a great leadership experience to add to your resume and college application. You will also receive free swag and VIP opportunities.

APPLICATION

First Name:

Last Name:

Email:

Why are you interested in joining the Project LIT leadership team?

What strengths, talents, skills, and so on. will you contribute to our team?

What would you like to see our Project LIT chapter accomplish this year?

INTERESTS – CHECK ALL THAT APPLY

_____Facilitate and lead our book clubs

_____Plan field trips and special events

_____Read to and mentor our LIT buddies

_____Create social media content

_____Create lit-inspired artwork

_____Beautify our classroom library and bulletin boards

_____Design and promote Project LIT swag/merch

_____Write book reviews

_____Build and/or distribute our LIT libraries

_____Engage in community outreach and public speaking

_____Serve as reading role models/ambassadors

_____Collaborate with other Project LIT chapters

_____Other (please describe) _____

_____

What areas from the list above are you most interested in, and why?

COMMITMENT & AVAILABILITY: Much of this work will take place outside of our normal class time. Describe your willingness and availability to complete tasks and attend Project LIT events (PLT, after school, weekends, etc.). We understand that your schedule may vary throughout the year!

Our first semester was a smashing success. We cooked empanadas after reading Elizabeth Acevedo's *With the Fire on High*, FaceTimed with Tiffany D. Jackson after reading *Monday's Not Coming*, and welcomed Pablo Cartaya for an author visit. Our custom, student-designed hoodies arrived just in time for our field trip to watch *Just Mercy* (another one of our book club selections). And then, just like that, a tornado tore through Nashville. A virus arrived shortly thereafter, sending everyone home and cutting our season short. As I reflect on those first seven months, though, it's clear that this is the Project LIT model that we can all replicate moving forward.

LEADING A PROJECT LIT CHAPTER

The two graphics below help us understand what it looks like to lead a Project LIT chapter from both an educator and student perspective and how we can all "level up" and expand the impact of our commitment to independent reading. This list is a menu of options—choose what's right for your students, your school, and your local community.

Our blog post about Project LIT

FIGURE 8.8 ● Project LIT Chapter Leader Graphic

Project LIT Chapter Leaders

- ❑ Encourage students to read and discuss Project LIT titles of their choice during daily independent reading
- ❑ Nurture authentic reading and writing identities by celebrating and promoting literacy every day
- ❑ Increase access to high-quality, culturally sustaining books that affirm and value all students
- ❑ Encourage students to create and publish poems, stories, artwork, etc. of their own
- ❑ Advocate for anti-racist literacy policies and practices
- ❑ Facilitate LIT circles and whole-class reads of Project LIT titles
- ❑ Design student-centered lessons and units featuring Project LIT titles
- ❑ Empower students to lead our Project LIT chapter and serve as LIT leaders in our community
- ❑ Host regular Project LIT Book Club events that bring students, educators, families, and community members together
- ❑ Create safe spaces to have courageous conversations as we strive to better ourselves, our schools, and our communities
- ❑ Connect, collaborate, and celebrate with fellow Project LIT students, educators, and authors (locally, nationally, globally)

#ProjectLITBookClub   @projectLITcomm

FIGURE 8.9 ● Project LIT Student Leaders Graphic

Project LIT Student Leaders

- ❑ Lead **Project LIT Book Club** events (classroom, school, community, etc.)
- ❑ Plan **field trips and special events** (book drive, author visit, poetry slam, reading marathon, movie, college trip, community service, etc.)
- ❑ Read to and mentor our **LIT buddies**
- ❑ Create **social media** content (YouTube, IG, Tik Tok, Podcast, etc.)
- ❑ Create **lit-inspired artwork** (murals, drawings, sketches, paintings, etc.)
- ❑ Beautify our **classroom library and bulletin boards**
- ❑ Design and promote **Project LIT swag/merch** (hats, shirts, hoodies, stickers, buttons, etc.)
- ❑ Write **book reviews** and share book recommendations
- ❑ Build, decorate, deliver, and/or steward our **LIT libraries**
- ❑ Lead **community outreach and recruitment** (public speaking)
- ❑ Serve as reading **role models and LIT ambassadors**
- ❑ **Collaborate** with fellow Project LIT leaders around the world
- ❑ Anything else you can think of!

#ProjectLITBookClub   @projectLITcomm

Become a Project LIT chapter leader here!

Whether your founding Project LIT team includes five, fifteen, or perhaps fifty incredible humans, the next step is to discuss goals and priorities. Perhaps you will decide to organize monthly or quarterly book clubs open to the entire grade, school, and/or community. Perhaps you will lead literacy-centered art and service projects, whether it's painting book spines on lockers, launching a book drive, or building a Little Free Library. Perhaps you will start a "Lit Buddies" program, where your middle or high school students will read to students at a nearby elementary school. Perhaps you will fundraise to bring one of your favorite authors to your school (or connect with them on Zoom). Perhaps you will start a teen writer's group, where students share original poetry and prose with one another. Perhaps your students will start sharing book reviews on student-led podcasts and YouTube channels. Perhaps your students will design and promote merchandise and swag (t-shirts, hoodies, hats, stickers, water bottles, etc.) to spread a love of reading and develop entrepreneurial skills. Perhaps you will collaborate with local colleges, universities, businesses, and nonprofits, or connect with fellow Project LIT leaders around the world. Or perhaps you will simply meet regularly as a group to eat bagels and talk about life and the books you're reading.

Again, this work doesn't need to be flashy or time-consuming or expensive. We don't need to be perfect. We don't need to reach a hundred or a thousand students right away (or ever). We don't need to blast everything on social media, especially when there are hateful "followers" lurking and looking to discredit the work we're doing. The key is that you and I, that all of us, continue to do *something* to encourage our students to "just read it"—and to carry their love of literacy forward into life and community.

HOW HAVE YOU GROWN AS A READER THROUGH PROJECT LIT?

PROJECT LIT FOUNDERS, SPRING 2019

- If I'm bored now, I want to pick up a book instead of watching TV. Books have become my new outlet.
- I went from not owning a single book to having my own mini library at home.
- Project LIT has increased my passion for reading. I would read but not as much as I should have. Project LIT has made it fun to read.
- I learned to love reading.
- I used to skim through books, and now I actually read them.
- I've always been a reader, but I'm glad that my love of books didn't fade in high school.
- I hated reading, but now I can read anything, even something I'm not interested in.
- Instead of being forced to read books for class, Project LIT has got me into the habit of enjoying the books I read instead of doing it just because I have to.
- I am more likely to pick up a book during my free time rather than waste my time.
- Now I enjoy reading and see it as a calming outlet for me.
- I have read more books than I thought I could.
- I have been able to read longer and higher-level books.
- I have applied what I've read to real-life situations.
- Before Project LIT, I feel like it took me a few weeks to finish a book as to now it only takes me a few days.
- I've started to read more books and longer books than I used to.
- I began to read more, and the books become more enjoyable.
- As a reader, I feel like I have broadened my horizons.
- I gradually fell in love the more books I read. Despite the work behind the books, I feel like I got to fully enjoy each one. Books have become more than just words. They have become more like moments away from life, making me feel more at peace with myself.

FIGURE 8.10 ● Project LIT Survey 1

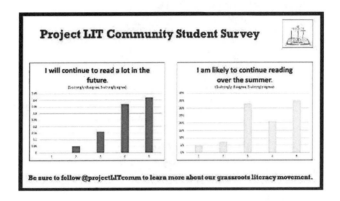

FIGURE 8.11 ● Project LIT Survey 2

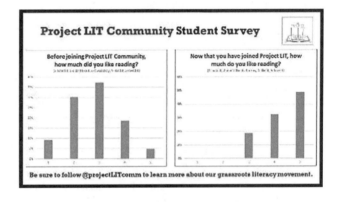

HOW HAVE YOU GROWN AS A PERSON THROUGH PROJECT LIT?

PROJECT LIT FOUNDERS, SPRING 201

- I'm more open minded.
- I have become more of a leader and a more determined person. It made me more organized as well as a harder worker.
- Getting to know people in my community and giving back to my area.
- Yes, since the many book clubs, field trips, and videos I participated in, it helped me come out of my quiet shell and expanded my thinking.
- I've started to work well with others.
- It taught me to not be afraid to speak out about anything you're passionate about.

- I've learned to be helpful and more generous toward people.
- I am now aware of how many connections you can make with literature.
- Project LIT has helped mold me into the person I am today. My reading and communication skills have grown tremendously.
- Project LIT taught me how to work in a group and the importance of patience.
- I've become a more critical thinker. I'm able to see different views of a situation.
- I'm calmer.
- I've gotten way better at my communication skills and being the first to speak up.
- I've overcome challenges that I thought I would never overcome, like speaking in front of a lot of people.
- I can do anything if I believe.
- It's helped me with my leadership and public speaking skills.
- I've definitely opened up more to others. I've actually become comfortable sitting through panels or interviews because with Project LIT, I'm allowed to be myself in my natural way without being judged.
- I became more confident in myself and started interacting with more people outside of my school.
- I used to be more by myself, but after being in Project LIT, I'm more people oriented, and it makes me want to be more social and outgoing.
- Project LIT has helped me grow as a person because not only did it teach me responsibility, it also taught me that everybody is different, and we should respect them and appreciate them for who they are.
- I value simple things in life now. I know I'm blessed to be in the position I'm in now. I know if I want to do something in life to help my community, I could and would.
- I've never been good at communicating with people because I never really had to. Being a part of Project LIT has encouraged me to share my opinions with others and listen to what they have to say also. It's really helped me learn a lot about the topics we'd discussed and how the people felt about them.
- This gives me the chance to be an example to not only my generation but to younger kids as well.
- I no longer let others influence my actions.
- Project L.I.T has made me more aware of the community problems. I have become a more caring person.
- I would say that I've grown to love helping people. I had previously loved being kindhearted and a good helper; however, Project LIT has opened my eyes to bigger possibilities.
- Since I joined Project Lit, I read much better than I used to, and it made me want to help people more. I like being able to make a change in the community. This year, I think I have become a better person.

PROJECT LIT HAS TAUGHT ME . . .

PROJECT LIT FOUNDERS, SPRING 2019

- to be yourself.
- that you can do anything as long as you put your mind to it.
- reading is important.
- to love reading more.
- how to connect with others through a book.
- how to be a leader.
- that there's more to life than phones. You can connect through books.
- how to be helpful and generous to people.
- communication skills.
- leadership and public speaking skills.
- that books can give you knowledge.
- to be grateful, to be loving, and to be kind.
- time management.
- how to speak publicly and be confident in myself.
- how to make the best of what I have.
- to strive and make my community better.
- how to make connections.
- to take leadership.
- how to communicate.
- how to stay dedicated and remain true to one thing.
- how to be a leader and a better reader.
- that you're going to have to step out of your comfort zone in order to get things you want accomplished.
- to make a change and do something productive.
- the importance of reading and how it can bring people together.
- how to stay organized and to appreciate everything you have.
- how to be open minded to others' opinions and to think deeper about books.

Overtime

I want to leave you with three quick stories. The first is from December 2013, halfway through my fifth year of teaching. After a few years of trial and lots of error, my friend and colleague Mr. Rogen and I had finally figured some things out. The work was difficult, but man, our students were *reading*. In fact, I recently revisited an old Instagram post from that year. In the picture, you can see our students holding up a massive banner full of colorful index cards arranged to spell out *JB (heart shape) READING*. The caption reads: "JBMS 8th graders love reading so much they've already read more than 1,000 books."

There's much I've forgotten from that school year. However, I can still recall the sense of pride and excitement we felt that winter. With some groups, it's hard to tell if we're making a difference (even though we usually are), but with that group, it was obvious. The progress was visible. We could all sense it. And as any proud teacher would do, I wanted to recognize and reward students for their individual and collective effort. *What if we sent every student home with a new book before winter break? How awesome would that be?* And so that's what we did. Here's how Mr. Rogen described it years later (via a Twitter [now X] thread):

(Ten) years ago, winter break, (Amato) and I were at JBMS, and I think we were figuring out more and more the power of getting more books into our kids' hands. So one day, Amato starts reaching out to all sorts of people to get books for our kids on holiday. Being Amato, he's successful, and we get like 300–400 books for the kids. He decides that just giving the kids books isn't enough. It has to be special for them. And so, he has to wrap up a few books for each kid in our grade. But understand, it's the day before, and so he would have to wrap up hundreds and hundreds of books. Impossible. But he still wants to do it. So what does he do? Uses his sick day. Comes into work. Wraps up hundreds and hundreds of books while "not working." End of the day, he hands each kid a special gift of several books to read over the break. Kids have a blast opening/trading and then reading the books. All because he was willing to trade his days for them.

After the break, kids were talking about what books they read, swapping books, etc. The culture of reading was being built.

It's hard to believe that more than a decade has passed since that moment. In many places, including that very middle school, our literacy crisis has only intensified—through no fault of our students or educators. Sure, the pandemic is partly to blame, but the inequities have always existed.

For example, in January 2019, before the phrase "learning loss" was tossed around like a football at recess, I was back in the JBMS library for one of the first times since I left the middle school in 2015. All literacy teachers in our East Nashville cluster were there for our district's required "professional development" day. As I browsed the beautiful shelves and made small talk with fellow educators during a break, I discovered that JBMS no longer had a librarian. (And not just any librarian, one of the best. Mrs. Davis was incredible. Students *loved* her and the space she created for them. She showed me and so many others what it looked like to truly celebrate reading and our readers.)

Even more tragic, I learned the library was literally off limits for kids. (If I recall, all classrooms were moved to the first floor due to the declining enrollment while the library sat deserted on the second floor.) Yet, there we were, expected to spend seven hours listening to how the latest scripted curriculum was going to be the answer to all of our literacy challenges. (Spoiler alert: It was not.) I was devastated. I was furious. I turned to Twitter (now X) to share my frustrations.

Does anyone in Nashville know that a school in a literal book desert no longer has a librarian? Does anyone care? I know that solving our city's literacy crisis is hard, complicated work, but why can't we do the simple things? Do we really want ALL students to become lifelong readers?

As I review the thread today, I stand by all of it. And the answer to that final question, sadly, is no. There are parents and politicians across our country who want "their children" to become readers but not "those children." Who want to protect "their children" but not "those children." Who believe in choice for "their children" but not "those children." What happened to standing up for *all* children?

While the book bans in states like Florida and Texas and Tennessee make the headlines, scenes like the one I just described have been happening far more frequently and for much longer than some realize. The quiet censorship, the devaluing of school libraries and librarians, the push for scripted curriculum, the lack of autonomy, the emphasis on high-stakes testing—all of it is harmful.

In simple terms, it means there are more educators like Mrs. Davis and Mr. Rogen—the knowledgeable, dedicated librarians and teachers you and I (and most Americans) want for our children—leaving the profession than there are entering it. Make no mistake: it's 100 percent intentional. And it's going to have profoundly negative effects that we are only just beginning to feel.

I don't pretend to have all the answers, but I do know this: We cannot afford to sit this one out. Like I said in the opening, our students need you. They need us! You don't need to rewrite your school's curriculum overnight. You don't need a thousand students to join your book club. You don't need to stay in your classroom until 6 p.m. grading essays. You definitely don't need to write a book (trust me on this one).

You just need to continue to be you. Keep that fire. Keep that spirit. Keep being the educator who gives a damn, who cares about the well-being of every student in your classroom, and who tries to do and be a little bit better every day.

Whether you are preparing for your first year in education, gearing up for one of your last, or, like me, find yourself somewhere in between, thank you. Thank you for the work you have done and for the work you will continue to do alongside and on behalf of our young people. My hope is that this book will help you reach even more readers, particularly those who are often overlooked in our classrooms and communities.

I decided to title this final chapter "Overtime" as a nod to Kwame Alexander's *The Crossover*. The book holds a special place in my heart for a few reasons. As you now know, the novel in verse was our first ever Project LIT Book Club selection. It was the book that started a movement. I believe *The Crossover* exemplifies everything our English classrooms should be about—at times, fun, fast-paced, and playful; at others, serious, emotional, and heartfelt. In one moment, students are laughing out loud at Filthy's killer rhymes, and in the next, they are analyzing author's craft and discussing how to deal with grief. Books like *The Crossover* are magical.

On a personal note, this book helped me heal. I've read *The Crossover* dozens of times, but I'll never forget listening to Kwame Alexander read it aloud on Instagram Live. It was early in quarantine, the spring of 2020. It was one of the first times I had opened the book since losing my dad.

> Basketball Rule #10
>
> A loss is inevitable,
>
> like snow in winter.
>
> True champions
>
> learn
>
> to dance
>
> through
>
> the storm.

As Kwame read page after page from a library in London, and I followed along from my desk in Nashville, I remember thinking: *He's speaking to me! Kwame understands.* I remember, in that moment, feeling less alone. I cried. And then I smiled. That's the power of a great book. And that's why, despite the challenges, I absolutely love being an English teacher.

I can't tell you how many times I've had a classroom conversation unfold like this one (and it never gets old):

"I don't want to read today."

"Why not?"

"I'm just not in the mood."

"I don't blame you, but I have a feeling you'll like this one."

"What is it?"

"*The Crossover*."

"What's it about?"

"Here. Just read it."

Appendix

Spring 2022 Annual Literacy Report – Dr. Amato's 10th Grade English Students

	1	2	3	4	5
In general, how do you feel about reading? (1-hate it, 5-love it)	0%	2.3%	9.3%	**60.5%**	**27.9%**
How often do you read outside of school? (1-never, 5-all the time)	4.7%	**23.3%**	**41.9%**	18.6%	11.6%
Reading is cool. (1-strongly disagree, 5-strongly agree)	0%	0%	11.6%	**44.2%**	**44.2%**
Reading is boring. (1-strongly disagree, 5-strongly agree)	**37.2%**	**37.2%**	23.3%	2.3%	0%
Reading is important. (1-strongly disagree, 5-strongly agree)	0%	0%	2.3%	**20.9%**	**76.7%**
I appreciate that we have choice in what we read in class. (1-strongly disagree, 5-strongly agree)	0%	0%	2.3%	**9.3%**	88.4%
I appreciate that we have daily time to read in class. (1-strongly disagree, 5-strongly agree)	0%	0%	4.7%	**18.6%**	**76.7%**
I consider reading to be a hobby. (1-strongly disagree, 5-strongly agree)	4.7%	4.7%	18.6%	**46.5%**	**25.6%**
I plan to continue reading this summer. (1-strongly disagree, 5-strongly agree)	2.3%	7.0%	23.3%	**34.9%**	**32.6%**
I have improved as a reader this year. (1-strongly disagree, 5-strongly agree)	2.3%	7.0%	11.6%	**25.6%**	**53.5%**

Approximately how many books did you read this school year?

Our collective average was approximately **eleven books per student** during the 2021–2022 school year. This was a massive victory, especially in comparison to the previous year. During our fall 2021 survey, when asked "How many books did you read during the 2020–2021 school year?," the collective average was **just under four books** per student. In other words, each student read, on average, **seven more books** than they did the previous year. Approximately one-third of our students reported reading zero to two books during the 2020–2021 school year. During the 2021–2022 school year, every student read at least five.

What genres did you read this year? (Check all that apply)

The three most popular genres were **realistic fiction, graphic novels,** and **mystery/thriller.** The next three were **romance, fantasy,** and **nonfiction.**

What is the best book you read this year?

Students shared so many great titles. Too many to list here.

How have your reading habits/routines changed over the course of this school year, especially in comparison to previous years? (Complete sentences here!)

- Ever since you made us read at the beginning of class, I find myself actually reading. I became interested in books and having you there to guide me towards different genres and books was really helpful.

- Before this year I never read a lot. Now I read almost every day and even read at home on my free time. I never thought I could read a single full book.

- I haven't really read much in my life so me reading 9 books is a lot and it really surprised me.

- I started reading a lot more often in comparison to last year; however, a bit less than I did in 6th/7th grade.

- I have gotten my love for reading back. I have read more books this school year than freshman year and 8th grade. I've incorporated it in my life either when I wake up or right before bed. It's helped me relax and stimulate my mind.

- My habits changed because I actually finish books now instead of dropping them in the middle of it.

- Before this school year, I only read books when I was told to. I used to never just pick up a book for the simple source of entertainment. Now, I can find love in reading! I can pick up a book with joy and not sorrow.

The answers above are even more worthy of applause when compared to our students' responses from the fall of 2021.

- Not very good and I kind of drifted away from reading because I couldn't really find something good to read.

- My reading routine has decreased over the past year.

- Nothing too noticeable? I've always enjoyed reading or writing but I don't have the attention span to enjoy most books that I really wanna read so I don't.

- It is absolutely hard for me to focus when it comes to reading.

- No, I have never liked reading and only read when necessary.

- Very much. I've been reading less, and my motivation has been iffy. I am trying to get back into reading, though.

- I pretty much stopped reading.

- It got bad because I didn't have books I liked reading and the library was closed.

- I don't read as much sadly.

How would you evaluate your performance as a reader this year?

- I'm mainly proud of the number of books that I have read this year and the different genres that I explored.

- I figured out how to find new books to read. And I've started getting back into reading which I am proud of. I'm still very picky though.

- I think I have improved as a reader. I am very proud that every book I started, with the exception of one, I finished. I definitely want to read more books. My favorite genre is poetry/novel in verse, and I hope to write my own book of poems over the summer.

- I am proud of myself for actually finishing books and enjoying them. I used to read like 3 books in a school year so just reading more in itself is something I'm proud of.

- I feel my performance has been the same for a very long time, however I have found myself reading challenging books, and I am more comfortable there than I used to be.

- I discovered some new authors that I really like and so I will continue to follow their journey.

- I'm proud of my dive into different genres I typically wouldn't explore. It has opened my mind and made me want to try other things. I want to improve how much I read outside of school.

- I am most proud of my personal growth. Reading has helped shape me into a better individual. I have a better mindset and brain thanks to the incredible books I was able to read.

- I think I'm most proud of myself trying new genres. I am also proud I read more. I want to broaden my vocabulary and read more challenging books. I think my takeaway for this year is reading is still fun no matter my age. I learned I really love to read poetry, and I like to read about books that I can relate to. I also learned I always cry at the end of books no matter the end.

- I think I've started thinking deeper and recognizing more complex themes.

What will you remember most about our class?

- I will mainly remember the monthly nature walks.

- The jokes and laughs.

- Our walks are probably the most memorable. The poems we wrote after the walks. Our class discussions, just the overall vibe of tranquility in this class.

- The greatest memories of this class was the laughs we had and the deep and random conversations. You've added a new definition to learning is and can be fun.

- That we had choice in how we spent our time.

- Independent reading time. I'm going to miss it as it was something I always looked forward to :(

- I will remember the off-topic conversations and the structure. I enjoy classes that have that. The freedom that came with reading was also really great and most of the writing topics were too :)

- I will remember our monthly walks most of anything.

- What I will remember more about this class is my funny classmates and my cool teacher and what he has taught me.

- How we would read every morning

- I will remember our class conversations before class began. I really enjoyed our conversations about food and overall advice and events that would happen.

- I will remember all of the meaningful conversations we had about EVERYTHING!

- The simple walks. Sometimes getting outside was the best part of my day. I will forever cherish them.

- Being freely able to do most things.

- I think I'll remember all the jokes we made. I'll also remember the amazing constructive criticism. I love how we all had fun times, but we also had amazing learning experiences. I think this is the English class I've learned the most.

References

Bethea, C. (2023, February 7). Why some florida schools are removing books from their libraries. *The New Yorker.* https://www.newyorker.com/news/letter-from-the-south/why-some-florida-schools-are-removing-books-from-their-libraries

Hanft, A. (2019, January 15). Boston marathon data analysis, Part 1. *Medium.* https://ade3.medium.com/boston-marathon-data-analysis-part-1-4891d1832eba

Hoffman Institute Foundation. (n.d.). *Feelings list.* Hoffman Institute. https://www.hoffmaninstitute.org/wp-content/uploads/Practices-FeelingsSensations.pdf

Knight, L., Reynolds, J., & Blackman, M. (2022, December 17). "I've been banned since the beginning": Jason Reynolds talks to Joseph Coelho. *The Guardian.* https://www.theguardian.com/books/2022/dec/17/ive-been-banned-since-the-beginning-jason-reynolds-talks-to-joseph-coelho

Medina, M. (2021, October 30). *Stop the madness: Banning books is not the answer.* Meg Medina. https://megmedina.com/2021/10/stop-the-madness-banning-books-is-not-the-answer/

National Council of Teachers of English (NCTE). (2019, November 7). *Statement on independent reading.* https://ncte.org/statement/independent-reading/

Noah, T. (2018, January 23). *Jason Reynolds —Serving young readers with "Long Way Down"* - The Daily Show with Trevor Noah. Comedy Central. https://www.cc.com/video/avk8pe/the-daily-show-with-trevor-noah-jason-reynolds-serving-young-readers-with-long-way-down

Now Spark Creativity. (2018, February 15). *One pagers: The simplest way to success.* Spark Creativity. https://nowsparkcreativity.com/2018/02/one-pagers-simplest-way-to-success.html

Proulx, N. (2021, January 12). Getting to know each other with "My Ten,". *The New York Times.* https://www.nytimes.com/2021/01/12/learning/getting-to-know-each-other-with-my-ten.html

Qasim, N. (2021, April 15). The books that made me: 8 writers on their literary inspirations. *The New York Times.* https://www.nytimes.com/2021/04/15/books/the-books-that-made-me-8-writers-on-their-literary-inspirations.html

Reynolds, J. (2018, May 28). *Ten things I've been meaning to say to you.* Powell's Books. https://www.powells.com/post/lists/ten-things-ive-been-meaning-to-say-to-you

Serrano, S. (2016, July 21). A teacher's reward. *The Ringer.* https://www.theringer.com/2016/7/21/16042010/a-teachers-reward-the-secret-power-of-being-an-educator-b7c5c901dea0

Stone, N. (2018, September 27). Nic stone's letter to her younger self is an important reminder that you don't have to fit in just one box. *Teen Vogue.* https://www.teenvogue.com/story/nic-stone-letter-younger-self-odd-one-out

Tolin, L., & Coates, T.-N. (2023, May 9). *Ta-nehisi coates at the world voices festival.* PEN America. https://pen.org/ta-nehisi-coates-book-bans/

Willingham, D. T. (2018, December 8). Is listening to a book the same thing as reading it? *The New York Times.* https://www.nytimes.com/2018/12/08/opinion/sunday/audiobooks-reading-cheating-listening.html

Wong, A. (2016, July 14). Where books are all but nonexistent. *The Atlantic.* https://www.theatlantic.com/education/archive/2016/07/where-books-are-nonexistent/491282/

Index

Because...
ALL TEACHERS ARE LEADERS

AFRIKA AFENI MILLS

This guide explores why racial identity work is crucial, especially for White-identifying students and teachers, and guides educators to provide opportunities for antiracist learning.

ALLISON SKERRETT, PETER SMAGORINSKY

Engage students in critical thinking, literacy activities, and inquiry using the personal and social issues of pressing importance to today's students.

MARIA WALTHER

This resource offers a scaffolding for moving from teacher-led demonstration of read alouds to student-led discovery of literacy skills—across the bridge of shared reading.

VERA AHIYYA

Spark courageous conversations with children about race, identity, and social justice using read alouds as an entry point.

To order your copies, visit corwin.com/literacy

At Corwin Literacy we have put together a collection of just-in-time, classroom-tested, practical resources from trusted experts that allow you to quickly find the information you need when you need it.

DOUGLAS FISHER, NANCY FREY, DIANE LAPP

Like an animated encyclopedia, this book delivers the latest evidence-based practices in 13 interactive modules that will transform your instruction and reenergize your career.

JUSTIN M. STYGLES

Learn how to build relationships so shame-bound readers trust enough to risk enough to grow.

GRETCHEN BERNABEI, JAYNE HOVER

Use these lessons and concrete text structures designed to help students write self-generated commentary in response to reading.

CHRISTINA NOSEK, MELANIE MEEHAN, MATTHEW JOHNSON, MATTHEW R. KAY, DAVE STUART JR.

This series offers actionable answers to your most pressing questions about teaching reading, writing, and ELA.

CL22153261

A Sage Company